T0323620

G   U   I   D   E

Prospective Financial Information

WITH CONFORMING CHANGES AS OF
NOVEMBER 1, 2012

edition of the AICPA Guide *Prospective Financial Information*, which was originally issued in 1993,
een modified by the AICPA staff to include certain changes necessary because of the issuance of authoritative
ouncements since the guide was originally issued and other changes necessary to keep the guide current on
try and regulatory matters. The appendix "Schedule of Changes Made to the Text From the Previous Edition"
ifies all changes made in this edition of the guide. The changes do *not* include all those that might be considered
ssary if the guide were subjected to a comprehensive review and revision.

1 2 3 4 5 6 7 8 9 0 AAP 1 9 8 7 6 5 4 3

ISBN 978-1-93735-185-4

Notice to Readers

This AICPA Guide, which contains attestation guidance, is an interpretive publication pursuant to AT section 50, *SSAE Hierarchy* (AICPA, *Professional Standards*). Interpretive publications include recommendations on the application of Statements on Standards for Attestation Engagements (SSAEs) in specific circumstances, including engagements for entities in specialized industries. Interpretive publications are issued under the authority of the Auditing Standards Board (ASB). The members of the ASB have found this guide to be consistent with existing SSAEs.

A practitioner should be aware of and consider interpretive publications applicable to his or her attestation engagement. If a practitioner does not apply the attestation guidance included in an applicable AICPA Guide, the practitioner should be prepared to explain how he or she complied with the SSAE provisions addressed by such attestation guidance.

The guide also includes descriptions and recommendations regarding presentation and disclosure of prospective financial information. It is intended to be helpful in determining whether prospective financial information is presented in conformity with AICPA presentation guidelines. Rule 102, *Integrity and Objectivity* (AICPA, *Professional Standards*, ET sec. 102 par. 01), of the AICPA Code of Professional Conduct prohibits members from knowingly misrepresenting facts to others. A member who issues a report indicating the accompanying prospective financial information has been prepared in conformity with guidelines established by the AICPA would be held in violation of Rule 102 if it was determined that the guidelines were not followed.

Recognition

Darrel R. Schubert, *Chair*
Auditing Standards Board

Financial Forecasts and Projections Task Force (1986)

Robert K. Elliott, *Chair*	Carl P. Gross
Saul Braverman	John M. Kohlmeier
Phillip W. Crawford	Norman A. Lavin
Kenneth J. Dirkes	Dale G. Neuhaus

Financial Forecasts and Projections Task Force (1993)

Kenneth J. Dirkes, *Chair*	James W. Ledwith
Richard Dieter	Don M. Pallais
Harvey J. Gitel	Ernest L. Ten Eyck
John M. Hollenbeck	

Financial Forecasts and Projections Conforming Changes Task Force (1997)

Don M. Pallais, *Chair*   Glenn Johnson

Kenneth J. Dirkes

AICPA Staff

Liese B. Faircloth
Technical Manager
Accounting and Auditing Publications

Reviewers

The AICPA gratefully acknowledges Don M. Pallais for his review of this guide.

Guidance Considered in This Edition

This edition of the guide has been modified by the AICPA staff to include certain changes necessary due to the issuance of authoritative guidance since the guide was originally issued, and other revisions as deemed appropriate. Authoritative guidance issued through November 1, 2012, has been considered in the development of this edition of the guide.

This guide includes relevant guidance issued up to and including the following:

- Financial Accounting Standards Board (FASB) Accounting Standards Updates issued through September 30, 2012

- Statement on Auditing Standards (SAS) No. 126, *The Auditor's Consideration of an Entity's Ability to Continue as a Going Concern* (AICPA, *Professional Standards*, AU-C sec. 570)

- SSAE No. 17, *Reporting on Compiled Prospective Financial Statements When the Practitioner's Independence is Impaired* (AICPA, *Professional Standards*, AT sec. 301 par. .23)

- Statement on Standards for Accounting and Review Services No. 20, *Revised Applicability of Statements on Standards for Accounting and Review Services* (AICPA, *Professional Standards*, AR sec. 90)

- Interpretation No. 17, "Required Supplementary Information That Accompanies Compiled Financial Statements," of AR section 80, *Compilation of Financial Statements* (AICPA, *Professional Standards*, AR sec. 9080 par. .63–.68)

- Interpretation No. 11, "Required Supplementary Information That Accompanies Compiled Financial Statements," of AR section 90, *Review of Financial Statements* (AICPA, *Professional Standards*, AR sec. 9090 par. .41–.44)

Users of this guide should consider guidance issued subsequent to those items listed previously to determine their effect on entities covered by this guide. In determining the applicability of a pronouncement, its effective date should also be considered.

The changes made to this edition of the guide are identified in appendix E, "Schedule of Changes Made to the Text From the Previous Edition." The changes do not include all those that might be considered necessary if the guide were subjected to a comprehensive review and revision.

References to Professional Standards

In citing generally accepted auditing standards and their related interpretations, references use section numbers within the codification of currently effective SASs and not the original statement number, as appropriate. In those sections of the guides that refer to specific auditing standards of the Public Company Accounting Oversight Board, references are made to the AICPA's *PCAOB Standards and Related Rules* publication.

AICPA.org Website

The AICPA encourages you to visit the website at www.aicpa.org, and the new Financial Reporting Center at www.aicpa.org/FRC. The Financial Reporting Center was created to support members in the execution of high quality financial reporting. Whether you are a financial statement preparer or a member in public practice, this center provides exclusive member-only resources for the entire financial reporting process and provides timely and relevant news, guidance, and examples supporting the financial reporting process, including accounting, preparing financial statements, and performing compilation, review, audit, attest, or assurance and advisory engagements. Certain content on the AICPA's websites referenced in this guide may be restricted to AICPA members only.

Preface

Purpose and Applicability

This AICPA Guide supersedes the AICPA *Guide for Prospective Financial Statements*, which was originally issued in 1986, and subsequent editions of that guide with conforming changes made by the AICPA staff.

Public Accounting Firms Registered With the Public Company Accounting Oversight Board

Subject to the Securities and Exchange Commission (SEC) oversight, Section 103 of the Sarbanes-Oxley Act of 2002 (act) authorizes the Public Company Accounting Oversight Board (PCAOB) to establish auditing and related attestation, quality control, ethics, and independence standards to be used by registered public accounting firms in the preparation and issuance of audit reports as required by the act or the rules of the SEC. Accordingly, public accounting firms registered with the PCAOB are required to adhere to all PCAOB standards in the audits of issuers, as defined by the act, and other entities when prescribed by the rules of the SEC.

GUIDE FOR PROSPECTIVE FINANCIAL INFORMATION
FLOWCHART OF TYPES OF PROSPECTIVE PRESENTATIONS[1]

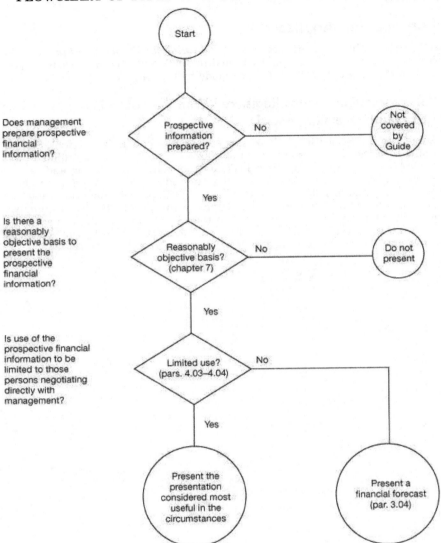

Does management prepare prospective financial information?

Is there a reasonably objective basis to present the prospective financial information?

Is use of the prospective financial information to be limited to those persons negotiating directly with management?

---

[1] Presentation could be a financial forecast (paragraph 3.04), financial projection (paragraph 3.05), or a partial presentation (paragraph 3.06).

GUIDE FOR PROSPECTIVE FINANCIAL INFORMATION
FLOWCHART
OF PRACTITIONERS' SERVICES

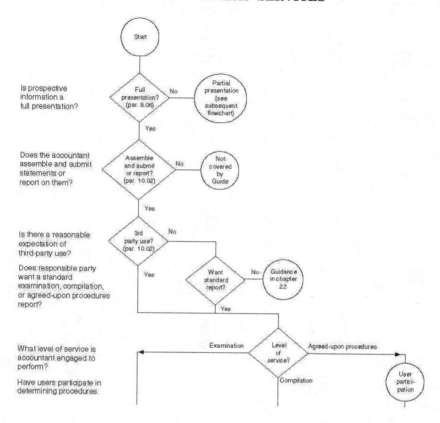

Is prospective information a full presentation?

Does the accountant assemble and submit statements or report on them?

Is there a reasonable expectation of third-party use?

Does responsible party want a standard examination, compilation, or agreed-upon procedures report?

What level of service is accountant engaged to perform?

Have users participate in determining procedures.

x

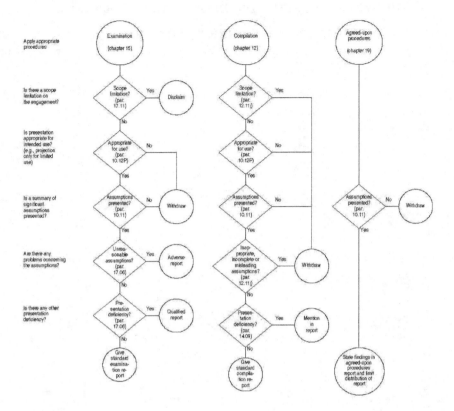

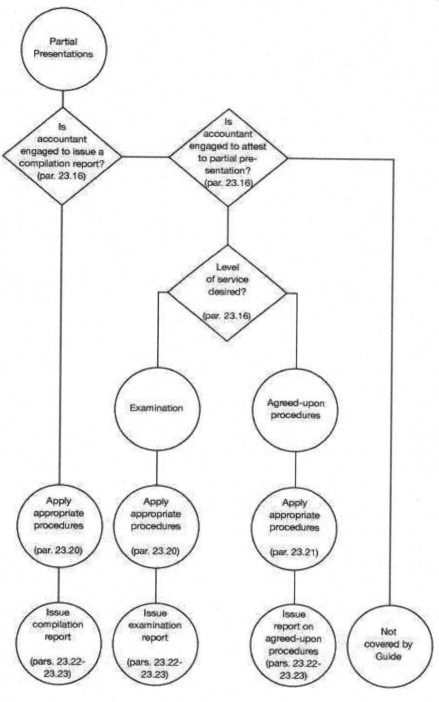

TABLE OF CONTENTS

Contents

Contents

Part 1

General Guidance Regarding Prospective Financial Information

Chapter 1

Introduction

1.01 Prospective financial information is of interest to a broad spectrum of parties, including management, present or potential owners of equity interests, credit grantors, and other informed third parties, government agencies, and the public.

1.02 This Audit and Accounting Guide establishes guidelines for the preparation and presentation of financial forecasts and projections (referred to as *prospective financial statements*). Chapter 23, "Partial Presentations of Prospective Financial Information," describes how these guidelines apply to the unique aspects of partial presentations of prospective financial information. This guide also is intended to assist the practitioner in performing professional services on and reporting on such information.

1.03 Prospective financial statements are based on assumptions regarding future events. The assumptions are in turn based on a combination of available information and judgment, in which both history and plans play a part.

1.04 Because no one can know the future, and because prospective financial information may be affected by many factors both internal and external to the entity, the Statements on Standards for Attestation Engagements (SSAEs) require the practitioner to exercise professional judgment. This judgment may be used to estimate when and how conditions are likely to change. These judgments subsequently may prove to be unrepresentative of future conditions; thus, the achievability and reliability of prospective financial information can never be guaranteed.

1.05 Prospective financial information is less amenable to objective verification than is historical data. When working with or using prospective information, it is essential to understand its inherent limitations.

Structure of the Guide

1.06 Although the guide covers both financial forecasts and financial projections, its primary focus is on forecasts because they more closely parallel historical financial statements, which are intended to provide the financial information needed by persons making financial decisions who have access to neither the entity's financial records nor its management. Financial forecasts provide a framework from which principles for financial projections are derived. Thus, the guide first presents the principles relating to financial forecasts and then shows how those principles are modified for financial projections.

1.07 The guidance on forecasted financial information contained in chapters 6–23 generally also applies to projected financial information. Certain paragraphs in those chapters, however, do not apply—partially or fully—to projections. In those instances, readers interested in financial projections should refer to the corresponding *italicized* paragraphs (which bear the same paragraph numbers followed by the letter P) and consider the modifications discussed in those paragraphs in conjunction with the paragraphs that precede them.

Relationship to Other Literature

1.08 In January 2001, the Auditing Standards Board (ASB) issued SSAE No. 10, *Attestation Standards: Revision and Recodification* (AICPA, *Professional Standards*). AT section 301, *Financial Forecasts and Projections* (AICPA, *Professional Standards*), establishes standards for practitioners' services on prospective financial information. This guide incorporates those standards in the sections on practitioners' services (parts 3 and 4 of this guide). Accordingly, a practitioner who complies with this guide will also be in compliance with the SSAE. The guide also provides additional explanatory and illustrative material to aid the practitioner in applying the SSAE.

1.09 This guide also incorporates the guidance in AT sections 101–701, *Attestation Standards: Revision and Recodification* (AICPA, *Professional Standards*), issued in September 2002; AT section 20, *Defining Professional Requirements in Statements on Standards for Attestation Engagements* (AICPA, *Professional Standards*), issued in December 2005; and AT section 50, *SSAE Hierarchy* (AICPA, *Professional Standards*), issued in November 2006.

1.10 Previous editions of this guide have been superseded but nonetheless provide the basis for much of the guide's content. The superseded editions are

- *Guide for Prospective Financial Statements* (1986), which was based on the Statement on Standards for Accountants' Services on Prospective Financial Information, "Financial Forecasts and Projections," issued by the ASB in 1985.

- *Guide for Prospective Financial Information* (1993), which incorporated three Statements of Position (SOPs) issued at the time by the ASB's Financial Forecasts and Projections Task Force: SOP 89-3, *Questions Concerning Accountants' Services on Prospective Financial Statements*; SOP 90-1, *Accountants' Services on Prospective Financial Statements for Internal Use Only and Partial Presentations*; and SOP 92-2, *Questions and Answers on the Term* Reasonably Objective Basis *and Other Issues Affecting Prospective Financial Statements*.

- *Guide for Prospective Financial Information* (1997), which revised the 1993 edition to recognize the implications of the Private Securities Litigation Act of 1995 (see paragraph 1.12). The 1997 edition was updated in 1999 to incorporate a number of changes needed to conform to authoritative pronouncements issued after 1997.

1.11 The Securities and Exchange Commission (SEC) permits the publication of prospective financial information under certain conditions and has adopted the general policy of encouraging such publication. The SEC has indicated that companies that include prospective financial information in SEC filings or annual reports should meet certain broad standards and disclosure requirements. In addition, the SEC adopted a rule that essentially provides a safe harbor against SEC actions for statements made by or on behalf of companies that issue prospective information or by an independent accountant, unless such statements were (*a*) made other than in good faith or (*b*) disclosed without a reasonable basis. See the SEC policies that appear as appendixes A,

"SEC Policy on Projections," and B, "SEC Safe Harbor Rule for Projections," of this guide.[1]

1.12 The Private Securities Litigation Reform Act of 1995, in addition to other provisions, amends the Securities Act of 1933 and the Securities Exchange Act of 1934 by creating a new safe harbor for forward-looking statements made by an issuer, persons acting on behalf of such issuer, and any outside reviewer retained by such issuer to make a statement on behalf of such issuer. The act reshapes securities laws that professional investors and some class-action lawyers have used against corporations, practitioners, and securities underwriters. The law encourages voluntary disclosure of forward-looking information to investors by establishing a carefully designed safe harbor. Forward-looking statements that include meaningful and cautionary disclosures that identify factors that could alter forecasted results are protected by the safe harbor. However, there are certain notable exclusions to the safe harbor provisions of the act. See appendix D, "Private Securities Litigation Reform Act of 1995," for the safe harbor provisions of that act.[2]

1.13 The Department of the Treasury has issued regulations on tax shelter opinions. The regulations provide that if the practitioner provides a *tax shelter opinion,* the practitioner should, if possible, provide (*a*) an opinion on whether it is more likely than not that an investor will prevail on the merits of each material tax issue and (*b*) an overall evaluation of the extent to which the material tax benefits are likely to be realized in the aggregate. Those regulations indicate that, if a practitioner provides services on a financial forecast or projection included in tax shelter offering materials, the practitioner may be deemed to have issued a tax shelter opinion. The Treasury Department's regulations in Circular 230, *Regulations Governing Practice before the Internal Revenue Service,* are included as appendix C, "IRS Regulations Regarding Tax Shelter Opinions (Circular 230)," of this guide.

Effective Date

1.14 The presentation guidelines in the original guide are effective for prospective financial statements prepared on or after September 30, 1986. The guidance on accountants' services appearing in the original guide is effective for engagements in which the date of completion of the accountants' services on prospective financial statements is September 30, 1986, or later except for the guidance on agreed-upon procedures in chapters 19–21, which is effective for reports dated after April 30, 1996. The guidance incorporated from SSAE No. 10 is effective for practitioners' reports issued on or after June 1, 2001. SSAE No. 11, *Attest Documentation* (AICPA, *Professional Standards,* AT sec. 101) (discussed in paragraphs 12.11–.18, 15.41–.48, and 19.11–.18), which expanded the documentation requirements for attestation engagements, is effective for services on prospective financial information for periods ending on or after December 15, 2002. The guidance incorporated from SSAE No. 17, *Reporting on Compiled Prospective Financial Statements When the Practitioner's Independence is Impaired* (AICPA, *Professional Standards,* AT sec. 301 par. .23), is effective for prospective financial statements for periods ending on or after

---

[1] AT section 701, *Management's Discussion and Analysis* (AICPA, *Professional Standards*), sets forth attestation standards and provides guidance concerning the performance of an attest engagement with respect to management's discussion and analysis (MD&A) prepared pursuant to the rules and regulations adopted by the Securities and Exchange Commission. Paragraphs .25–.26 of AT section 701 discuss the practitioner's responsibility when the MD&A presentation includes forward-looking information.

[2] See footnote 1.

December 15, 2010. SSAE No. 17 updated paragraph .23 of AT sec. 301 by permitting accountants to disclose the reason(s) for an independence impairment in a report on compiled prospective financial information (discussed in paragraph 14.05).

Chapter 2

Scope

Presentations

2.01 Prospective financial statements[1] may comprise a complete prospective presentation of financial position, results of operations, cash flows, and summaries of significant assumptions and significant accounting policies, or they may be limited to the items listed in paragraph 8.06. Chapters 1–22 of the guide apply to these prospective presentations. A presentation that does not include the applicable minimum items in paragraph 8.06, including presentations limited to specified elements or accounts, is considered to be a partial presentation. Chapter 23, "Partial Presentations of Prospective Financial Information," describes how the guidance in chapters 6–22 applies to the unique aspects of partial presentations.

2.02 Prospective financial information may be referred to by a number of different names, such as forecasts, projections, feasibility studies, break-even analyses, and budgets. Whatever such information is called, it is considered to be prospective financial statements if the presentation fits the description of prospective financial statements.

2.03 The objective of some financial presentations, commonly called *pro forma information*, is to show what the significant effects on historical financial information might have been, had a consummated or proposed transaction (or event) occurred at an earlier date. Although the transactions in question may be prospective and such presentations may look like those described in the guide, the guide does not apply to those presentations because they are essentially historical statements and do not purport to be prospective financial statements.

Practitioners' Services

2.04 Practitioners are sometimes engaged for the expressed purpose of compiling, examining, or applying agreed-upon procedures to prospective financial statements. Often, however, they are engaged to assist their clients in other areas. Examples are obtaining financing, deciding whether to lease or buy an asset, consummating a merger or acquisition, determining the tax consequences of future actions, or planning future operations. In providing such services, practitioners become involved with prospective financial statements. Regardless of the objective of the engagement, this guide covers the professional services that practitioners may provide on prospective financial statements for third-party use: compilation, examination, and application of agreed-upon procedures.

2.05 Practitioners may also be engaged to provide the types of services described in the preceding paragraph in connection with prospective financial statements for internal use only and for partial presentations. Chapter 22, "Guidance on the Practitioner's Services and Reports on Prospective Financial Statements for Internal Use Only," provides guidance on the practitioner's

---

[1] See the definition of *prospective financial statements* that is presented in paragraph 3.03.

services and reports on prospective financial statements for internal use only. Chapter 23 describes how the guidance in chapters 6–22 applies to the unique aspects of partial presentations.

2.06 The practitioner may perform procedures to achieve the engagement's objectives that exceed the procedures discussed in this guide. For example, the guide is not intended to cover all aspects of performing financial feasibility studies, although such studies usually contain prospective financial statements. However, if a practitioner provides a service on a feasibility study that includes prospective financial statements, then this guide applies to that service and resulting report. (Paragraph 17.27 illustrates a report on an examination of a financial forecast contained in a feasibility study.)

2.07 Practitioners may be engaged to provide a variety of services relating to prospective financial information, such as providing assistance in developing forecasting systems and identifying factors to be considered in developing prospective financial statements. This guide is not intended to provide comprehensive guidance regarding such services.[2]

2.08 Sometimes, practitioners are associated with prospective financial information that may be used in a pending or potential formal legal proceeding before a trier of fact in connection with the resolution of a dispute between two or more parties. These services are often called litigation support services.

2.09 This guide does not apply to engagements involving prospective financial information used solely in connection with litigation support services. A practitioner may, however, look to this guide because it provides helpful guidance for many aspects of such engagements and may be referred to as useful guidance in such engagements. Litigation support services are engagements involving pending or potential formal legal proceedings before a trier of fact in connection with the resolution of a dispute between two or more parties, for example, when a practitioner acts as an expert witness. This exception is provided, because, among other things, the practitioner's work in such proceedings is ordinarily subject to detailed analysis and challenge by each party to the dispute. This exception does not apply, however, if either of the following occurs (see paragraph 10.03):

a. The practitioner is specifically engaged to issue or does issue an examination, a compilation, or an agreed-upon procedures report on prospective financial statements.

b. The prospective financial statements are for use by third parties who, under the rules of the proceedings, do not have the opportunity for analysis and challenge by each party to a dispute in a legal proceeding.

For example, creditors may not have such opportunities when prospective financial statements are submitted to them to secure their agreement to a plan of reorganization.

2.10 According to paragraph .06 of AT section 301, *Financial Forecasts and Projections* (AICPA, *Professional Standards*), occasionally, a practitioner may be engaged to prepare a financial analysis of a potential project where the engagement includes obtaining the information, making appropriate assumptions, and assembling the presentation. Such an analysis is not, and should not be characterized as, forecasted or projected information and would not be

---

[2] However, this guide may include information that would be useful to the practitioner when providing such services (see chapter 10, "Types of Practitioners' Services").

appropriate for general use unless a responsible party reviewed and adopted the assumptions and presentation and presented it as a financial forecast (see paragraph 10.13).

Chapter 3

Definitions

3.01 Certain terms are defined as follows for the purposes of this guide.

3.02 *Prospective financial information.* Any financial information about the future. The information may be presented as complete financial statements or limited to one or more elements, items, or accounts.

3.03 *Prospective financial statements.* Prospective financial information that presents financial position, results of operations, and cash flows. They are either financial forecasts or financial projections including the summaries of significant assumptions and accounting policies. Although prospective financial statements may cover a period that has partially expired, statements for periods that have completely expired are not considered to be prospective financial statements. Pro forma financial statements[1] and partial presentations are not considered to be prospective financial statements.

3.04 *Financial forecast.* Prospective financial statements that present, to the best of the responsible party's knowledge and belief, an entity's expected financial position, results of operations, and cash flows. A financial forecast is based on the responsible party's assumptions reflecting conditions it expects to exist and the course of action it expects to take. A financial forecast may be expressed in specific monetary amounts as a single-point estimate of forecasted results or as a range, where the responsible party selects key assumptions to form a range within which it reasonably expects, to the best of its knowledge and belief, the item or items subject to the assumptions to actually fall. If a forecast contains a range, the range is not selected in a biased or misleading manner (for example, a range in which one end is significantly less expected than the other). Minimum presentation guidelines for a financial forecast are set forth in paragraph 8.06.

3.05 *Financial projection.* Prospective financial statements that present, to the best of the responsible party's knowledge and belief, given one or more hypothetical assumptions, an entity's expected financial position, results of operations, and cash flows. A financial projection is sometimes prepared to present one or more hypothetical courses of action for evaluation, as in response to a question that begins for instance, "What would happen if . . . ?" A financial projection is based on the responsible party's assumptions reflecting conditions it expects would exist and the course of action it expects would be taken, given one or more hypothetical assumptions. A projection, like a forecast, may contain a range. Minimum presentation guidelines for a financial projection are set forth in paragraph 8.06.

3.06 *Partial presentation.* A presentation of prospective financial information that excludes one or more of the applicable items required for prospective financial statements set forth in paragraph 8.06.

3.07 *Entity.* Any unit, existing or to be formed, for which financial statements could be prepared in accordance with generally accepted accounting

---

[1] See paragraph 2.03 for a description of pro forma financial statements.

principles or special purpose frameworks.[2] For example, an entity can be an individual, partnership, corporation, trust, estate, association, or governmental unit.

3.08 *Hypothetical assumption.* An assumption used in a financial projection or in a partial presentation of projected information to present a condition or course of action that is not necessarily expected to occur, but is consistent with the purpose of the presentation.

3.09 *Responsible party.* The person or persons who are responsible for the assumptions underlying the prospective financial information. The responsible party usually is management, but it can be persons outside the entity who currently do not have the authority to direct operations (for example, a party considering acquiring the entity).[3]

3.10 *Management.* Those persons who are expected to direct the operations of the entity during the prospective period. Management typically refers to those persons at the highest level of authority within the entity.[4]

3.11 *Key factors.* The significant matters on which an entity's future results are expected to depend. Such factors are basic to the entity's operations and thus encompass matters that affect, among other things, the entity's sales, production, service, and financing activities. Key factors serve as a foundation for prospective financial information and are the bases for the assumptions.

3.12 *General use.* Use of prospective financial statements by persons with whom the responsible party is *not* negotiating directly.

3.13 *Limited use.* Use of prospective financial information by the responsible party alone or by persons with whom the responsible party *is* negotiating directly.

3.14 *Examination of prospective financial information.* A professional service that involves (*a*) evaluation of the preparation of the prospective financial information, the support underlying the assumptions, and the presentation of the prospective financial information for conformity with AICPA presentation guidelines, and (*b*) issuance of an examination report.

3.15 *Compilation of prospective financial information.* A professional service that involves assembly, to the extent necessary, of prospective financial information; consideration of whether the assumptions or presentation are obviously inappropriate; and issuance of a compilation report in which the practitioner expresses no conclusion or any other assurance.

3.16 *Assembly.* The manual or computer processing of mathematical or other clerical functions related to the presentation of the prospective financial information. Assembly does not refer to the mere reproduction and collation of such statements or to the responsible party's use of the practitioner's computer processing hardware or software.

---

[2] AU-C section 800, *Special Considerations—Audits of Financial Statements Prepared in Accordance With Special Purpose Frameworks* (AICPA, *Professional Standards*), discusses special purpose frameworks, commonly called *other comprehensive bases of accounting* or *OCBOA*).

[3] See chapter 5, "Responsibility for Prospective Financial Information."

[4] If the entity is to be formed in the future, the term *management* includes the promoters or other individuals who expect to be responsible for directing the operations of the entity.

Chapter 4

Types of Prospective Financial Information and Their Uses

4.01 Entities prepare prospective financial information for a variety of reasons. For example, an entity may want to obtain external financing, consider a change in operations or accounting, or prepare a budget. The reason for which the prospective financial information is prepared determines the type of prospective information developed.

4.02 Prospective financial information is for either *general use* or *limited use.* This chapter discusses the differences between the two uses and the types of presentations that are appropriate for those uses.

4.03 *General use* of prospective financial statements refers to use of the statements by persons with whom the responsible party is not negotiating directly, for example, in an offering statement of an entity's debt or equity interests. Because recipients of prospective financial statements distributed for general use are unable to ask the responsible party directly about the presentation, the presentation most useful to them is one that portrays, to the best of the responsible party's knowledge and belief, the expected results. Thus, only a financial forecast is appropriate for general use.

4.04 *Limited use* of prospective financial information refers to use of prospective financial information by the responsible party alone or by the responsible party and third parties with whom the responsible party is negotiating directly. Examples include use in negotiations for a bank loan, submission to a regulatory agency,[1] and use solely within the entity. Third-party recipients of prospective financial information intended for limited use can ask questions of the responsible party and negotiate the terms or structure of a transaction directly with such party. Any type of prospective financial information that would be useful in the circumstances would normally be appropriate for limited use. Thus, the presentation may be a financial forecast, a financial projection, or a partial presentation.

4.05 Because a financial projection is not appropriate for general use, it should not be distributed to those who will not be negotiating directly with the responsible party (for example, in an offering statement of an entity's debt or equity interests), unless the projection is used to supplement a financial forecast and is for a period covered by the forecast.

4.06 A partial presentation also may be appropriate in many limited-use situations. For example, a responsible party may prepare a partial presentation to analyze whether to lease or buy a piece of equipment or to evaluate the income tax implications of a given election because it may only be necessary to assess the impact on one aspect of financial results rather than on the financial statements taken as a whole. Therefore, a partial presentation is often appropriate for use by third parties who will be negotiating directly with the responsible party. However, a partial presentation is not ordinarily appropriate for general use.

---

[1] Submission to a regulatory agency is considered *limited use* even though, by law or regulation, the practitioner's report may be made a matter of public record.

4.07 The classification of prospective financial information use as either general or limited is not dependent on the number of users. Rather, the use is considered limited if each of the users negotiates directly with the responsible party; the use is considered to be general if the users do not. Thus, prospective financial information to be used by even one passive user would be considered general use, whereas use by a number of persons who all negotiate directly with the responsible party would be considered limited use.

4.08 The responsible party should have a reasonably objective basis to present a financial forecast in order for it to be appropriate for general use. Because users expect financial forecasts to present the responsible party's *best estimate*, the term *reasonably objective basis* is intended to communicate to responsible parties a measure of the quality of information necessary to present a forecast. The responsible party has a reasonably objective basis to present a forecast if sufficiently objective assumptions can be developed for each key factor. In some instances, the nature of one or more assumptions may be so subjective that the responsible party could have no reasonably objective basis to present a forecast (see paragraph 7.03). In that case, the responsible party generally should not present prospective financial statements for general use.

4.09 If the responsible party does not have a reasonably objective basis for one or more assumptions, it nonetheless may be able to present prospective financial information for limited use. For example, it might be appropriate for the responsible party to (*a*) establish hypothetical assumptions that have no reasonably objective basis and present a financial projection (see paragraph 7.01P) or (*b*) present a partial presentation (see chapter 23, "Partial Presentations of Prospective Financial Information") that omits the element, item, or account that does not have a reasonably objective basis.

Chapter 5

Responsibility for Prospective Financial Information

5.01 Prospective financial information, including the underlying assumptions, is the responsibility of the entity's *responsible party*.[1] The responsible party cannot guarantee the achievement of the financial results set forth in the prospective financial information because achievability depends on many factors that are outside of its control. However, the responsible party may influence the operations of an entity through planning, organizing, controlling, and directing its activities and, therefore, is in a position to develop reasonable or appropriate assumptions with respect to key factors.

5.02 The responsible party may enlist the assistance of outside parties in preparing prospective financial information. For example, a practitioner may provide such assistance by helping the responsible party to identify key factors, develop assumptions, gather information, or assemble the information. The practitioner may also be engaged to develop a financial model so the responsible party or others may consider the results by using a variety of assumptions. Such activities ordinarily would not affect the practitioner's objectivity in examining the prospective financial information.[2]

5.03 According to paragraph .06 of AT section 301, *Financial Forecasts and Projections* (AICPA, *Professional Standards*), regardless of the extent of the practitioner's participation, the assumptions remain the responsibility of the responsible party. The practitioner may assist in the formulation of assumptions, but the responsible party is nonetheless responsible for the preparation and presentation of the prospective financial statements because the prospective financial statements are dependent on the actions, plans, and assumptions of the responsible party, and only it can take responsibility for the assumptions. That should include evaluating the assumptions, making key decisions, and adopting and presenting the assumptions as its own.

5.04 Since the practitioner does not take responsibility for the assumptions, services on an entity's prospective financial information would not, per se, affect independence with regard to services on the entity's historical financial statements.

5.05 Occasionally, a practitioner may be engaged to prepare a financial analysis of a potential project in which the engagement includes obtaining information, making appropriate assumptions, and assembling the presentation. Such an analysis is not, and should not be, characterized as forecasted or projected information, and would not be appropriate for general use unless a responsible party reviewed and adopted the assumptions and presentation and presented it as a financial forecast (see paragraph 10.13).

---

[1] See the definition of *responsible party* in paragraph 3.09.

[2] Some of these services may not be appropriate if the practitioner is to be named in a filing with the Securities and Exchange Commission (SEC). The SEC and Public Company Accounting Oversight Board have different independence rules. Therefore, when providing services for public companies, the practitioner should be aware of those rules.

Part 2

Guidance for Entities That Issue Prospective Financial Statements

Chapter 6

Preparation Guidelines

Because financial forecasts and projections are similar in many respects, separate guidance for projections is provided only to the extent that it differs from that for forecasts. *Italicized* paragraphs in this chapter show how the guidance presented for forecasts should be modified for projections. Any plain-text paragraph not followed by an italicized paragraph applies to both forecasts and projections, even though it uses only the term *forecast*.

6.01 This chapter provides guidance to the responsible party for preparing financial forecasts. These guidelines are applicable in general, but the organizational and procedural means of applying them may differ from case to case because of the circumstances involved.

6.02 An entity can prepare financial forecasts without adhering to all the guidelines in this chapter. Using a process that incorporates these guidelines, however, often results in the development of more reliable prospective data than preparing financial forecasts without such a process. In addition to providing better management data, the use of such a process facilitates an independent practitioner's examination of the resulting financial forecasts.

6.03 A process for preparing financial forecasts may be any of the following:

    a. A formal system

    b. Performance of a work program that outlines the steps followed in preparation

    c. Documented procedures, methods, and practices used in preparation

The type of process used in preparing financial forecasts normally depends on the circumstances. In some cases, the complexity of the data involved or the regular use of the process may require a formal system. In many cases, however, the cost of a formal system exceeds the benefits derived from it, and an entity can satisfactorily prepare financial forecasts using either of the other processes. The three types of processes are discussed in the following paragraphs.

6.04 Financial forecasts may be prepared as the output of a formal system. A formal system consists of a set of policies, procedures, methods, and practices systematically applied by qualified personnel. It embraces inputs, processing, and outputs of the system and includes the collection, recording, analysis, interpretation, processing, and review of information concerning all elements of the enterprise.

6.05 A formal system also consists of a set of related policies, procedures, methods, and practices that are used to prepare financial forecasts, monitor attained results relative to the forecasts, and prepare revisions to or otherwise update, the forecasts.

6.06 Financial forecasts may also be prepared without a formal system. A formal work program outlining the steps followed in the preparation of the financial forecasts (which may be refined as work progresses), or a documentation of procedures, methods, and practices used in preparation, may take the place of a formal system and still conform to these guidelines. If a work program is used, it provides for adequate definition of the procedures, methods, and practices to be employed.

6.07 The guidelines in this chapter represent the elements that generally should be included in a process to develop financial forecasts. However, the guidelines may not apply to immaterial items.

6.08 The following is a summary of the guidelines for preparation of financial forecasts. These guidelines are discussed in the following paragraphs:

Paragraphs	*Guidelines an Entity Should Generally Apply*
6.09–.10P	Financial forecasts are prepared in good faith.
6.11–.14	Financial forecasts are prepared with appropriate care by qualified personnel.
6.15–.19	Financial forecasts are prepared using appropriate accounting principles.
6.20–.25	The process used to develop financial forecasts provides for seeking out the best information that is reasonably available at the time.
6.26–.27	The information used in preparing financial forecasts is consistent with the plans of the entity.
6.28–.29	Key factors are identified as a basis for assumptions.
6.30–.36	Assumptions used in preparing financial forecasts are appropriate.
6.37–.38	The process used to develop financial forecasts provides the means to determine the relative effect of variations on the major underlying assumptions.
6.39–.41	The process used to develop financial forecasts provides adequate documentation of both the financial forecasts and the process used to develop them.
6.42–.43	The process used to develop financial forecasts includes, where appropriate, the regular comparison of the financial forecasts with the attained results.
6.44–.46	The process used to prepare financial forecasts includes adequate review and approval by the responsible party at the appropriate levels of authority.

Financial forecasts are prepared in good faith.

6.09 The potential to mislead a third-party reader of financial forecasts is greater than that for historical financial statements. Preparation of financial forecasts necessitates the use of judgment, and the responsible party should make a good-faith effort in preparing such statements. Good faith in this context includes making a diligent effort to develop appropriate assumptions (see paragraphs 6.20–.38). Good faith also includes exercising care not to mislead a third-party reader. Accordingly, financial forecasts should be presented in conformity with the presentation guidelines in chapter 8, "Presentation Guidelines," of this guide, including appropriate disclosures.

6.10 Because a financial forecast reflects the responsible party's estimate of financial results based on its plans, good faith precludes preparing it with either undue optimism or pessimism.

6.10P *Although a financial forecast prepared in good faith is neither unduly optimistic nor pessimistic, the purpose of a financial projection may require optimism or pessimism. For example, a break-even analysis may be prepared by a real estate developer who expects to realize income. Accordingly, the hypothetical assumptions used in a financial projection should be consistent with the purpose of the projection; the other assumptions, including assumed courses of action, should be consistent with events expected to occur given the hypothetical assumptions.*

Financial forecasts are prepared with appropriate care by qualified personnel.

6.11 *Appropriate care* means that diligence and proper attention should be exercised in the preparation of the financial forecasts.

6.12 The preparation of financial forecasts ordinarily involves the use of large amounts of data and requires a great many calculations. These data may be processed without the benefit of the checks and balances inherent in a historical accounting system, which makes the preparation of financial forecasts particularly susceptible to clerical error. Established procedures will facilitate the prevention, detection, and correction of such errors.

6.13 The use of qualified personnel ensures that appropriate knowledge and competence are present or are acquired while developing the financial forecasts. Personnel having competence in marketing, operations, finance, research and engineering, and other technical areas as appropriate under the circumstances may participate in the development of the financial forecasts.

6.14 Analytical capability and expertise may be needed to analyze and interpret relevant historical data. In some circumstances, expertise in technical forecasting techniques and methods may be required.

Financial forecasts are prepared using appropriate accounting principles.

6.15 The accounting treatment applied to events and transactions contemplated in financial forecasts should be the same as the accounting treatment expected to be applied in recording the events when or if they occur.

6.16 Occasionally, in a financial forecast, a basis of accounting is used that is different from that used for historical financial statements. For example, a cash-basis statement may be prepared to determine cash flow. In these situations the process used to develop the financial forecast provides a means for reconciling the prospective results with those that would be obtained by using the basis of accounting used in historical financial statements.

6.17 From time to time, entities change the accounting principles they use. Such changes should be reflected in financial forecasts as they would be in historical financial statements. (Financial Accounting Standards Board [FASB]

Accounting Standards Codification [ASC] 250, *Accounting Changes and Error Corrections*, states that there is a presumption made in preparing financial statements that an accounting principle, once adopted, should not be changed in accounting for events and transactions of a similar type. According to FASB ASC 250-10-45-2, that presumption may be overcome only if the change is required by a newly issued codification update or the entity can justify the use of an alternative acceptable accounting principle on the basis that it is preferable.)

6.18 Because a financial forecast reflects an estimate of the entity's expected results, an accounting change should be reflected in the forecast only if the responsible party expects to make the change in the historical statements.

6.18P There are instances in which changes in accounting principles reflected in financial projections need not be expected to occur in the historical financial statements. For example, a projection may be prepared for the purpose of estimating an entity's financial results based on a change in the method by which inventories are valued. These may be prepared for analytical purposes with no intention of actually changing the method of inventory valuation.

6.19 If such changes in accounting treatment are contemplated, the process used to develop financial forecasts includes a means to reconcile the prospective results with those that would be obtained by using the accounting principles used in prior historical financial statements.

The process used to develop financial forecasts provides for seeking out the best information that is reasonably available at the time.

6.20 Information relevant to financial forecasts comes from many sources, both inside and outside an entity. An effective process to develop financial forecasts provides for searching out the best information that is reasonably available relevant to developing assumptions that are appropriate in relation to the presentation. The information used would include any relevant historical information.

6.20P Although this guideline applies to financial projections, it need not be applied to hypothetical assumptions selected to analyze alternative courses of action. However, the assumptions other than the hypothetical ones should be developed by the responsible party using the best information that is reasonably available at the time, given the hypothetical assumptions. For example, a financial projection might show results using several sales prices for the entity's product. The assumptions relating to semivariable costs (for example, commissions) should be developed based on the best information that is reasonably available for each sales price and consistent with the expected course of action at each sales price.

6.21 The acquisition of information ordinarily involves a cost, which is commensurate with the anticipated benefits to be derived from the information. For example, the cost of making a survey may far exceed any potential benefit, even though the survey might provide the most precise information available. This section does not intend that information be acquired regardless of cost, although cost alone is not sufficient reason not to acquire needed information.

6.22 Financial forecasts can be based only on information that is reasonably available at the time they are prepared. Often, pertinent information becomes available only after financial forecasts have been completed or disclosed, or after the prospective period has expired. The fact that information existed does not necessarily mean that it was available to the preparers of the financial forecasts.

6.23 Different sources of information involve different degrees of reliability. The reliability of the basic data should be considered in the process of preparing the financial forecasts.

6.24 A key consideration in the preparation of financial forecasts is the use of an appropriate level of detail. In certain situations, the use of more detail may improve the reliability of financial forecasts. For example, forecasting sales by product line rather than in the aggregate may improve the reliability of the sales forecasts, especially if the products sold are in different markets.

6.25 However, situations also exist in which the use of less detail or a more aggregated approach may improve reliability. For example, forecasting the cost for a common component contained in various product lines may be determined more effectively by grouping the product lines to ascertain the total quantity of the component expected to be used.

The information used in preparing financial forecasts is consistent with the plans of the entity.

6.26 Financial forecasts should be consistent with the expected economic effects of anticipated strategies, programs, and actions, including those being planned in response to expected future conditions.

6.26P *Financial projections need not necessarily be consistent with the plans of the responsible party but, instead, may represent alternatives based on a special purpose contemplated in preparing the presentation. The alternatives should reflect the responsible party's expected actions given the actual occurrence of the hypothetical event. For example, a manufacturing company that does not lay off workers during slow periods should not treat labor as a variable expense if the hypothetical event is a temporary reduction in production levels. The presentation should reflect the course of action consistent with its purpose.*

6.27 An indication of the responsible party's plans can often be found in its budgets, goals, and policies. These pertinent sources of information should be considered in the preparation of financial forecasts. In considering these sources of information, the entity determines whether they are unduly optimistic or pessimistic, and if they are, that fact should be taken into account when preparing financial forecasts. Plans and budgets are more reliable and credible when developed through the use of effective planning and control systems. Sound, timely reporting according to functional responsibility, together with effective planning and budgeting, form the foundation of a process that develops financial forecasts.

Key factors are identified as a basis for assumptions.

6.28 Key factors are those significant matters upon which an entity's future results are expected to depend. These factors are basic to the entity's operations and serve as the foundation for the prospective financial statements. Key factors vary by entity and industry.

6.29 All key factors should be identified in preparing financial forecasts. After such identification, assumptions should be developed for those key factors. For example, if a key factor is manufacturing labor, assumptions might be developed regarding manpower requirements and labor rates.

Assumptions used in preparing financial forecasts are appropriate.

6.30 Assumptions are the essence of developing financial forecasts and are the single most important determinant of such statements. The quality of the underlying assumptions largely determines the quality of financial forecasts.

6.31 The attention devoted to the appropriateness of a particular assumption should be commensurate with the likely relative impact of that assumption on the prospective results. Assumptions with greater impact should receive more attention than those with less impact.

6.32 The assumptions should be reasonable and suitably supported. The level of support should be persuasive, although there are times when a number of assumptions within a narrow range of possibilities may appear equally likely.

6.32P *Hypothetical assumptions need not be reasonable but should be appropriate in light of the purpose for which the financial projection is prepared. All other assumptions should be reasonable, given the hypothetical assumptions, and be consistent with the hypothetical assumptions and with each other. That is, the other assumptions should be developed to depict conditions based on the hypothetical assumptions. For example, if a financial projection is prepared to show the effect of the construction of a new production facility that is partially financed, the presentation should include the effect of the related debt service. Furthermore, hypothetical assumptions need not be supported, as they relate to the special purpose of the presentation. The other assumptions, however, should be suitably supported given the hypothetical assumptions.*

6.33 The nature of a business enterprise is such that many underlying assumptions are interrelated, and certain of their elements may have multiple effects. For example, a slowdown in economic activity typically will not only cause a slowdown in sales volume, but may also affect sales prices and the availability and cost of resources. The conditions assumed in arriving at the prospective sales or revenue data should be consistent with those assumed in developing the prospective financial data for the cost of operations. The entity should exercise care to ensure that appropriate costs and revenues have been considered, that sufficient capacity and resources would be available to produce the forecasted revenues, that capital expenditures have been recognized as appropriate, that provision has been made for applicable taxes, and that the need for financing has been considered.

6.34 Support for assumptions might include market surveys; general economic indicators; trends and patterns developed from the entity's operating history, such as historical sales trends; and internal data and analyses, such as obligations under union contracts for labor rates.

6.35 In analyzing alternative assumptions, care should be exercised to assess the situation objectively. Relating assumptions to past or present conditions often is a useful approach for checking reasonableness or appropriateness; however, trends are not necessarily reliable indicators of the future. The entity should consider paying particular attention to the possibility of changes in conditions, which rest mainly on theory and on an understanding of the basic causal factors.

6.36 It is ordinarily not feasible to exhaustively document and support all the assumptions underlying financial forecasts. It is nevertheless necessary to seek out and to identify explicitly the information that forms a basis for the most significant assumptions; although, frequently, the most basic assumptions with enormous potential impact, such as those relating to war or peace conditions, are not addressed explicitly. Despite precautions, hindsight will often reveal assumptions that have been overlooked or that, in light of later circumstances, received inadequate treatment. Furthermore, the nature of developing financial forecasts is such that some assumptions may not materialize, and unanticipated events and circumstances may occur no matter what effort, analysis, or support may be applied.

The process used to develop financial forecasts provides the means to determine the relative effect of variations in the major underlying assumptions.

6.37 Prospective financial results are relatively more sensitive to certain assumptions and less sensitive to others. Small changes in certain assumed conditions can result in relatively large variations in the prospective results, while relatively large changes in other assumptions cause only minor shifts in the prospective results.

6.38 In developing financial forecasts, an understanding of the relative sensitivity of the results to the assumed conditions permits the allocation of analysis and study, as well as review by persons of higher authority, to those areas with the most significant effects. The entity should consider paying particular attention to those assumptions (*a*) to which the attainment of forecasted results is particularly sensitive (that is, those in which a small variation in the assumptions would have a large effect on forecasted results) and (*b*) for which the probability of variation is high.

The process used to develop financial forecasts provides adequate documentation of both the financial forecasts and the process used to develop them.

6.39 Documentation makes possible the review and approval of financial forecasts by the responsible party. It facilitates the comparison of the financial forecasts with the actual financial results, and it provides the discipline necessary for developing reliable financial forecasts. Documentation enables the responsible party to analyze the key factors on which its assumptions are based, thereby allowing for the identification of changes in these factors and their anticipated effects, on a timely basis.

6.40 Documentation involves recording the underlying assumptions as well as summarizing the supporting evidence for the assumptions. Documentation also provides the ability to trace forecasted results back to the support for the basic underlying assumptions.

6.41 Adequate documentation makes it possible for persons who are experienced and qualified to develop financial forecasts to reconstruct the financial forecasts. Documentation covers the process, as well as the individual financial forecasts, and provides an organized record of both that can be maintained and made available for subsequent use.

The process used to develop financial forecasts includes, where appropriate, the regular comparison of the financial forecasts with the attained results.

6.42 The objective of financial forecasts is to estimate financial results, for one or more future periods, under expected conditions. The comparison of prospective financial results with actual results for the prospective period and for prior periods for which financial forecasts were prepared provides a historical measure of success in developing financial forecasts and may also be useful as an indication of the likely reliability of future financial forecasts. Regular comparison with actual results and analysis of deviations also provide a basis for making improvements in the methods and approaches used in developing financial forecasts; however, if there is no intention to prepare financial forecasts in the future, there may be no need for such comparisons and analyses.

6.43 If prospective results are compared to actual results, the comparison should not be limited to overall financial results but should also include comparison of the key factors and assumptions, such as sales volumes, prices, and production rates.

The process used to prepare financial forecasts includes adequate review and approval by the responsible party at the appropriate levels of authority.

6.44 Financial forecasts are important statements of the future financial results of an entity. The ultimate responsibility for financial forecasts rests with the responsible party at the highest level of authority, the same level as for historical financial statements.

6.45 Adequate review means that the review is conducted in sufficient depth to assure the responsible party of the soundness of the process used to develop the financial forecasts, and that the financial forecasts and subsequent revisions were prepared in accordance with the guidelines for the preparation of financial forecasts. The responsible party ordinarily would have access to the financial forecasts and supporting documentation in order to adequately review and approve the financial forecasts.

6.46 Review by the responsible party at intermediate levels of authority, including such functions as marketing, operations, engineering, and finance, enables the financial forecasts to be evaluated from several vantage points by those who will be responsible for the subsequent operations.

Chapter 7

Reasonably Objective Basis

> Because financial forecasts and projections are similar in many respects, separate guidance for projections is provided only to the extent that it differs from that for forecasts. *Italicized* paragraphs, with paragraph numbers that include a "P" in this chapter show how the guidance presented for forecasts should be modified for projections. Any plain-text paragraph not followed by an italicized paragraph applies to both forecasts and projections even though it uses only the term *forecast.*

7.01 The responsible party should have a reasonably objective basis to present a financial forecast. Because financial forecasts are presentations of information about the future, they are inherently less precise than information about past events. That "softness" of forecasted data is communicated to users of financial forecasts, in the introduction to the summary of significant assumptions, by including a caveat that the forecasted results may not be achieved.[1] Nevertheless, financial forecasts present, to the best of the responsible party's knowledge and belief, the entity's expected financial position, results of operations, and cash flows. The term *reasonably objective basis* communicates to responsible parties a measure of the quality of information that is necessary to present a financial forecast.

7.01P For a projection, the responsible party need not have a reasonably objective basis for the hypothetical assumptions, although, as noted in paragraph 3.08, the hypothetical assumptions should be consistent with the purpose of the projection. As the hypothetical assumptions increase in number, significance, or both, it may not be appropriate to present a projection.

7.02 Considerable judgment is required to evaluate whether a reasonably objective basis exists to present a financial forecast. Sufficient knowledge of the entity's business and industry is essential in making the evaluation.

7.03 The responsible party has a reasonably objective basis to present a financial forecast if sufficiently objective assumptions can be developed for each key factor. (Paragraph 3.11 defines *key factors* as the significant matters on which the entity's future results are expected to depend. Such factors are basic to the entity's operations and thus encompass matters that affect, among other things, the entity's sales, production, service, and financing activities.) The following matters should be considered when evaluating whether such assumptions can be developed:

- Can facts be obtained and informed judgments made about past and future events or circumstances in support of the underlying assumptions?

- Are any of the significant assumptions so subjective that no reasonably objective basis could exist to present a financial forecast? (For example, the responsible party might not have a reasonably objective

---

[1] Paragraph 8.29 illustrates the type of caveat to be included: "There will usually be differences between the forecasted and actual results, because events and circumstances frequently do not occur as expected, and those differences may be material."

basis to present a forecast that includes royalty income from products not yet invented or revenue from a thoroughbred being reared to race. In such cases, it would be inappropriate to present a forecast because of the lack of a reasonably objective basis.)

- Would people knowledgeable in the entity's business and industry select materially similar assumptions?

- Is the length of the forecast period appropriate? (See paragraphs 8.32–.34.)

Other matters that responsible parties may consider when evaluating whether sufficiently objective assumptions can be developed are shown in exhibit 7-1.

7.04 The evaluation of whether sufficiently objective assumptions can be developed for each key factor should be made within the following context:

- A factor is evaluated by considering its significance to the entity's plans and the dollar magnitude and pervasiveness of the related assumption's potential effect on forecasted results (for example, whether assumptions developed would materially affect the amounts and presentation of numerous forecasted amounts).

  The responsible party's consideration of which key factors have the greatest potential impact on forecasted results is a matter of judgment and is influenced by the responsible party's perception of the needs of a reasonable person who will rely on the financial forecast. A key factor having the greatest potential impact on forecasted results is one in which omission or misstatement of the related assumption would probably, in light of surrounding circumstances, change or influence the judgment of a reasonable person relying on the financial forecast. (The more likely an assumption will have a significant impact on the overall forecasted results, and the more likely the factors that relate to the assumption indicate a less objective basis, the more likely a judgment should be made that there is no reasonably objective basis to present a financial forecast.)

- The responsible party should seek out the best information that is available in order to develop the assumptions. Cost alone is an insufficient reason not to acquire needed information. However, the cost of incremental information should be commensurate with the anticipated benefit to be derived.

- A conclusion that a reasonably objective basis exists for a forecast might be easier to support if the forecast were presented as a range.

Exhibit 7-1

Sufficiently Objective Assumptions—Matters to Consider

Basis	Less Objective	More Objective
Economy	Subject to uncertainty	Relatively stable
Industry	Emerging or unstable; high rate of business failure	Mature or relatively stable
Entity:		
• Operating history	Little or no operating history	Seasoned company; relatively stable operating history
• Customer base	Diverse, changing customer group	Relatively stable customer group
• Financial condition	Weak financial position; poor operating results	Strong financial position; good operating results
Management's experience with:		
• Industry	Inexperienced management	Experienced management
• The business and its products	Inexperienced management; high turnover of key personnel	Experienced management
Products or services:		
• Market	New or uncertain market	Existing or relatively stable market
• Technology	Rapidly changing technology	Relatively stable technology
• Experience	New products or expanding product line	Relatively stable products
Competing assumptions	Wide range of possible outcomes	Relatively narrow range of possible outcomes
Dependency of assumptions on the outcome of the forecasted results[1]	More dependency	Less dependency

[1] Assumptions that depend on the achievement of other forecasted results. For example, the sales price of a real estate property in a forecast might be estimated by applying a capitalization rate to forecasted cash flows.

7.05 In addition to a reasonably objective basis, paragraphs 6.30–.36 call for the responsible party to develop appropriate assumptions to present a financial forecast. When evaluating whether assumptions underlying the financial forecast are appropriate, the responsible party should consider numerous factors, including whether

- there appears to be a rational relationship between the assumptions and the underlying facts and circumstances (that is, whether the assumptions are consistent with past and current conditions).

- the assumptions are complete (that is, assumptions have been developed for each key factor).

- it appears that the assumptions were developed without undue optimism or pessimism.

- the assumptions are consistent with the entity's plans and expectations.

- the assumptions are consistent with each other.

- the assumptions, in the aggregate, make sense in the context of the forecast taken as a whole.

7.06 Assumptions that have no material impact on the presentation may not have to be individually evaluated; however, the aggregate impact of individually insignificant assumptions should be considered in making an overall evaluation of whether the assumptions underlying the forecast are appropriate.

7.07 Paragraphs 7.08–.41 describe the facts and circumstances considered by the responsible party when evaluating whether there was a reasonably objective basis to present a financial forecast in each of three different examples:

- Paragraphs 7.08–.14 discuss a real estate developer who wants to forecast a proposed refinancing.

- Paragraphs 7.15–.30 describe a high-tech company that wants to forecast sales of a new product line.

- Paragraphs 7.31–.41 present a start-up company that wants to forecast its first two years of operations.

7.08 Example 1. An established builder of single-family homes has built two garden-apartment complexes in the last three years. He plans to build another garden-apartment complex and wants to syndicate the project. Both of the existing garden-apartment complexes are approaching full occupancy. The local economy is strong and has a diversified base. Furthermore, real estate in the area generally appreciates in value. There has been significant development in the area and, if it continues, supply will exceed demand within four years. The developer has appropriately considered this factor, as well as the associated cost of maintaining the proposed facility, in planning the project and developing the forecast.

7.09 In the past, the developer has financed each of his projects for 5 years at the maximum amount allowed by local financial institutions. Forecasts for the previous 2 projects assumed a 5-year financing period and a hypothetical sale of the property at the end of the forecast period. For the proposed development, the developer has obtained a commitment for a 3-year interest-only loan for an amount equal to 70 percent of the project's estimated cost. Current discussions with bankers have indicated a willingness to convert that loan to long-term financing for the project after rental stabilization, which is consistent with normal lending practices. The developer has indicated that he plans to refinance the committed loan after 3 years for an amount that exceeds the loan by approximately 76 percent. Such additional amounts (net of refinancing costs) are to be returned to the investors as a cash distribution. The developer's other resources are not sufficient to provide a meaningful guarantee of the refinancing. The forecast will be for 5 years, and will include a projection illustrating a hypothetical sale at the end of the forecast period. The facts can be summarized as follows.

	(In thousands)
• Estimated cost of the development to the partnership	$ 10,000
• Committed financing (interest-only loans) at 70 percent of the estimated cost	$ 7,000
• Proposed limited partnership investment	$ 3,000
• Amount of proposed refinancing:	
— Long-term refinancing of the three-year committed loan	$ 7,000
— Additional financing for payments to limited partners	5,000
— Cost of refinancing	300
	$ 12,300
• Forecasted cash flow before debt service for the fourth year	$ 1,500
• Capitalization rate (considered in this example to be acceptable under the circumstances)	9%
• Capitalized value at the end of the third year	$ 16,700

7.10 Question. Does the developer (the responsible party) have a reasonably objective basis to forecast the proposed refinancing?[2]

7.11 Answer.[3] This question can be divided into two further questions:

    a. Can the developer forecast a refinancing?

    b. Are the assumptions about the amount and terms of the refinancing sufficiently objective?

7.12 *Forecast of refinancing.* The developer has obtained a financing commitment for three years, based on local lending practices, and bankers have indicated a willingness to provide permanent financing in a manner that is consistent with these lending practices. Accordingly, it appears that the developer would have a reasonably objective basis for forecasting the project's

---

[2] Paragraphs 12.11*j* and 10.14–.15 include a discussion of a practitioner's responsibility to evaluate whether a responsible party has a reasonably objective basis for a financial forecast when engaged to compile or examine the forecast.

[3] This response is based on information presented in the question. Other information, such as that about the size and strength of the local economy, the precise locality of the project, local planning regulations, and the availability of third-party guarantees on the proposed refinancing, could change the response.

refinancing for a comparable amount in three years.[4] At that time, the building will still be considered relatively new and, based on maintenance plans, should be in good condition. Furthermore, real estate in the area generally is expected to appreciate in value, and forecasted cash flows (before debt service) are consistent with a refinancing assumption.

7.13 *Amount and terms of refinancing.* Although the developer may have a reasonably objective basis for a forecast that includes a refinancing for an amount approximating the original loan, it is not clear that such a basis exists for one that includes a refinancing significantly in excess of that amount. The following factors should be considered:[5]

- Although the local economy is strong and diversified, competing developments are being built and, in fact, there is some risk that supply could exceed demand.

- The developer has factored the effect of an increase in the supply of competing housing units into the forecast and may point to an estimated value of the project at the end of the third year, based on the application of a current capitalization rate to forecasted cash flows. However, capitalization rates may vary over time, and estimated values derived from the application of capitalization rates depend on the achievement of prospective cash flows.

- The developer is an experienced builder; however, he has limited experience in larger projects and has limited resources.

7.14 Based on the facts presented, it appears that the developer's basis for refinancing the project at an amount significantly greater than the original loan would be highly dependent on future events and circumstances such as anticipated cash flows, economic conditions, lending practices, and capitalization rates. Although forecasted results may be used as a basis for a refinancing assumption, in the absence of other supporting information, such results ordinarily would not provide a responsible party with a basis for concluding that the refinancing assumption was sufficiently objective. In this case, the developer's limited resources and the length of time until the refinancing would take place are all risk factors that mitigate reliance on forecasted results to provide support for the developer's assertion that a reasonably objective basis exists for the refinancing. Accordingly, in the absence of additional information, the facts in this case do not appear to support the developer's assertion that a reasonably objective basis exists for a forecast that includes the proposed refinancing assumption.[6]

7.15 Example 2. ACTech, Inc. was established to produce a line of flat-panel, AC-plasma computer-display products for use when, because of their

---

[4] Support for forecasted interest rates may exist in the form of interest-rate forecasts and current interest-rate trends. If interest-rate fluctuations are a concern, a conclusion that sufficiently objective interest assumptions could be developed may be easier to support if forecasted results are presented as a range (through the use of a range forecast).

[5] These items were developed by reference to the factors included in exhibit 7-1.

[6] In this example, the developer could consider including a refinancing for the committed amount ($7,000,000) in the forecast, and supplementing the forecast with a financial projection illustrating prospective results if the permanent financing obtained were for the greater amount ($12,300,000).

bulk and thickness, cathode-ray tubes (CRTs) would not be suitable.[7] The company was incorporated in 20X0 by former members of a management team (the founders), who designed the product and operated the business as a division of BigCo. The founders have purchased equipment and certain technology at a significant discount from BigCo with $1 million of funds raised from private investors. ACTech's goal is to become a leader in the production and sale of AC-plasma-display products by using newly developed but unproven technology to lower the cost of production and thereby compete more effectively with DC-plasma-display products. DC products are currently in common use due to their lower unit cost, but they are inferior to AC-plasma-display products in brightness and resolution.

7.16 *Product line and competition.* The mainstay of the ACTech product line will be a "plasma display system," which combines the AC-plasma-display panels with new low-cost drive circuitry. When compared to the most competitive product, the DC-plasma-display, ACTech's product is three times as bright with no flicker, consumes half the power for an equivalent level of light output, has a wider viewing angle, can be produced in much larger sizes, and has a longer life. DC panels are currently cheaper to produce, but with ACTech's circuitry and manufacturing expertise, management hopes to close the cost gap. ACTech is currently working on the implementation of its new technology. Prototypes have been successfully produced, but management estimates that, by using the equipment purchased from BigCo, it will need about a year to design and install a high volume production line.

7.17 Competition from other AC-plasma-display manufacturers will come primarily from ACpan, a very large manufacturer that uses most of its output in its own products. ACpan AC-plasma-displays have been available for the past five years and are comparable in quality to those of ACTech. Despite continued efforts, ACpan has achieved very little market penetration because, like ACTech and other producers of AC-plasma-displays, ACpan has not been able to successfully design and install a high volume production line. If successfully developed, ACTech's manufacturing process and the low-cost drive circuits will permit it to compete advantageously with ACpan. Other manufacturers of AC-plasma-displays charge prices that are higher than those of the ACpan products and that cater to military and specialty markets. In the market for large-screen sizes, management believes that there is no effective flat-panel competition.

7.18 Additionally, ACTech has received oral assurances from BigCo that it will purchase plasma displays from ACTech in sufficient quantities to meet its needs, which would account for about 5 percent of ACTech's estimated sales.

7.19 *Sales and marketing.* ACTech will sell primarily to equipment manufacturers via an internal sales force. Additionally, ACTech will use manufacturers' representatives or sales organizations to penetrate selected foreign markets. ACTech's products will be demonstrated at various trade shows and will be advertised in the appropriate trade journals.

7.20 ACTech has targeted specific markets for its primary growth. These markets include those for (*a*) mainframe interactive applications (ACTech, when it was a division of BigCo, had already established a small market in this

---

[7] Although flat-screen monitors are now common, when this example was developed for a 1992 Statement of Position they had not yet been economically mass-produced. The example is still useful because it illustrates the types of considerations used to determine whether there is a reasonably objective basis for new products or technologies. Considering these factors for flat-screen monitors in light of today's technology might yield a different conclusion.

area), (*b*) portable personal computers (ACTech is currently involved in discussions with several large companies in this market), (*c*) CAD/CAM/CAE workstations (ACTech is currently involved in discussions with producers serving both financial and design markets), and (*d*) manufacturing control products (ACTech is working with a company that uses a plasma panel with a touch screen to support the manufacturing process).

7.21 ACTech has estimated sales of approximately $600,000 in 20X2; $16 million in 20X3; and $40 million in 20X4. At anticipated levels of industry growth (provided from an outside source), these sales figures represent 0.3 percent, 6 percent, and 11 percent of the plasma-panel market, respectively.

7.22 *Product manufacture.* Management believes that the equipment purchased from BigCo by the founders is state of the art. ACTech is in the process of relocating the equipment to a new facility and setting up a modern, automated production facility. This new facility, which requires some renovation, will allow ACTech to begin production on a limited scale in about six months. Ample room exists for future expansion. No significant problems are expected in relocating and setting up the new facility, assuming that design problems related to high volume production can be overcome.

7.23 Production is expected to be at 500 AC-plasma-display-system units in 20X2, growing to 36,000 in 20X3, and 115,000 in 20X4.

7.24 *Management and personnel.* The ACTech management team is recognized throughout the computer industry as a leader in plasma-display technology and manufacturing. Together, the 4 founders have over 50 years of experience in the field of flat-panel displays. In addition, the founders have demonstrated significant academic and manufacturing achievements in the field of display technology. At present, ACTech has 3 full-time and 11 part-time employees. Management plans to hire an additional 35 employees during 20X2, including 3 marketing and sales employees.

7.25 Management expects employment to grow to about 250 by 20X4. Although production employees must be hired and trained, the labor market is sufficient to supply an adequate labor force with the basic technical skills needed to perform the required tasks, and management has experience in training. Further, management has had discussions with several candidates for the sales positions and does not anticipate difficulties in hiring qualified staff.

7.26 Question. Does management have a reasonably objective basis to present a financial forecast?[8]

7.27 Answer.[9] ACTech, Inc.'s financial forecast is based on two primary assumptions: (1) the successful design and installation of a high volume production line that would enable the company to reduce unit costs significantly, and (2) the timing and quantity of sales.

7.28 *High volume production.* ACTech is planning to manufacture and sell AC-plasma-display products for use in computer terminals. Its success will be highly dependent on its ability to produce those products in large quantities for sale at prices competitive with DC plasma products. Although prototypes of the company's products have been produced, circuitry compatible with high volume

---

[8] See footnote 2.

[9] This response is based on the information presented in the question. Other information about the status of engineering plans, the preproduction models, and marketing results could change the response. The response was developed by reference to the factors included in exhibit 7-1.

production has been developed, and experienced management has been hired, the company has yet to design and install the planned high volume production line. As indicated previously, management's current estimate is that it will be at least 12 months before that work is completed. Furthermore, the facts presented indicate that other manufacturers of AC-plasma-display units have not been successful in reducing production costs. BigCo's willingness to sell off its AC-plasma-display division may also indicate uncertainty about its ability to reduce production costs.

7.29 For the reasons discussed in the preceding paragraph, management's assumption that it will be able to achieve high volume, low cost production is relatively subjective. That assumption is critical to the company's sales assumptions, which depend on the reduction of production costs to a level that permits a pricing structure competitive with the pricing of DC-plasma units. Without a competitive pricing structure, the company's sales assumptions do not appear to be valid. Accordingly, ACTech does not appear to have a reasonably objective basis for presenting a financial forecast.

7.30 *Other matters.* If the feasibility of a high volume production line capable of producing AC-plasma units at a cost that permits ACTech to competitively price its product could be reasonably assured, a reasonably objective basis might exist for presenting a financial forecast. Before that conclusion can be reached, consideration should be given to ACTech's assumptions regarding market penetration. ACTech has developed a sales and marketing plan; however, questions exist concerning its assumptions of an aggressive market penetration (for example, capturing 11 percent of the plasma-panel market by the end of 20X4). There are several factors that appear to support its sales assumptions: the technological superiority of its products, competitive pricing, management's experience with its products, and the acceptability of the product to current users, such as BigCo. Nevertheless, it would be appropriate to gather additional information concerning marketing results to date before concluding whether a sufficiently objective basis exists for the assumptions regarding market penetration. Further, uncertainty concerning the company's sales assumptions may indicate that such assumptions would be easier to support if a range forecast were presented. (Exhibits 9-4 and 9-5 illustrate range forecasts.)

7.31 Example 3. As indicated in paragraph 8.33, it may be difficult to support an assertion that a reasonably objective basis exists to present a financial forecast for start-up companies. The following example illustrates a situation where a two-year forecast for a start-up company might be appropriate.

7.32 Newco was established to manufacture wall panels with self-contained insulation for use in commercial and industrial projects. The panels provide a lightweight interior and exterior wall combination. The company was incorporated in 20X0 by a former executive of one of the leaders in the wall-panel market, and by an individual who helped to develop the original technology 10 years ago (the founders). The founders have invested $1,000,000, which was used to order initial equipment and lease a building. Newco has sufficient capital to operate during the forecast period.

7.33 Although more expensive than those using traditional materials, the panels have proven to be easier to install than rolled or blown-in insulation and wall surface combinations. Therefore, the use of the insulated wall panels in construction has been increasing. Competition in the wall-panel market includes two divisions of publicly held corporations that produce the panels, along with a variety of other construction materials, in a number of plants. These competitors generally service the large-project market and are known to have significant backlogs. From interviews with industry sources, it has been determined that these companies have been unable to respond to small or rush orders. Newco believes that, as an entrepreneurial company having low overhead and specializing in one product, it can service the small-order market effectively and profitably.

7.34 Sales would be generated through bid contracts advertised by a clearinghouse that provides information to contractors and through the establishment of long-term relationships with engineering and architectural professionals. After lengthy correspondence with these professionals, Newco has obtained commitments for approximately 5 percent of its production capacity for 20X1 and 20X2 (about 25 percent and 15 percent of forecasted sales in 20X1 and 20X2, respectively). In addition, the initial equipment installation has allowed Newco to respond to selected advertised bids and obtain contracts for one-third of the opportunities pursued. These contracts account for 10 percent to 12 percent of the plant's capacity and extend through 20X2 (representing 50 percent and 35 percent of forecasted sales in 20X1 and 20X2, respectively). Newco plans to expand its sales force to enable it to respond to additional opportunities.

7.35 In estimating its sales, Newco considered the growth in the construction market, the increasing conversion to manufactured wall panels, its success rate in bidding opportunities, the planned growth of its sales force, and the number of orders received to date. Newco has estimated sales of approximately 20 percent and 33 percent of production capacity in 20X1 and 20X2, respectively. These sales figures would represent market shares of 2 percent to 3 percent of the bid market for insulated wall panels. In addition to clearinghouse data used to assess market growth and size, management has considered industry sources that provide significant information on construction and usage potentials in making its sales estimates.

7.36 The application of the technology involved in the production process continues to serve as a deterrent to entering into the small-order market. Newco's initial investment has allowed for limited-scale production, and no significant problems are expected in obtaining the additional equipment and achieving forecasted capacity. Further, the company has been able to manufacture a quality product within its range of estimated costs.

7.37 The founders are recognized within the industry for their technological and manufacturing expertise. Management has hired financial and production management executives, and is in the process of making its selection of three additional salespeople from a number of candidates experienced in the industry. Although additional production employees must be hired and trained, the labor market is sufficient to supply an adequate labor force with the basic technical skills needed to perform the required tasks.

7.38 Question. Does management have a reasonably objective basis to present a financial forecast for 20X1 and 20X2?[10]

---

[10] See footnote 2.

7.39 Answer.[11] Yes. Given the facts in this case, it appears that Newco has a reasonably objective basis to forecast its operations for the years 20X1 and 20X2.

7.40 Newco's product currently exists in the market and represents a technologically proven alternative that competes with similar technology and alternatives based upon price. Furthermore, the quality of its production and costs incurred to date have been in line with management's expectations. Accordingly, Newco's ability to forecast operating results depends on the primary assumption of the timing and quantity of sales.

7.41 Management's ability to identify competitors, analyze customer buying motives, and evaluate the market as well as the potential end usage demand are important determinants in forecasting sales. However, it is management's demonstrated success in identifying and establishing a specific customer base and in establishing a bidding track record that provides an important validation of its assessments of competition, pricing, and industry practices; it also provides the basis for management's sales forecast capabilities. Current contracts and commitments would account for a substantial portion of forecasted sales for 20X1 and 20X2, and the company's bidding success rate, coupled with the imminent hiring of experienced sales personnel, appears to provide a basis for estimated increases in sales during those years.

---

[11] This response is based on information presented in the question. Other information, such as that about the economy and its effect on Newco's industry and its forecasted results, may change this response. The response was developed by reference to the factors included in exhibit 7-1.

Chapter 8

Presentation Guidelines[1]

> Because financial forecasts and projections are similar in many respects, separate guidance for projections is provided only to the extent that it differs from that for forecasts. *Italicized* paragraphs in this chapter that include a "P" in the paragraph number show how the guidance presented for forecasts should be modified for projections. Any plain-text paragraph not followed by an italicized paragraph applies to both forecasts and projections even though it uses only the term *forecast.*

8.01 This chapter provides presentation guidelines for entities that issue financial forecasts.

Uses of a Financial Forecast

8.02 As explained in chapter 4, "Types of Prospective Financial Information and Their Uses," a financial forecast may be either for general use or for limited use. Because users of forecasts for general use may not have the opportunity to negotiate directly with the responsible party, they are best served by a presentation that presents, to the best of the responsible party's knowledge and belief, its expected financial position, results of operations, and cash flows,[2] that is, a financial forecast.

8.02P *As explained in chapter 4, financial projections are limited-use presentations and thus should not be submitted to those who do not have the opportunity to negotiate directly with the responsible party.*

Responsibility for Financial Forecasts

8.03 The responsibility for presentation of a financial forecast in conformity with these guidelines is analogous to that for the presentation of historical financial statements; that is, it is the responsibility of the *responsible party.*[3] The responsible party may enlist the assistance of outside parties to meet these presentation guidelines.

8.04 As discussed in chapter 7, "Reasonably Objective Basis," the responsible party should have a reasonably objective basis to present a financial forecast.

---

[1] Although this chapter presents guidelines for entities preparing prospective financial statements, AT sections are noted throughout where applicable so that the entity is aware of the requirements and guidelines placed upon practitioners examining prospective financial statements.

[2] A financial forecast may be summarized or condensed. Paragraph 8.06 describes the minimum items that constitute a forecast.

[3] See the definition of *responsible party* in paragraph 3.09.

Title

8.05 The title used for a financial forecast should describe the nature of the presentation and should include the word *forecast* or *forecasted*.

8.05P   Statement titles in financial projections are descriptive of the presentation. Accordingly, they do not imply that the presentation is a forecast. In addition, titles describe or refer to any significant hypothetical assumptions. For example, a break-even analysis might be titled "Projected Results of Operations and Cash Flows at Break-Even Sales Volume."

Format

8.06 Prospective information presented in the format of historical financial statements facilitates comparisons with financial position, results of operations, and cash flows of prior periods, as well as those actually achieved for the prospective period. Accordingly, prospective financial information preferably should be in the format of the historical financial statements that would be issued for the period(s) covered unless there is an agreement between the responsible party and potential users specifying another format. Financial forecasts may take the form of complete basic financial statements[4] or may be limited to the following items (where such items would be presented for historical financial statements for the period):[5]

    a. Sales or gross revenues

    b. Gross profit or cost of sales

    c. Unusual or infrequently occurring items

    d. Provision for income taxes

    e. Income from continuing operations

    f. Discontinued operations or extraordinary items

    g. Net income

    h. Basic and diluted earnings per share

    i. Significant changes in financial position[6]

    j. A description of what the responsible party intends for the financial forecast to present, a statement that the assumptions are based on

---

[4] The details of each statement may be summarized or condensed so that only the major items in each are presented. The usual footnotes associated with historical financial statements need not be included as such. However, items (*j*), (*k*), and (*l*) generally should be included.

[5] Similar types of financial information generally should be presented for entities for which these terms do not describe operations, as illustrated in paragraph 9.02. Furthermore, similar items generally should be presented if a different financial reporting framework is used to present the forecast. For example, if the forecast is presented on the cash basis, item (*a*) would be cash receipts. The basis of accounting on which the forecast is presented generally should be appropriate for the use of the forecast.

[6] The responsible party should disclose significant cash flows and other significant changes in balance sheet accounts during the period. However, neither a balance sheet nor a statement of cash flows, as described in Financial Accounting Standards Board (FASB) *Accounting Standards Codification* (ASC) 230, *Statement of Cash Flows*, is required. Furthermore, none of the specific captions or disclosures required by FASB ASC 230 are required. Significant changes disclosed will depend on the circumstances; however, such disclosures will often include cash flows from operations. Exhibits 9-2 and 9-6 illustrate alternative methods of presenting significant changes in financial position.

the responsible party's judgment at the time the prospective information was prepared, and a caveat that the forecasted results may not be achieved

k. Summary of significant assumptions

l. Summary of significant accounting policies

8.07 Items (a)–(i) in paragraph 8.06 represent the minimum items that constitute a financial forecast. A presentation that omits one or more of those that are applicable[7] is a partial presentation, which would not ordinarily be appropriate for general use.[8] If the omitted applicable item is derivable from the information presented, the presentation would *not* be deemed to be a partial presentation.

8.08 Items (j)–(l) in paragraph 8.06 are disclosures that should accompany the forecast, whether the presentation is limited to applicable minimum items or presents more detail. The omission of item (j), (k), or (l) from a presentation that contains at least the applicable minimum items would not make it a partial presentation; it would be a deficient presentation because of the lack of required disclosures.

8.09 The guidelines for preparation of financial forecasts (chapter 6, "Preparation Guidelines") apply even if the presentation is limited to the minimum items in the previous list. Therefore, the underlying data used in the preparation of financial forecasts should be sufficient to allow presentation of detailed statements, even though only the minimum are to be presented.[9]

8.10 Each page of a financial forecast should contain a statement that directs the reader to the summaries of significant assumptions and accounting policies.

Date

8.11 The date of completion of the preparation of a financial forecast should be disclosed. The responsible party should be satisfied that the assumptions are appropriate as of this date, even though the underlying information may have been accumulated over a period of time. Such a disclosure assists users in determining how current the presentation is and serves as a warning when such statements were prepared some time ago. Paragraph 8.29 (an example introduction to the summary of significant assumptions) illustrates such a disclosure.

Accounting Principles and Policies

8.12 A summary of significant accounting policies used in preparing the financial forecast should be disclosed. If a financial forecast is included in a document that contains some of this information, disclosure can be accomplished by cross-referencing.

---

[7] An applicable item is one that is presented for historical financial statements. For example, earnings per share is not an applicable item for a non public entity because earnings per share is not required to be presented for historical financial statements for such entities.

[8] See chapter 23, "Partial Presentations of Prospective Financial Information," for a discussion of partial presentations.

[9] This level of detail should ordinarily be comparable to that presented in historical financial statements.

8.13 Financial forecasts usually should be prepared on a basis consistent with the accounting principles expected to be used in the historical financial statements covering the prospective period (see paragraphs 6.15–.19).

8.13P Although ordinarily a financial projection should use the accounting principles expected to be used in the historical statements, sometimes the special purpose of the presentation requires that it be prepared based on other accounting principles. In such cases, the use of different accounting principles should be disclosed. Differences in financial position and results of operations arising from the use of different accounting principles may be reconciled and disclosed. An example of such a disclosure follows.

> *The projection assumes that inventory will be valued on the last-in, first-out method, whereas the company has historically used the first-in, first-out method. If the latter method were used in this projection, inventory and income before income taxes would be increased by $XX, provision for income taxes would be increased and other working capital decreased by $XX, and net income and shareholders' equity would be increased by $XX.*

8.14 If the historical financial statements for the prospective period are expected to be prepared in conformity with a financial reporting framework other than generally accepted accounting principles, the financial forecast preferably should be prepared on that basis of accounting, and the specific information required to be presented adapted as appropriate for the basis of accounting used. The basis of accounting used should be disclosed, along with the fact that the disclosed basis is different than generally accepted accounting principles

8.15 Ideally, prospective financial statements and historical financial statements should be available to users on the same basis of accounting. Occasionally, a different financial reporting framework is used for a financial forecast than that to be used for the historical financial statements for the prospective period. In such situations, the use of a different basis should be disclosed, and differences in results of operations and changes in financial position or cash flows resulting from the use of a different basis usually would be reconciled in the financial forecast. In some circumstances, such as certain tax shelters, a detailed reconciliation would not be useful. In such a case, a general description of the differences resulting from the use of different bases should be presented. Exhibit 9-6 illustrates a reconciliation in the case of a cash-basis projection where the historical financial statements are expected to be prepared in conformity with generally accepted accounting principles.[10]

8.16 If a financial forecast gives effect to a change in accounting principles from one used in prior-period historical financial statements, the change should be reported in the financial forecast for the period in which it is expected to be made, as would be required in reporting such an accounting change in historical financial statements.[11]

Materiality

8.17 The concept of materiality applies to financial forecasts; thus, the provisions of this chapter need not be applied to immaterial items. Materiality

---

[10] Although the example shown is a financial projection, the reconciliation in that example would be applicable to a financial forecast as well.

[11] See FASB ASC 250, *Accounting Changes and Error Corrections*, for guidance relevant to accounting for and disclosing changes in accounting principles (see paragraph 6.17).

is a concept that is judged in light of the expected range of reasonableness of the information, and therefore prospective information (information about events that have not yet occurred) is not expected to be as precise as historical information.

Presentation of Amounts

8.18 Financial forecasts are normally expressed in specific monetary amounts as a single-point estimate of forecasted results, but also can be expressed as a range if the responsible party selects key assumptions to form a range within which it reasonably expects, to the best of its knowledge and belief, the item or items subject to the assumptions actually to fall. The tentative nature of financial forecasts may be emphasized if the amounts representing the key measures (for example, sales and interest expense) were supplemented by analysis of the sensitivity of the forecast to variations. If a forecast contains a range, the range should not be selected in a biased or misleading manner (for example, a range in which one end is significantly less expected than the other).

8.19 If a forecast contains a range, the width of the range generally indicates the responsible party's relative uncertainty about the forecast. As the uncertainty surrounding the forecast increases, the range ordinarily would widen. However, if the range becomes too wide, the presentation may not be meaningful to users.

8.20 Financial forecasts may be supplemented by financial projections (*a*) for the same period, to indicate differences in results of operations and financial position resulting from assumptions other than those expected to materialize (for example, different levels of sales volume or occupancy rates), or (*b*) for additional periods, in the case of limited-use presentations. If financial forecasts and projections are presented together, each should be clearly labeled.

8.21 If a presentation that is other than a single-point estimate is issued, there should be a clear indication that the presentation does not necessarily represent either the best or worst possible alternatives.

Assumptions

8.22 The disclosure of significant assumptions is essential to the reader's understanding of the financial forecast; accordingly, the responsible party should disclose those assumptions deemed to be significant to the statements. The basis or rationale for the assumptions should preferably be disclosed to assist the user of the financial forecast to understand the presentation and make an informed judgment about it.

8.23 Identifying those assumptions that, at the time of preparation, appear to be significant to the financial forecast requires the careful exercise of judgment by the responsible party. By nature, financial forecasts embody a large number of assumptions, especially for a complex enterprise, and an attempt to communicate all assumptions is inherently not feasible. Furthermore, questions may arise after the fact regarding certain assumptions that were not disclosed, and unforeseen changes may make certain assumptions significant that previously were considered unimportant. The assumptions disclosed should include

a. assumptions about which there is a reasonable possibility of the occurrence of a variation that may significantly affect the prospective results; that is, sensitive assumptions.

b. assumptions about anticipated conditions that are expected to be significantly different from current conditions, which are not otherwise reasonably apparent (see paragraph 8.26).

c. other matters deemed important to the prospective information or its interpretation.

8.23P *In addition to those assumptions discussed in paragraph 8.23, the responsible party should identify which assumptions in the projection are hypothetical. In addition, the disclosure should indicate whether the hypothetical assumptions are improbable.*

8.24 The presentation should indicate which assumptions disclosed appeared particularly sensitive at the time of preparation. Although the responsible party should try to identify particularly sensitive assumptions, hindsight may reveal sensitive assumptions that did not appear to be particularly sensitive earlier (see paragraph 6.22).

8.25 Particularly sensitive assumptions are those assumptions having a relatively high probability of variation that would materially affect the financial forecast. The impact on the financial forecast might result from either (a) an assumption with a relatively high probability of a sizable variation or (b) an assumption for which the probability of a sizable variation is not as high but for which a small variation would have a large impact. Not all significant assumptions are particularly sensitive. For example, an assumption regarding the federal income tax rate may be significant but not particularly sensitive, whereas the assumption about the interest rate of a new debt issue may be both significant and particularly sensitive. The disclosure of particularly sensitive assumptions need not include a quantification of the potential effects of variations in those assumptions. The illustrative prospective financial statements in chapter 9, "Illustrative Prospective Financial Statements," include examples of disclosures of assumptions that are particularly sensitive. The following situations illustrate situations involving particularly sensitive assumptions:[12]

A forecast might assume that an entity will lose no customers that would have a significant effect on prospective results. If, however, there is a small number of customers that each account for a significant portion of sales, the retention of all of them might be a particularly sensitive assumption. The need for a disclosure would depend on the magnitude of the effect on the forecast of the loss of the customer(s) and the likelihood of losing them.

A forecast might assume sales of a product that a governmental agency has not yet approved for sale. The approval might be a particularly sensitive assumption if it or its timing is uncertain and the effect on the forecast of a failure to approve the product is significant.

---

[12] The judicially created "bespeaks caution" doctrine, in general, provides that forward-looking information is not actionable if it is accompanied by appropriate cautionary language. Disclosures of particularly sensitive assumptions, including matters such as those included in this paragraph, may help the responsible party in responding to litigation that challenges its prospective financial information. Further, the responsible party may give consideration to whether the quantification of particularly sensitive assumptions may be useful to users in evaluating the prospective financial information.

Other examples of particularly sensitive assumptions might be those that involve the potential effects of legislation, integration problems associated with a forecasted acquisition, and potential impediments to operations resulting from uncertainties related to licensing or permits.

8.26 Frequently, a basic assumption that current conditions having enormous potential impact will continue to prevail is considered to be implicit in the financial forecast. Examples are conditions of peace and the absence of natural disasters. Such assumptions need be disclosed only if there is a reasonable possibility that the current conditions will not prevail.

8.27 Although all significant assumptions should be disclosed, they need not be presented in such a manner or in such detail as would adversely affect the competitive position of the entity.

8.28 An introduction preceding the summary of assumptions should be provided to make clear that the assumptions disclosed are not an all-inclusive list of those used in the preparation of the prospective information, and that they were based on the responsible party's judgment at the time the prospective information was prepared. This introduction should describe what the responsible party intends the financial forecast to present, should include a statement that the assumptions are based on the responsible party's judgment at the time the prospective information was prepared, and should include a caveat that the prospective results may not be attained.

8.29 The introduction for a financial forecast that does not contain a range should be similar to the following:

> This financial forecast presents, to the best of management's[13] knowledge and belief, the Company's expected financial position, results of operations, and cash flows for the forecast period. Accordingly, the forecast reflects its judgment as of [*date*], the date of this forecast, of the expected conditions and its expected course of action. The assumptions disclosed herein are those that management believes are significant to the forecast. There will usually be differences between the forecasted and actual results, because events and circumstances frequently do not occur as expected, and those differences may be material.

8.29P *The introduction preceding the summary of significant assumptions for a financial projection should, in addition, clearly explain any special purpose and limitation of the usefulness of the statements. For example, the introduction preceding the summary of assumptions for a presentation of results with sales at maximum productive capacity would be similar to the following. This example illustrates the introduction for a presentation with an improbable hypothetical assumption; the example should be modified as appropriate in the circumstances.*

> *This financial projection is based on sales volume at maximum productive capacity and presents, to the best of management's[14] knowledge and belief, the Company's expected financial position, results of operations, and cash flows for the projection period if such sales volume were attained. Accordingly, the projection reflects its judgment*

---

[13] If the responsible party is other than management, the reference to management in the introduction should generally be to the party who assumes responsibility for the assumptions.

[14] *If the responsible party is other than management, this reference should generally be to the party who assumes responsibility for the assumptions.*

as of [date], the date of this projection, of the expected conditions and its expected course of action if such sales volume were experienced. The presentation is designed to provide information to the Company's board of directors concerning the maximum profitability that might be achieved if current production were expanded through the addition of a third production shift, and should not be considered to be a presentation of expected future results. Accordingly, this projection may not be useful for other purposes. The assumptions disclosed herein are those that management believes are significant to the projection. Management considers it highly unlikely that the stated sales volume will be experienced during the projection period. Furthermore, even if the stated sales volume were attained, there will usually be differences between projected and actual results, because events and circumstances frequently do not occur as expected, and those differences may be material.

8.30 The following is an example of an introduction for a forecast that contains a range. In the situation illustrated, the responsible party does not make a point estimate of occupancy of its apartment building but expects, to the best of its knowledge and belief, that actual occupancy will be between 75 percent and 95 percent of the available apartments.

This financial forecast presents, to the best of management's knowledge and belief, the Company's expected financial position, results of operations, and cash flows for the forecast period at occupancy rates of 75 percent and 95 percent of available apartments. Accordingly, the forecast reflects its judgment as of *[date]*, the date of this forecast, of the expected conditions and its expected course of action at each occupancy rate. The assumptions disclosed herein are those that management believes are significant to the forecast. Management reasonably expects, to the best of its knowledge and belief, that the actual occupancy rate achieved will be within the range shown; however, there can be no assurance that it will. Further, even if the actual occupancy rate is within the range shown, there will usually be differences between forecasted and actual results, because events and circumstances frequently do not occur as expected, and those differences may be material, and the actual results may be outside the range presented by the forecast.

8.31 Examples of disclosures of assumptions appear in the illustrative financial forecasts in chapter 9.

Period to Be Covered

8.32 When evaluating the period to be covered by a financial forecast, the responsible party should balance the information needs of users with its ability to estimate prospective results; however, a reasonably objective basis should exist for each forecasted period (month, quarter, year) presented.

8.33 Ordinarily, to be meaningful to users, the presentation of a financial forecast should include at least one full year of normal operations (for example, an entity forecasting a major acquisition would present at least the first full year following the acquisition, and a newly formed entity would include at least the first full year of normal operations in addition to the start-up period).[15] However, the degree of uncertainty generally increases with the time span of the forecast and, at some point, the underlying assumptions may become so subjective that a reasonably objective basis may not exist to present a financial forecast. It ordinarily would be difficult to establish that a reasonably objective basis exists for a financial forecast extending beyond three to five years[16] and, depending on the circumstances, a shorter period may be appropriate (for example, for certain start-up or high tech companies, it may be difficult to support an assertion that a reasonably objective basis exists to present a financial forecast and, if so, for more than one year).

8.34 Although the degree of uncertainty generally increases with the time span, short-term financial forecasts may not be meaningful in (a) industries with a lengthy operating cycle or (b) situations in which long-term results are necessary in order to evaluate the investment consequences involved. However, it may not be practical in all situations to present financial forecasts for enough future periods to demonstrate the long-term results. In those circumstances, the presentation should include a description of the potential effects of such results.

Disclosures at the End of the Forecast Period

8.35 Sometimes, the potential effects of long-term results are disclosed at the end of the forecast period. For example, if a real estate entity's forecast does not extend to the period in which the entity's investment is expected to be liquidated, the disclosures would include a discussion of the effects of a liquidation at the end of the forecast period. Such a hypothetical sale of the entity's real estate may be presented in the notes to the financial forecast or in a separate statement presented as part of the forecast. Such presentations should be appropriately labeled and accompanied by applicable disclosures, including the significant assumptions, an indication of which of those assumptions are hypothetical, and a statement that describes the purpose of the presentation. Exhibit 9-3 illustrates a presentation that may be appropriate for disclosing the long-term results of certain real estate projects. The illustration includes a projection that discloses the effect on limited partners of a hypothetical sale of property at the end of the forecast period.

8.36 In rare cases, the responsible party may forecast the sale of its real estate investment during the forecast period. In such circumstances, the sale is not hypothetical and is included in the financial forecast with other operating results and cash flows.

8.37 As stated in paragraph *7.01P*, the responsible party need not have a reasonably objective basis for the hypothetical assumptions used in a projection (for example, the assumptions used to project the effects of a hypothetical sale of real estate at the end of the forecast period). However, the assumptions should be consistent with the purpose of the disclosures—to provide users with meaningful information about the long-term results of their investment decisions.

---

[15] Securities and Exchange Commission (SEC) Regulation S-K, 229.10(b)(2) states that, for certain companies in certain industries, a forecast covering a two- or three-period may be entirely reasonable. Other companies may not have a reasonable basis for forecasts beyond the current year. Accordingly, the responsible party should generally select the period most appropriate in the circumstances.

[16] Financial forecasts for longer periods may be appropriate, for example, when long-term leases or other contracts exist that specify the timing and amount of revenues and costs can be controlled within reasonable limits.

8.38 Typically, when disclosing the effects of a hypothetical sale of an entity's real estate investment at the end of the forecast period, the sales price is based on a specified capitalization rate of forecasted cash flows. To be consistent with the purpose of the disclosures, the capitalization rate assumed should be consistent with the assumptions used in the forecast as well as with the entity's or industry's experience. If the capitalization rate assumed is not consistent with the entity's or industry's experience, the responsible party should consider whether the resulting projected sales price is appropriate because it may result in a presentation that is inconsistent with the objective of providing users with meaningful information about the long-term results of their investment decisions.[17]

8.39 Other sale prices also may be consistent with the purpose of the projection. For example, if significant nonrecourse debt is involved, the sales price assumed is often the existing mortgage balance or the existing mortgage balance plus original capital contributions.[18] Such assumed sales prices provide meaningful information that helps investors analyze their investment risk.

Disclosures About Periods Beyond the Forecast Period

8.40 Sometimes, the potential effects of long-term results are included in disclosures related to periods beyond the forecast period.[19] Specific plans, events, or circumstances that might be disclosed include the following:

- Scheduled increases in loan principal
- A planned refinancing
- Existing plans for future expansion of production or operating facilities or for the introduction of new products
- Expiration of a significant patent or contract
- The expected sale of a major portion of an entity's assets
- Scheduled or anticipated taxes that have adverse consequences for investors

8.41 Because it is not possible to anticipate all the circumstances that might arise, this guide does not contain a standard format for disclosures intended to demonstrate operating or other results beyond the forecast period. However, such disclosures should be based on the responsible party's plans and knowledge of specific events and circumstances, at the date of the forecast, that are expected to have a material effect on results beyond the forecast period.

8.42 Disclosures may be limited to a narrative discussion of the responsible party's plans, or they may include estimates of expected effects of future transactions or events. In all cases, however, the disclosure should be included in or incorporated by reference to the summary of significant assumptions and accounting policies. It also should

---

[17] Paragraph 8.22 states that the basis or rationale for the assumptions preferably should generally be disclosed to assist the user of the financial forecast in understanding the forecast and making an informed judgment about it.

[18] Paragraph *8.23P* states that "the responsible party should generally identify which assumptions in the projection are hypothetical."

[19] As previously discussed, disclosures about the long-term effects of investment decisions may be presented in a general-use document as a financial projection only if the projection is used to supplement a financial forecast and is for a period covered by the forecast. (Exhibit 9-3 illustrates such disclosures.) The disclosures described previously differ from those that might be included in such a financial projection because they are for a period beyond the forecast period.

- include a title that indicates that it presents information about periods beyond the financial forecast period.

- include an introduction indicating that the information presented does not constitute a financial forecast and indicating its purpose.

- disclose significant assumptions and identify those that are hypothetical, as well as the specific plans, events, or circumstances that are expected to have a material effect on results beyond the forecast period.

- state that (*a*) the information is presented for analysis purposes only, (*b*) there is no assurance that the events and circumstances described will occur, and (*c*) if applicable, the information is less reliable than the information presented in the financial forecast.

8.43 The purpose of these disclosures is to provide users with additional information that is useful in analyzing forecasted results. However, the information relates to periods beyond the forecast period, and management generally does not have a reasonably objective basis for presenting it as forecasted information. Accordingly, the disclosures are less reliable than those that are included in a financial forecast. Therefore, such disclosures should not be presented comparatively to forecasted results on the face of the financial forecast or in related summaries of results (for example, in a summary of investor benefits), or as a financial projection,[20] because such presentations could be misleading. The following examples illustrate the types of disclosures that may be appropriate.

---

[20] Paragraph 3.05 includes the definition of a financial projection. Paragraph 4.05 states that a financial projection is not appropriate for general use unless it supplements a financial forecast and is for a period covered by the forecast.

Example 1

Note A: Supplemental Information Related to the Three Years Ending December 31, 20X8[21]

Although management is unable to prepare a financial forecast for the three-year period ending December 31, 20X8, it believes that the following information is necessary for users to make a meaningful analysis of the forecasted results.

Management's forecast anticipates the operation of each of the three properties described therein during the five-year period ending December 31, 20X5. Current plans are to continue the operation of all three properties through December 31, 20X8, at which time the properties will be offered for sale. The following table illustrates the pretax effect to limited partners of a sale of properties at December 31, 20X8, and the subsequent liquidation of the partnership. The table is based on the following hypothetical assumptions:[22]

- Column A is based on the assumption that the property will be sold (or foreclosed) for the balance of the mortgage notes at December 31, 20X8.

- Columns B and C are based on the assumption that the properties will be sold at estimated market values, which are calculated by capitalizing estimated cash flows from operations for the year immediately preceding the sale at rates of 7 percent and 9 percent, respectively.

- The estimated balance of outstanding mortgage notes at December 31, 20X8, is based on the assumption that the partnership will continue to make payments in accordance with existing terms of the mortgage notes. Note 7 to the financial forecast describes the partnership's outstanding mortgage notes and related payment terms.

- Management has estimated net operating cash flow (in total and per unit) for the three-year period ending December 31, 20X8, using assumptions substantially the same as those used in its financial forecast for the five-year period ending December 31, 20X5. In preparing the estimate, 20X5 forecasted rental income and forecasted operating expenses and management fees were increased by 5 percent per year.

	A	B	C
	Sale for Existing Mortgage Balance	*Sale at a 7% Capitalization Rate*	*Sale at a 9% Capitalization Rate*
Cash distributions to limited partners			
For the forecast period	$XXX	$XXX	$XXX

---

[21] Exhibit 9-3 contains an alternate presentation of long-term results if a projection is used to supplement a financial forecast and is for the period covered by the forecast. It presents a projected sale of real estate property as if it were sold on the last day of the forecasted period.

[22] As discussed in paragraph 8.38, the capitalization rate assumed ordinarily should be consistent with the assumptions used in the forecast as well as the entity's and the industry's experience.

	A *Sale for Existing Mortgage Balance*	B *Sale at a 7% Capitalization Rate*	C *Sale at a 9% Capitalization Rate*
For the three-year period ending December 31, 20X8	XXX	XXX	XXX
Net from sale and dissolution	XXX	XXX	XXX
Less original capital contribution	(XXX)	(XXX)	(XXX)
Net pretax cash flow from partnership	$XXX	$XXX	$XXX
Taxable income			
For the forecast period	$XXX	$XXX	$XXX
For the three-year period ending December 31, 20X8	$XXX	$XXX	$XXX
From sale and dissolution	$XXX	$XXX	$XXX

This information is less reliable than the information presented in the financial forecast and, accordingly, is presented for analysis purposes only. Furthermore, there can be no assurance that the events and circumstances described in this analysis will occur.

Example 2

Note B: Supplemental Information Related to Periods Beyond the Forecast Period

Although management is unable to prepare a financial forecast for periods beyond 20X5, it believes that the following information is necessary in order for users to make a meaningful analysis of the forecasted results.

Management's forecast for the three-year period ending December 31, 20X5, anticipates sales of its Model 714 High Tech Laser Analyzers and related equipment in the amounts of $13,500,000, $14,000,000, and $14,500,000, respectively. Such sales represent approximately 50 percent of the Company's sales for the forecast period and were the major reason for the Company's growth in 20X0 and 20X1. The Company is currently a leader in laser technology, and its Model 714 is now widely used by the industry. However, the Company expects the sales of this product to peak in 20X5 and to decline in periods subsequent to the forecast period. The Company is currently developing the Model 714A High Tech Analyzer, which is an improvement on the Model 714 Analyzer, and an X series visual modulator and laser scanner.

This information is less reliable than the information presented in the financial forecast and, accordingly, is presented for analysis purposes only. Furthermore, there can be no assurance that the events and circumstances described in this analysis will occur.

Distinguishing From Historical Financial Statements

8.44 Financial forecasts should be clearly labeled to preclude a reader from confusing them with historical financial statements.

8.45 Prior-period information, such as historical results, and financial forecasts for prior periods may be presented alongside financial forecasts to facilitate comparison. If such prior-period information is presented, it should be clearly labeled and distinguished from the financial forecasts.

Correction and Updating of a Financial Forecast

8.46 Correction of a financial forecast refers to the modification of the forecast after issuance for an error that was made in preparing the forecast. Updating a financial forecast refers to changing the forecast to reflect changes in assumptions, actual results, or anticipated events and circumstances.

8.47 *Errors.* If the responsible party discovers that an error was made in preparing a financial forecast, they should determine whether any users currently rely or are likely to rely on the forecast and, if so, consider whether it is necessary to withdraw the forecast. If the responsible party concludes that it is necessary to withdraw the forecast, it should make a reasonable effort to inform any such users that the forecast is no longer to be relied upon and, if practical, to issue a corrected forecast. For examples of how such notification might be made, see paragraphs .15–.18 of AU-C section 560, *Subsequent Events and Subsequently Discovered Facts* (AICPA, *Professional Standards*).

8.48 *Updating.* It is not usually expected that forecasts will be updated and the responsible party may state in the presentation that it does not intend to update the forecast.[23] Nevertheless, there may be situations in which updating would be appropriate, for example, if a material event occurs while an entity's debt or equity interests are currently being offered for sale. In deciding whether it is appropriate to issue an updated financial forecast, the responsible party should consider whether users would expect prospective statements to be updated. Updating requires the reanalysis of key factors and assumptions and the preparation of a new financial forecast. The reasons for updating should be described in a note to the updated presentation.

8.49 The following is an example of an explicit statement regarding the inclusion of a financial forecast (that is not intended to be updated) in the summary of significant assumptions.

> The financial forecast was prepared as of March 30, 20XX, to assist the prospective bondholders in estimating whether the operations of the XYZ Company may be expected to support a $10,000,000 bond issue. Because it is contemplated that the entire bond issue will be sold within ninety days hereafter, management does not intend to revise this forecast to reflect changes in present circumstances or the occurrence of unanticipated events.

8.50 If the responsible party has decided that an updated forecast is appropriate but cannot be issued promptly, appropriate disclosure should be made to persons who currently rely or are likely to rely on the forecast. Such disclosure would include a description of the circumstances necessitating an

---

[23] However, see Regulation S-K, section 229.10(b)(3)(iii) (reprinted in appendix A, "SEC Policy on Projections"), in which registrants are reminded of their responsibility to update forecasts under SEC regulations.

updated financial forecast, along with a notification that the current forecast should not be used for any purpose and that an updated financial forecast will be issued upon its completion.

8.51 If, however, the responsible party decides that the current financial forecast should no longer be used for any purpose but that it is not appropriate to issue an updated forecast, this decision and the reason for it should be disclosed to persons who currently rely or are likely to rely on the forecast.

Chapter 9

Illustrative Prospective Financial Statements

9.01 This chapter illustrates prospective financial statements presented in conformity with the presentation guidelines in chapter 8, "Presentation Guidelines." The examples presented in this chapter were designed to illustrate forecasts and projections presented as full and minimum presentations, the use of different bases of accounting, and the use of a range. The unique features of each presentation are described in the following list:

a. Exhibits 9-1 and 9-2 are financial forecasts for a manufacturing or commercial type of entity. Although the preferable presentation of prospective financial statements ordinarily consists of a complete set of statements (similar to the entity's historical financial statements) as shown in exhibit 9-1, a presentation may be limited to the applicable minimum items described in paragraph 8.06, as shown in exhibit 9-2.

b. Exhibit 9-3 illustrates a financial forecast presented on a tax basis of accounting typically used for limited partnership ventures. Such ventures do not normally prepare financial statements on other than a tax basis; accordingly, the minimum presentation items in paragraph 8.06 were adapted to fit a tax-basis presentation.

c. Exhibit 9-4 illustrates a financial forecast expressed in the form of a range representing two scenarios: one, a continued downturn in the economy, and the other, the beginning of recovery in the economy.

d. Exhibit 9-5 illustrates a financial forecast also expressed in the form of a range. The range forecast illustrates the expected range of net income and distributable cash based on increases in current market rates for rental properties and certain expenses of 4 percent and 6 percent annually. Unlike the presentation in exhibit 9-4, which is a side-by-side, columnar presentation, this forecast presents separate statements for each end of the range.

e. Exhibit 9-6 illustrates a financial projection. The example shown is a cash-flow projection that assumes the construction of an additional plant. Because of the hypothetical assumption (the construction of the plant), the presentation can be expected to be useful only to the responsible party and the party with whom the entity is dealing directly in regard to the construction or financing of the plant.

9.02 Paragraph 8.06 indicates that the minimum disclosure items need be presented only if applicable but should be adapted as necessary to portray operations. Exhibit 9-3 illustrates how the minimum items might be adapted in the case of an entity in the business of renting property. The example meets the minimum presentation guidelines as follows:

Minimum Disclosure Item	Exhibit 9-3 Presentation
a. Sales or gross revenue	Rental income
b. Gross profit or cost of sales	Not applicable
c. Unusual or infrequently occurring items	Not applicable
d. Provision for income taxes	Not applicable
e. Income from continuing operations	Same as item g; not separately presented
f. Discontinued operations or extraordinary items	Not applicable
g. Net income	Taxable income (loss)
h. Basic and diluted earnings per share	Share of taxable income (loss) per unit
i. Significant changes in financial position	• Investment by limited partners • Financing • Construction expenditures • Repayments of principal • Cash distributions
j. A description of what the responsible party intends the financial forecast to present, a statement that the assumptions are based upon the responsible party's judgment at the time the prospective information was prepared, and a caveat that the forecasted results may not be attained.	Introduction to the forecast
k. Summary of significant assumptions	Summary of significant forecast assumptions
l. Summary of significant accounting policies	Not illustrated

9.03 Exhibit 9-3 includes disclosure of the potential tax consequences should the property be sold at the end of the forecast period, as an aid to users in evaluating long-term investment consequences, because the forecast does not extend to the period in which the property is expected to be sold.

9.04 The example of a financial projection (exhibit 9-6) illustrates a reconciliation from net income using the accrual method of accounting, which is to be used to prepare the historical financial statements for the prospective period, to net increase (decrease) in cash (as specified in paragraph 8.15).

9.05 The illustrations presented are consistent with the guidance in chapter 8, although other presentation formats could also be consistent. For instance, although all of the examples present the summary of significant assumptions and accounting policies after the presentation of prospective amounts, it would also be appropriate to present them first. Furthermore, it may be appropriate to commingle the disclosures of assumptions and accounting policies rather than present them separately. It may also be appropriate to present them in a less formal manner than illustrated, such as computer-printed output (indicating data and relationships) from electronic spreadsheet and general-purpose financial modeling software, as long as the responsible party believes that the disclosures and assumptions can be understood by the users. The appropriateness of any format depends upon individual circumstances.

Exhibit 9-1

XYZ COMPANY, INC.

Forecasted Statement of Income and Retained Earnings
Year Ending December 31, 20X3

(in thousands except per-share amounts)

	Forecasted	Comparative Historical Information	
	20X3	20X2	20X1
Net sales	$101,200	$91,449	$79,871
Cost of sales	77,500	70,140	60,463
Gross profit	23,700	21,309	19,408
Selling, general, and administrative expenses	15,100	13,143	11,014
Operating income	8,600	8,166	8,394
Other income (deductions):			
Miscellaneous	1,700	964	(308)
Interest expense	(2,400)	(1,914)	(1,943)
	(700)	(950)	(2,251)
Income before income taxes	7,900	7,216	6,143
Income taxes	3,400	3,267	2,929
Net income	4,500	3,949	3,214
Retained earnings at beginning of year	10,500	7,803	5,543
Dividend (per share 20X3: $1.50; 20X2: $1.35; 20X1: $1.00)	(1,400)	(1,288)	(954)
Retained earnings at end of year	$13,600	$10,464	$7,803
Basic earnings per share	$4.73	$4.14	$3.37

See accompanying Summary of Significant Forecast Assumptions and Accounting Policies.

XYZ COMPANY, INC.

Forecasted Statement of Cash Flows
Year Ending December 31, 20X3

(in thousands)

	Forecasted	Comparative Historical Information	
	20X3	20X2	20X1
Cash flows from operating activities:			
Net earnings	$4,500	$3,949	$3,214
Adjustments to reconcile net income to net cash provided by operating activities:			
Depreciation expense	2,800	2,422	2,181
Changes in:			
Accounts receivable	(2,500)	(1,430)	(483)
Inventory	(100)	(3,995)	(1,431)
Other current assets	(1,700)	(350)	(62)
Accounts payable and accrued expenses	1,100	1,696	846
Other current liabilities	—	811	161
Net cash provided by operating activities	4,100	3,103	4,426
Cash flows (used for) investing activities:			
Additions to property and equipment	(4,400)	(2,907)	(2,114)
Other assets	(2,200)	(600)	(83)
Net cash used for investing activities	(6,600)	(3,507)	(2,197)
Cash flows from (used for) financing activities:			
Dividends paid	(1,400)	(1,288)	(954)
Proceeds from bank loans	1,500	100	(300)
Proceeds from long-term borrowings	6,000	4,100	2,000
Principal payments of long-term debt	(2,200)	(2,842)	(1,958)
Net cash from (used in) financing activities	3,900	70	(1,212)
Net increase (decrease) in cash	1,400	(334)	1,017
Cash, beginning of year	1,900	2,196	1,179
Cash, end of year	$3,300	$1,862	$2,196

Income tax payments were $3,207 and $2,789 in 20X2 and 20X1, respectively, and are estimated to be $3,300 in 20X3. Interest payments related to borrowings were $1,756 and $2,155 in 20X2 and 20X1, respectively, and are estimated to be $2,620 in 20X3.

See accompanying Summary of Significant Forecast Assumptions and Accounting Policies.

XYZ COMPANY, INC.
Forecasted Balance Sheet
December 31, 20X3
(in thousands)

	Forecasted	Comparative Historical Information	
	20X3	20X2	20X1
ASSETS			
Current assets:			
Cash	$ 3,300	$ 1,862	$ 2,196
Accounts receivable (net)	14,900	12,438	11,008
Inventory	27,000	26,932	22,937
Other	3,500	1,813	1,463
Total current assets	48,700	43,045	37,604
Property, plant, and equipment	30,900	26,915	22,832
Less accumulated depreciation	17,300	14,912	11,314
Net property, plant, and equipment	13,600	12,003	11,518
Other assets	5,000	2,714	2,114
	$ 67,300	$ 57,762	$ 51,236
LIABILITIES AND STOCKHOLDERS' EQUITY			
Current Liabilities:			
Notes payable to bank	$ 4,600	$ 3,100	$ 3,000
Accounts payable and accrued expenses	12,300	11,193	9,497
Current installments of long-term debt	4,400	3,968	3,010
Other	900	925	114
Total current liabilities	22,200	19,186	15,621
Long-term debt, excluding current installments	20,100	16,700	16,400
Stockholders' equity:			
Capital stock	11,400	11,412	11,412
Retained earnings	13,600	10,464	7,803
Total stockholders' equity	25,000	21,876	19,215
	$ 67,300	$ 57,762	$ 51,236

See accompanying Summary of Significant Forecast Assumptions and Accounting Policies.

Exhibit 9-2

XYZ COMPANY, INC.

Summarized Financial Forecast
Year Ending December 31, 20X3

(in thousands except per-share amounts)

Exhibit 9-1 presents one format for prospective financial statements. However, a more summarized presentation may be given (see paragraph 8.06). Following is a summarized presentation that could be used in lieu of the preceding exhibit.

	Forecasted	Comparative Historical Information[1]	
	20X3	20X2	20X1
Sales	$ 101,200	$ 91,449	$ 79,871
Gross profit	23,700	21,309	19,408
Income tax expense	3,400	3,267	2,929
Net income	4,500	3,949	3,214
Basic earnings per share	4.73	4.14	3.37
Significant anticipated changes in financial position:			
Cash provided by operations	4,100	3,103	4,426
Net increase (decrease) in long-term borrowings	3,400	300	(300)
Dividend (per share 20X3: $1.50; 20X2: $1.35; 20X1: $1.00)	1,400	1,288	954
Additions to plant and equipment	4,400	2,907	2,114
Increase (decrease) in cash	1,400	(334)	1,017

See accompanying Summary of Significant Forecast Assumptions and Accounting Policies.

---

[1] Comparative historical information is not part of the minimum presentation described in paragraph 8.06.

XYZ COMPANY, INC.
Summary of Significant Forecast
Assumptions and Accounting Policies (Exhibits 9-1 and 9-2)
Year Ending December 31, 20X3

This financial forecast presents, to the best of management's knowledge and belief, the Company's expected financial position, results of operations, and cash flows for the forecast period.[2] Accordingly, the forecast reflects management's judgment as of February 17, 20X3, the date of this forecast, of the expected conditions and its expected course of action. The assumptions disclosed herein are those that management believes are significant to the forecast. There will usually be differences between forecasted and actual results, because events and circumstances frequently do not occur as expected, and those differences may be material. The comparative historical information for 20X1 and 20X2 is extracted from the Company's financial statements for those years. Those financial statements should be read for additional information.

a. **Summary of Significant Accounting Policies.** (not illustrated)

b. **Sales.** The overall market for the Company's products has grown over the past five years at an average rate of 2 percent above the actual increase in gross domestic product, and the Company's market share has remained steady at 14 percent to 16 percent. Based on a recent market study of demand for the Company's products, sales are forecasted to increase 11 percent from 20X2 (which is 2 percent above the Department of Commerce Bureau of Economic Analysis estimate of the rise in gross domestic product in the forecast period), with a market share of 15 percent and unit price increased to cover a significant portion of forecasted increases in cost of manufacturing.

c. **Cost of Sales**

> **Materials.** Materials used by the Company are expected to be readily available, and the Company has generally used producer associations' estimates of prices in the forecast period to forecast material costs. The price for copper, a major raw material in the Company's products, recently has been disrupted by political events in certain principal producer countries. As a result, industry estimates of copper prices in the forecast period range from 15 percent to 30 percent above 20X2 prices. The Company expects to be able to assure sufficient supplies and estimates that the cost of copper will increase by 22 percent over 20X2. However, due to the uncertainties noted above, the realization of the forecast is particularly sensitive to the actual price increase. A variation of five percentage points in the actual increase above or below the assumed increase would affect forecasted net earnings by approximately $485,000.

> **Labor.** The Company's labor union contract, which covers substantially all manufacturing personnel, was negotiated in 20X2 for a three-year period. Labor costs are forecasted based on the terms of that contract.

---

[2] For the presentation illustrated in exhibit 9-2, this would read ". . . summary of the Company's expected results of operations and changes in financial position . . . ."

d. **Plant and Equipment and Depreciation Expense.** Forecasted additions to plant and equipment, $4.4 million, comprise principally the regular periodic replacement of manufacturing plant and vehicles at suppliers' quoted estimated prices and do not involve a significant change in manufacturing capacity or processes. Depreciation is forecasted on an item-by-item basis.

e. **Selling, General, and Administrative Expenses.** The principal types of expense within this category are salaries, transportation costs, and sales promotion. Salaries are forecasted on an individual basis, using expected salary rates in the forecast period. Transportation costs comprise principally the use of contract carriers; volume is forecasted based on the sales and inventory forecasts (including forecasts by sales outlet), and rates are forecasted to rise by 16 percent over 20X2, based on trucking industry forecasts. Sales promotion costs are expected to increase by approximately 14 percent above the level of 20X2 in order to meet increased competition and to maintain market share. The level of other expenses is expected to remain the same as in 20X2, adjusted for expected increases in line with the consumer price index (assumed to rise 9 percent on the mean of [*several widely used estimates*]).

f. **Miscellaneous Income.** The forecast assumes royalty income of $950,000 will be received based on an agreement under which the Company is to receive a minimum of $950,000 for the first 10,000,000 units produced under its patented die casting process and $.05 per unit above that level. Management believes it is unlikely that production will exceed 10,000,000 units. The balance of miscellaneous income is assumed to come from investment of excess cash and other sources.

g. **Bank Borrowings and Interest Expense.** The forecast assumes that the Company will obtain an extension of existing short-term lines of credit at terms comparable to those in effect in 20X2 (2 percent over prime rate). The Company used the arithmetic mean of [*three widely used estimates*] of bank prime rate during the forecast period (ranging from 12 percent to 14 percent) to estimate prime rate at 13 percent. However, because of recent volatility in the financial markets, short-term interest rates have been very unstable, ranging from 12 percent to 17 percent during 20X2.

The Company has forecasted additional long-term borrowings of $6 million and has entered into preliminary negotiations with its bankers for this financing. The borrowings are principally to fund purchases of plant and equipment and additions to other long-term assets and will be secured by such additions. Based on the preliminary negotiations, the Company has assumed that the additional long-term financing will bear interest at 14 percent.

h. **Income Taxes.** The provision for income taxes is computed using the statutory rates in effect during 20X2, which are not expected to change, and assuming investment tax credit on qualifying investments at rates in effect in 20X2.

i. **Dividend.** The Company's normal dividend policy is to pay out the previous year's dividend increased to the extent of at least one-third of any increase in profits over the previous year, provided the board of directors considers that the Company's cash and working capital position will not be adversely affected. The dividend has been forecasted at $1.50 per share, assuming an increased payout over 20X2 of one-third of the excess of forecasted net earnings for the year ending December 31, 20X3, above those of 20X2.

Exhibit 9-3

DEF ASSOCIATES, LTD.

(A Limited Partnership)

**Statement of Forecasted Taxable Income (Loss)
For Each Year in the Five-Year Period
Ending December 31, 20X5**

	Reference	20X1	20X2	20X3	20X4	20X5
Rental income	d	$ —	$105,000	$378,000	$438,165	$468,837
Operating expenses	f	—	46,216	133,596	144,426	149,947
Mortgage interest expense	h	—	83,950	172,003	185,500	183,000
Cash from operations		—	(25,166)	72,401	108,239	135,890
Depreciation	g	—	27,800	74,133	74,133	74,133
Taxable income (loss)		$ —	$(52,966)	$(1,732)	$34,106	$61,757
Limited partners' share of taxable income (loss)		$ —	$(22,966)	$(1,732)	$34,106	$61,757

See accompanying Summary of Significant Forecast Assumptions and Accounting Policies.

Note: The purpose of this presentation is to illustrate a limited partnership's financial forecast prepared on a tax basis. It also illustrates the hypothetical sale of real estate at the end of the forecast period. The body of tax law is in a continuous state of change. This financial forecast is not intended to reflect current or future tax laws.

DEF ASSOCIATES, LTD.
(A Limited Partnership)
Statement of Forecasted Sources and Uses of Cash
For Each Year in the Five-Year Period Ending December 31, 20X5

	Reference	20X1	20X2	20X3	20X4	20X5
Sources of cash						
Investment by general partner		$20,000	$30,000	$ —	$ —	$ —
Investment by limited partners	b	500,000	—	—	—	—
Outside financing	h	129,000	1,421,000	—	—	—
Cash from operations		—	(25,166)	72,401	108,239	135,890
Total sources		649,000	1,425,834	72,401	108,239	135,890
Uses of cash						
Rental and advertising expenses	e	7,000	33,800	—	—	—
Syndication costs		21,500	—	—	—	—
Construction costs	g	587,850	1,192,150	30,000	—	—
Construction period interest and taxes	e	17,650	211,000	—	—	—
Repayment of principal	h	—	—	14,862	18,355	20,888
Distributions to limited partners	c	—	—	24,474	89,884	115,002
Total uses		634,000	1,436,950	69,336	108,239	135,890
Change in cash		15,000	(11,116)	3,065	—	—
Cash balance, beginning of year		—	15,000	3,884	6,949	6,949
Cash balance, end of year		$15,000	$3,884	$6,949	$ 6,949	$ 6,949

See accompanying Summary of Significant Forecast Assumptions and Accounting Policies.

Note: The purpose of this presentation is to illustrate a limited partnership's financial forecast prepared on a tax basis. It also illustrates the hypothetical sale of real estate at the end of the forecast period. The body of tax law is in a continuous state of change. This financial forecast is not intended to reflect current or future tax laws.

DEF ASSOCIATES, LTD.

(A Limited Partnership)

**Statement of Forecasted Allocation of Limited Partner
Interest Per $5,000 Unit and Presentation of Tax Effects
Assuming a 31% Tax Bracket For Each Year in
the Five-Year Period Ending December 31, 20X5**

	Reference	20X1	20X2	20X3	20X4	20X5
Limited partner investment per unit	b	$ 5,000	$ —	$ —	$ —	$ —
Share of taxable income (loss)	c	$ —	$ (230)	$ (17)	$ 341	$ 618
Assumed tax bracket	i	31%	31%	31%	31%	31%
Tax benefit (cost)		—	71	5	(106)	(192)
Cash distributions	c	—	—	245	899	1,150
Total tax benefits and cash distributions		$ —	$ 71	$ 250	$ 793	$ 958
Cumulative cash flow excluding hypothetical sale		$ (5,000)	$ (4,929)	$ (4,679)	$ (3,886)	$ (2,928)

See accompanying Summary of Significant Forecast Assumptions and Accounting Policies.

Note: The purpose of this presentation is to illustrate a limited partnership's financial forecast prepared on a tax basis. It also illustrates the hypothetical sale of real estate at the end of the forecast period. The body of tax law is in a continuous state of change. This financial forecast is not intended to reflect current or future tax laws.

AAG-PRO 9.05

DEF ASSOCIATES, LTD.
Summary of Significant Forecast Assumptions and Accounting Policies
For Each Year in the Five-Year Period Ending December 31, 20X5

This financial forecast presents, to the best of management's knowledge and belief, the Partnership's expected results of operations and sources and uses of cash for the forecast period presented on the tax basis of accounting. Accordingly, the forecast reflects management's judgment as of June 30, 20X1, the date of this forecast, of the expected conditions and its expected course of action. The assumptions disclosed herein are those that management believes are significant to the forecast. There will usually be differences between the forecasted and actual results because events and circumstances frequently do not occur as expected and those differences may be material.

The body of tax law is in a continuous state of change. Accordingly, there could be developments, statutory or otherwise, that would alter the forecast. Because transactions are susceptible to varying interpretations under income tax law, rulings, and regulations, the Internal Revenue Service may not concur with the determinations of the factual issues and the interpretations of existing law, rulings, and regulations that served as the basis for the assumptions used by management to prepare the forecast. Such differences might alter the forecast. (See other comments on this subject on pages aa-bb of this offering memorandum.)

a. **Summary of Significant Accounting Policies.** (not illustrated)

b. **Description of the Project.** The proposed development, DEF Gardens, is a seventy-unit apartment complex to be constructed on an eight-and-one-quarter acre, residentially zoned parcel of land in Phoenix, Arizona, to be leased from the General Partner (see note **f**). Construction of the development is anticipated to begin on July 15, 20X1, and to be completed by August 1, 20X2 (see note **e**). Equity financing is proposed to be obtained from the sale of 100 limited partnership units at $ 5,000 per unit in July 20X1. The proceeds from the sale, together with anticipated bank financing, are expected to provide the necessary funding requirements for the project (see note **h**).

c. **Allocation of Income, Losses, and Cash Distributions.** The Partnership Agreement provides that the limited partners (as a group) are to receive 100 percent of all cash distributions, whether from operations or from the proceeds of refinancing or disposing of Partnership property, until they have received distributions equal to their original investments. Thereafter, the limited partners are to receive 65 percent of all distributions. Cash available for distributions will be reserved to the extent necessary to provide for normal operating needs.

Taxable income or loss is to be allocated among the partners according to their relative interests in the Partnership. Accordingly, the forecasted taxable income or loss is allocable to the partner who earns the corresponding economic benefit or bears the corresponding economic burden, as determined under applicable regulations.

Income or losses of the Partnership for a year are allocable to the partners pro rata to the portions of the year in which the respective partners were members of the Partnership. The forecast of the allocation of the net loss to be sustained for the year 20X2 is based on the assumption that all limited partners will acquire their interest in the Partnership as of July 1, 20X1.

d. **Rental Income.** Rental income is based on the General Partner's estimates that the apartment building will be available for occupancy on or before August 1, 20X2, and the number of units occupied, average rent per unit, and percentage occupancy will be as follows:

	8/1/X2 to 12/31/X2	20X3	20X4	20X5
Average number of units occupied	40	60	65	65
Average monthly rental per unit	$525	$525	$562	$601
Average percentage	57%	86%	93%	93%

The average monthly rental per unit is forecasted to increase 7 percent per year in 20X4 and 20X5 based upon the most recent experience in the area. Occupancy percentage is based on the General Partner's consideration of demand for the forecast period and is consistent with percentages currently obtained in similar apartment complexes managed by the General Partner. For each thirty-day period subsequent to August 2, 20X2, that occupancy is delayed, if any, rental income for 20X2 will be reduced by approximately $21,000.

e. **Construction Period Expenses.** Obligations incurred during the construction period (July 15, 20X1 to August 1, 20X2) consist of the following:

	20X1	20X2
Interest on construction loan	$16,900	$203,000
Real estate taxes	750	8,000
Rental and advertising expenses	$7,000	$33,800

Such expenses are based on the General Partner's most recent experience in similar apartment complexes in the area. Interest on the construction loan and real estate taxes incurred during the construction period will be capitalized as part of the cost of the building. For each thirty-day period subsequent to August 2, 20X2, that construction continues, construction period expenses for 20X2 (primarily interest) will increase by approximately $25,000.

f. **Operating Expenses.** Annual expenses for the operating of the Partnership's property are based on the General Partner's experience in similar apartment complexes. Operating expenses include salaries for the apartment manager, repairs and maintenance, cleaning, insurance, real estate taxes, and utilities. They also include a management fee of $10,000 per year to the General Partner and lease payments to the General Partner of $4,630 per month for the use of the land on which the apartment complex is to be constructed. The initial fixed term of the lease is for twenty-five years with an option to renew for an additional twenty-five years.

***g.* Construction Costs and Depreciation.** The forecasted construction costs are based on a fixed-price contract with the general contractor. The total estimated cost of constructing the project is $2,038,650, which includes $228,650 of construction period interest and taxes (see note **e**). Depreciation is computed according to the Accelerated Cost Recovery System using the straight-line method, the mid-month convention, and a recovery period of 27.5 years.

***h.* Financing Arrangements.** Construction of the seventy-unit apartment project and construction period expenses are to be financed by a $1,550,000 construction loan and capital contributions of $500,000 by the limited partners and $50,000 by the General Partner. It is anticipated that the loan will bear interest at an annual interest rate of 14 percent. Upon completion of construction, a permanent thirty-year nonrecourse mortgage loan will become effective at an anticipated annual interest rate of 13 percent, payable interest only for one year and principal amortization and interest payments thereafter. For each .25 percent variance in the actual interest rates obtained, the dollar amount of interest expense, and the resulting taxable income or loss will vary by approximately $2,000 in 20X2 and $4,000 in 20X3 through 20X5.

***i.* Tax Matters.** The Partnership is relying on an opinion from its legal counsel (included on pages xx-yy of this offering memorandum) that the investors more likely than not will prevail on the merits of each material tax issue, and that the material tax benefits in the aggregate are likely to be realized.

The forecast does not provide for state and local income taxes on the partners, nor does it provide for federal alternative minimum tax on federal limitations on deductions for passive losses. Each partner should consult his or her personal tax advisor in this regard.

***j.* Analysis of the Tax Effect and Cash Flow on the Sale of the Property at the End of the Forecast Period.** The following table illustrates the effect on limited partners of a hypothetical sale of the apartment complex at December 31, 20X5, given two different hypothetical sales prices, and the subsequent liquidation of the Partnership. This table is presented for analysis purposes only because it is not expected that the property will be sold at that date or for those hypothetical amounts. These illustrations are based on the following:

1. Column A is based on the hypothetical assumption that the property will be sold (or foreclosed) for the balance of the mortgage at December 31, 20X5.

2. Column B is based on the hypothetical assumption that the property will be sold for $500,000 net cash (the limited partners' original capital contributions), subject to the existing mortgage.

3. These illustrations do not reflect the effect of (*a*) capital losses from other transactions or (*b*) the alternative minimum tax in the year of sale, if any, because these factors would be dependent upon each individual partner's tax situation.

DEF ASSOCIATES, LTD.
(A Limited Partnership)
Statement of Effect on Limited Partners of Hypothetical Sale of Property and Liquidation of Partnership
December 31, 20X5

	A Sale for Balance of Mortgage Loan		B Sale for Balance of Mortgage Loan and Limited Partners' Capital Contribution	
	Total	Limited Partners' Share	Total	Limited Partners' Share
Net sales price	$ 1,495,895		$ 1,995,895	
Less adjusted basis	(1,829,251)		(1,829,251)	
Gain (loss) on sale	$ (333,356)	$ (333,356)	$ 166,644	$ 83,936
Cumulative ordinary income from operations	$ 41,165	$ 71,165	$ 41,165	$ 71,165
Gain (loss) on sale of building:				
Ordinary portion	—	—	—	—
Capital portion	(333,356)	(333,356)	166,644	83,936
Capital loss on liquidation	(21,500)	(1,500)	(21,500)	(1,500)
Cumulative taxable gain (loss)	$ (313,691)	$ (263,691)	$ 186,309	$ 153,601
Cumulative current distribution	$229,360	$ 229,360	$ 229,360	$ 229,360
Cumulative liquidating distribution	6,949	6,949	506,949	424,241
Less cumulative contributions	(550,000)	(500,000)	(550,000)	(500,000)
Cumulative net cash return (deficiency) before taxes	$(313,691)	$(263,691)	$ 186,309	$ 153,601

Note: The purpose of this presentation is to illustrate a limited partnership's financial forecast prepared on a tax basis. It also illustrates the hypothetical sale of real estate at the end of the forecast period. The body of tax law is in a continuous state of change. This financial forecast is not intended to reflect current or future tax laws.

Exhibit 9-4

JMK COMPANY, INC.

Consolidated Statements of Income and Retained Earnings

For Years Ending December 31, 20X5 (forecasted) and December 31, 20X4 and 20X3 (historical)

(in thousands except per-share amounts)

	Forecasted 20X5		Comparative Historical Information	
	Economy Begins Recovery	Continued Downturn in the Economy	20X4	20X3
Net sales	$ 639,000	$ 599,000	$ 619,008	$ 628,273
Costs and expenses:				
Costs of sales	510,000	488,500	490,091	487,607
Selling and advertising	31,420	32,060	31,324	28,775
General and administrative	33,600	33,500	31,255	27,752
Interest	1,700	1,650	2,818	2,839
Other (net)	1,030	1,030	(161)	352
Total	577,750	556,740	555,327	547,325
Income before income taxes	61,250	42,260	63,681	80,948
Income taxes	27,125	18,390	28,287	39,256
Net income	34,125	23,870	35,394	41,692
Retained earnings beginning of year	237,698	237,698	215,966	186,374
Cash dividends	16,758	15,613	13,662	12,100
Retained earnings end of year	$255,065	$245,955	$237,698	$215,966
Basic earnings per share	$3.50	$2.45	$3.63	$4.27

See accompanying Summary of Significant Forecast Assumptions and Accounting Policies.

Note: This presentation includes all the minimum items that constitute a financial forecast without presenting a balance sheet.

JMK COMPANY, INC.

Consolidated Statements of Cash Flows

For Years Ending December 31, 20X5 (forecasted) and December 31, 20X4 and 20X3 (historical)

(in thousands)

	Forecasted 20X5		Comparative Historical Information	
	Economy Begins Recovery	*Continued Downturn in the Economy*	*20X4*	*20X3*
Cash flows from operating activities:				
Net earnings	$ 34,125	$ 23,870	$ 35,394	$ 41,692
Depreciation expense	19,500	19,360	17,986	16,342
Amortization expense	2,170	2,170	225	227
Deferred compensation	2,080	1,980	1,637	274
Changes in:				
Accounts receivable	(3,000)	2,950	(7,586)	(11,794)
Inventories	(2,200)	11,260	8,059	(19,533)
Prepaid expenses	(550)	(550)	1,633	(3,831)
Accounts payable	2,000	1,620	1,682	2,730
Accrued liabilities	(3,600)	(3,465)	(1,611)	(4,328)
Income taxes	50	480	(3,979)	4,503
Other items	1,400	1,280	(17,980)	12,015
Net cash provided by operating activities	51,975	60,955	35,460	38,297
Cash flows from (used for) investing activities:				
Additions to property and equipment	(30,500)	(29,300)	(32,404)	(25,671)
Dispositions of property	528	528	783	758
Other assets	2,700	2,682	(5,672)	3,320
Net cash used for investing activities	(27,272)	(26,090)	(37,293)	(21,593)
Cash flows from (used for) financing activities:				
Dividends paid	(16,758)	(15,613)	(13,662)	(12,100)
Proceeds from notes receivable	(1,533)	(1,533)	(250)	(3,111)

	Forecasted 20X5		Comparative Historical Information	
	Economy Begins Recovery	Continued Downturn in the Economy	20X4	20X3
Reductions of long-term debt	3,588	(1,518)	(245)	(14,225)
Bond financing	—	—	15,500	—
Net cash from (used in) financing activities	(14,703)	(18,664)	1,343	(29,436)
Net increase (decrease) in cash	10,000	16,201	(490)	(12,732)
Cash, beginning of year	1,300	3,300	1,768	14,500
Cash, end of year	$ 11,300	$ 19,501	$ 1,278	$ 1,768

Income tax payments were $25,722 and $24,739 in 20X4 and 20X3, respectively, and are estimated to be $26,133 if the economy begins a recovery and $4,999 if there is a continued downturn in 20X5. Interest payments related to borrowings were $952 and $763 in 20X4 and 20X3, respectively, and are estimated to be $777 if the economy begins a recovery and $845 if there is a continued downturn in 20X5.

See accompanying Summary of Significant Forecast Assumptions and Accounting Policies.

Note: This presentation includes all the minimum items that constitute a financial forecast without presenting a balance sheet.

JMK COMPANY, INC.
Summary of Significant Forecast Assumptions and Accounting Policies
For the Year Ending December 31, 20X5

This financial forecast presents, to the best of management's knowledge and belief, the Company's expected consolidated statements of income and retained earnings and cash flows for the forecast period assuming either a recovery in the economy or a continued downturn in the economy. Accordingly, the forecast reflects management's judgment as of January 31, 20X5, the date of this forecast, of the expected conditions and its expected course of action under each scenario. The assumptions disclosed herein are those that management believes are significant to the forecast. Management reasonably expects, to the best of its knowledge and belief, that the level of economic activity will be within the range shown; however, there can be no assurance that it will. Furthermore, even if the level of economic activity is within the range shown, there will usually be differences between forecasted and actual results because events and circumstances frequently do not occur as expected, and those differences may be material, and the actual results may be outside the ranges presented.

    a. **Summary of Significant Accounting Policies.** (not illustrated)

    b. **Sales.** The sales of the Company have been closely related to the level of activity in the economy. Economists are currently divided in their forecasts of overall economic activity for 20X5. Consequently, management has prepared its forecast in the form of alternative scenarios: one, representing a continued downturn in the economy based on a 2 percent decrease in real GDP for the forecast period, and the other, a beginning of economic recovery based on a 2 percent increase in real GDP for the period. It is anticipated that many of the differences between the two scenarios would be concentrated in the automotive sector of the Company's business.

    c. **Cost of Sales.** The forecast assumes that management is able to maintain tight controls over manufacturing costs and inventory levels. If the downturn in the economy continues, management plans to continue substantial reduction in inventory levels. However, if the economy recovers, the Company will begin rebuilding the level of inventories.

    d. **Selling and Advertising.** The forecast assumes that cost control measures will allow the Company to maintain selling costs at a relatively constant level. The Company plans to spend more on promotional campaigns if the economic downturn persists.

    e. **General and Administrative Expense.** The forecast anticipates a $1.7 million increase in the level of general and administrative expense, due primarily to the development of new computer-based information systems to better control the Company's performance.

    f. **Income Taxes.** The provision for income taxes is computed using the rates currently in effect for 20X5.

    g. **Long-Term Debt.** The Company anticipates a modest reduction in long-term debt if the decline in the economy persists. However, if the economy turns around, the Company expects to increase long-term debt at an interest rate of 1 point above prime.

h. **Dividend.** The Company's policy is to pay out a predetermined portion of net income, and the forecasted dividend assumes continuation of that policy.

Exhibit 9-5

At 4 Percent Annual Increases in Rents and Certain Expenses
ABC REALTY FUND INCORPORATED

Forecasted Statement of Income (Loss)
For Each of the Four Years Ending December 31, 20X9
Presented as a Range

(000 omitted)

	Year Ending December 31,			
	20X6	20X7	20X8	20X9
Operating income:				
Rental income	$6,952	$ 9,231	$ 9,750	$10,138
Tenant reimbursements	791	796	826	848
Other income—parking	63	66	69	71
Gross income	7,806	10,093	10,645	11,057
Operating expenses:				
Property management fee	(204)	(212)	(223)	(232)
Real property taxes	(837)	(860)	(883)	(907)
Operating expenses	(1,064)	(1,107)	(1,151)	(1,197)
Ground rent	(53)	(52)	(52)	(52)
Total operating expenses	(2,158)	(2,231)	(2,309)	(2,388)
Operating income	5648	7862	8336	8669
Interest expense:				
Interest expense— mortgage loans	$ (903)	$ (887)	$(869)	$(850)
Interest expense— secured notes	(4,291)	(4,341)	(4,396)	(4,457)
Interest expense— convertible notes	(647)	(647)	(486)	0
	(5,841)	(5,875)	(5,751)	(5,307)
Other income (expenses):				
Base advisory fee	(550)	(587)	(593)	(621)
Administrative expenses	(260)	(270)	(281)	(292)
Interest income	123	125	127	139
Depreciation	(1,303)	(1,303)	(1,303)	(1,303)
Amortization	(282)	(326)	(439)	(475)
	(2,272)	(2,361)	(2,489)	(2,552)
Income (loss)	$(2,465)	$ (374)	$ 96	$ 810
Basic earnings per share	$(1.20)	$(0.20)	$0.03	$0.26
Diluted earnings per share	$(0.98)	$(0.15)	$0.03	$0.26

See accompanying Summary of Significant Forecast Assumptions and Accounting Policies.

At 6 Percent Annual Increases in Rents and Certain Expenses
ABC REALTY FUND INCORPORATED

Forecasted Statement of Income (Loss)
For Each of the Four Years Ending December 31 20X9
Presented as a Range

(000 omitted)

	Year Ending December 31,			
	20X6	*20X7*	*20X8*	*20X9*
Operating income:				
Rental income	$7,021	$ 9,442	$10,118	$10,720
Tenant reimbursements	814	842	883	916
Other income—parking	65	69	72	77
Gross income	7,900	10,353	11,073	11,713
Operating expenses:				
Property management fee	(206)	(218)	(233)	(247)
Real property taxes	(843)	(871)	(901)	(933)
Operating expenses	(1,085)	(1,150)	(1,219)	(1,292)
Ground rent	(52)	(52)	(52)	(52)
Total operating expenses	(2,186)	(2,291)	(2,405)	(2,524)
Operating income	5,714	8,062	8,668	9,189
Interest expense:				
Interest expense—mortgage loans	$ (903)	$ (887)	$ (869)	$ (850)
Interest expense—secured notes	(4,291)	(4,341)	(4,396)	(4,457)
Interest expense—convertible notes	(647)	(647)	(486)	0
	(5,841)	(5,875)	(5,751)	(5,307)
Other income (expenses):				
Base advisory fee	(555)	(601)	(614)	(657)
Administrative expenses	(265)	(281)	(298)	(315)
Interest income	125	125	135	152
Depreciation	(1,303)	(1,303)	(1,303)	(1,303)
Amortization	(280)	(326)	(456)	(504)
	(2,278)	(2,386)	(2,536)	(2,627)
Income (loss)	$ (2,405)	$ (199)	$ 381	$ 1,255
Basic earnings per share	$ (1.18)	$ (0.11)	$ 0.14	$ 0.40
Diluted earnings per share	$ (0.95)	$ (0.08)	$ 0.14	$ 0.40

See accompanying Summary of Significant Forecast Assumptions and Accounting Policies.

At 4 Percent Annual Increases in Rents and Certain Expenses
ABC REALTY FUND INCORPORATED

**Forecasted Statement of Distributable Cash
For Each of the Four Years Ending December 31 20X9
Presented as a Range**

(000 omitted)

| | *Year Ending December 31,* | | | |
	20X6	*20X7*	*20X8*	*20X9*
Cash from operations:				
Operating income	$ 5,648	$ 7,862	$ 8,336	$ 8,669
Master lease obligation	1,975	90	12	0
Leasing commissions	(136)	(76)	(232)	(219)
Tenant improvements	(151)	(57)	(213)	(174)
	7,336	7,819	7,903	8,276
Debt service (principal and interest):				
Mortgage loans	(1,067)	(1,067)	(1,067)	(1,067)
Secured notes	(3,838)	(3,838)	(3,838)	(3,838)
	(4,905)	(4,905)	(4,905)	(4,905)
Other income (expenses):				
Base advisory fee	(550)	(587)	(593)	(621)
Base advisory fee deferral	550	587	593	621
Administrative expenses	(260)	(270)	(281)	(292)
Stipulated cash amount	409	0	0	0
Interest income	123	125	127	139
	272	(145)	(154)	(153)
Distributable cash	$ 2,703	$ 2,769	$ 2,844	$ 3,218

See accompanying Summary of Significant Forecast Assumptions and Accounting Policies.

At 6 Percent Annual Increases in Rents and Certain Expenses

ABC REALTY FUND INCORPORATED

Forecasted Statement of Distributable Cash
For Each of the Four Years Ending December 31 20X9
Presented as a Range

(000 omitted)

	Year Ending December 31,			
	20X6	*20X7*	*20X8*	*20X9*
Cash from operations:				
Operating income	$ 5,714	$ 8,062	$ 8,668	$ 9,189
Master lease obligation	1,975	90	12	0
Leasing commissions	(130)	(78)	(259)	(234)
Tenant improvements	(152)	(60)	(238)	X
	7,407	8,014	8,183	8,766
Debt service (principal and interest):				
Mortgage loans	(1,067)	(1,067)	(1,067)	(1,067)
Secured notes	(3,838)	(3,838)	(3,838)	(3,838)
	(4,905)	(4,905)	(4,905)	(4,905)
Other income (expenses):				
Base advisory fee	(555)	(601)	(614)	(657)
Base advisory fee deferral	555	420	583	602
Administrative expenses	(265)	(281)	(298)	(315)
Stipulated cash amount	410	0	0	0
Interest income	125	125	135	152
	270	(337)	(194)	(218)
Distributable cash	$ 2,772	$ 2,772	$ 3,084	$ 3,643
Distributable cash per share	$ 1.10	$ 1.10	$ 1.15	$ 1.15

See accompanying Summary of Significant Forecast Assumptions and Accounting Policies.

ABC REALTY FUND INCORPORATED

Summary of Significant Forecast
Assumptions and Accounting Policies
For Each of the Four Years Ending December 31, 20X9

This financial forecast presents, to the best of the Advisor's (management's) knowledge and belief, the Company's expected range of net income (loss) and distributable cash for the forecast period (assuming increases in current market rates for rental properties and certain expenses of 4 percent and 6 percent annually). Accordingly, the forecast reflects the Advisor's judgment, as of December 4, 20X5, the date of this forecast, of the expected conditions and its expected course of action based on the increases in rents and certain expenses reflected in the forecast. The assumptions disclosed herein are those that the Advisor believes are significant to the forecast. Management reasonably expects, to the best of its knowledge and belief, that the actual increases in rents and certain expenses will be within the range shown; however, there can be no assurance that they will. Furthermore, even if the increases in rents and certain expenses are within the range shown, there will usually be differences between forecasted and actual results, because events and circumstances frequently do not occur as expected, and those differences may be material, and the actual results may be outside the ranges presented.

ABC Realty Fund Incorporated ("the Company") is a newly organized corporation that intends to qualify as a real estate investment trust under the Internal Revenue Code.

a. Summary of Significant Accounting Policies

Acquisition

The Company has been established to acquire 10 commercial real estate projects from affiliates of ABC at cost plus carrying costs to date of sale (January 1, 20X6) and an acquisition fee (see note **j**). The purchase price for the properties being acquired are as follows:

Properties	Purchase Prices
CD Business Park	$ 2,680,000
Bank of Toledo Building	10,180,000
Sky Industrial Park	3,380,000
Erie Centre	15,400,000
Lake Business Center	7,550,000
Lake Plaza	4,320,000
Inverness Business Center	9,190,000
Inverness Plaza	3,730,000
Ford Business Park	14,650,000
American Business Park I	4,470,000
	$75,550,000

Capitalization

Source of funds:

Mortgage loans	$ 9,383,000
Secured notes	40,400,000
Common stock	25,200,000
Convertible notes	6,475,000
TOTAL	$81,458,000

Use of funds:

Purchase price	$75,550,000
Issuance cost—stock	2,000,000
Issuance cost—secured notes	1,010,000
Organization costs	200,000
Acquisition fee to Advisor	755,500
Loan commitment fees	404,000
Other offering costs	700,000
Working capital reserve	838,500
TOTAL	$81,458,000

The secured notes and convertible notes have been committed to by third parties, subject to the completion of the common stock offering as discussed in the offering circular.

Basis of Accounting

The forecast has been prepared using generally accepted accounting principles that the Company expects to use when preparing its historical financial statements.

Depreciation and Amortization

The forecast assumes that the Company will depreciate its buildings and capital improvements using the straight-line method over forty years. For depreciation purposes, the cost of the properties consists of the purchase price of $75,550,000 and the property acquisition fee to the Advisor of $755,500, less expected rents due under the master lease of $5,086,100 and the stipulated cash amount of $721,100, and is allocated as follows:

Land	$18,393,300
Buildings and improvements	52,105,000
	$70,498,300

Master Lease Revenues and Stipulated Cash Amount

Rents under the master lease and stipulated cash amounts to be received by the company under agreements with the Advisor are to be credited to the cost of the properties as a reduction of the purchase price, thereby affecting subsequent depreciation.

Leasing Commissions and Tenant Improvement Costs

Leasing commissions and tenant improvement costs paid by the Company are to be amortized over the terms of the respective leases, using the straight-line method.

Issuance Costs

Issuance costs and other offering costs relating to the sale of the stock will be charged directly against stockholders' equity. Issuance costs and other offering costs relating to the sale of the secured notes will be amortized over the term of the secured notes.

Loan Commitment Fees

Loan commitment fees will be amortized over the term of the secured notes.

Income Taxes

The Company will elect to be treated as a real estate investment trust under the provisions of the Code. It assumes the trust will distribute all of its taxable income to the stockholders within the prescribed time limits. Therefore, no provision has been made for federal income taxes.

b. Rental Income

	(A) Range of Existing Rental Rates Under Present Leases Per Sq. Ft.	(A) Forecasted 20X6 Market Rental Rates Per Sq. Ft.	Base Mgmt. Fee	Total Improvement Costs Per Sq. Ft.
CD Business Park	$.32–$.38	$.38–$.40	2%	$ .15
Bank of Toledo	$.56–$1.65	$1.25–$1.65	4%	$3.50
Sky Industrial Park	$.33–$.38	$.38–$.40	2%	$.15
Erie Centre	$1.00–$1.20	$1.00	3%	$1.75
Lake Business Center	$.47–$.87	$.56–$.87	3%	$.75
Lake Plaza	$1.24–$1.47	$1.29	3%	$3.50
Inverness Business Center	$.42–$.83	$.62–$1.06	3%	$.75
Inverness Plaza	$.81	$1.00	3%	$3.50
Ford Business Park	$.75–$.90	$1.07	3%	$1.75
American Business Park I	$.33–$.58	$.38–$.46	5%	$.50

(A) Calculated using net rentable square feet, on a monthly basis. Future leases for CD Business Park, Inverness Plaza and Ford Business Park are assumed to be triple net leases. Leases for Sky Industrial Park and Erie Centre are assumed to be a combination of triple net and gross leases. All other properties are assumed to have gross leases.

Leases in effect on December 31, 20X5, serve as the basis for all rental calculations in the forecast. It is expected that existing tenants will exercise available options upon the expiration of the original lease terms. It is also forecasted that new tenants, including any old tenants whose leases, including renewals, have expired, will sign leases at the forecasted market rental rate. The forecast is presented assuming that the market rental rate escalates 4 percent and 6 percent annually beginning January 1, 20X6.

The forecast gives effect to the master lease with the Advisor ("master lease") covering buildings that are less than 95 percent leased as of the commencement date, under which the Advisor will lease sufficient space such that each building is 95 percent leased. The rental rates for such space are equal to the rental income and reimbursable expense assumptions included in the forecast. The master lease is to have a term of forty months and will address only space that is unoccupied as of the commencement date plus 126,446 square feet of space presently occupied by two major tenants in Lake Business Center, Inverness Business Center, and Inverness Plaza, should such space become vacant during the term of the master lease. Leased space, other than that noted above, as of the commencement date that is vacated later, is not covered by this master lease.

Rental payments due under the master lease by the Advisor during the forty-month term are assumed to aggregate approximately $14,200,000, although the Advisor estimates that approximately $9,113,900 will be obtained from substitute lessees to reduce the obligation of the Advisor under the master lease to approximately $5,086,100.

Based upon historical experience for similar properties, it is expected that 75 percent of existing tenants will renew upon expiration of their leases (including renewal periods), while 25 percent will vacate. New lease terms are generally expected to be three to five years.

c. Tenant Reimbursements

Tenants in certain properties are required to pay their pro rata share (based on square footage occupied) of certain reimbursable expenses in excess of the defined base year costs ("expense stop"). All other tenants are required to pay all operating expenses related to their leased premises (triple net leases).

The "expense stops" are recalculated upon lease expiration using the turnover year as the base year. The new "expense stop" rate is assumed to apply to the released space. The same method is used for space under the master lease beginning in 20X6, using 20X5 as a base year for calculation.

d. Vacancy Reserve, Credit, and Turnover Loss

A vacancy factor of 5 percent of total rental income, including tax and expense reimbursements and parking income, is forecasted. The vacancy factor allows for vacant space that is assumed to exist between the expiration of a lease and the re-leasing of the space, rent concession on re-leasing, and collection losses.

e. Tenant Improvements and Leasing Commissions

Tenant improvements represent the Advisor's estimate of the per square foot cost of making space ready for occupancy by new tenants for spaces vacated by existing tenants. One-half of this amount is forecasted to be paid by the Company for tenants renewing existing leases. The cost per square foot detailed by property in note **b** is escalated 4 percent and 6 percent annually beginning in 20X6.

Leasing commissions represent approximately 5 percent of aggregate future rentals to be received from replacement tenants and 2.5 percent of the aggregate future rentals from renewal tenants. For purposes of the forecast, it is generally assumed that 75 percent of the existing tenants will renew, and 25 percent will leave upon the expiration of their lease terms (including renewal periods). This estimate is consistent with the prior experience of the Advisor based on comparable properties.

f. Operating Expenses

Real Estate Taxes

Real estate taxes are based on a review of prior taxes, current local tax laws and discussion with local tax assessors, and have been escalated 4 percent and 6 percent annually.

Operating Expenses

Operating expenses are the Advisor's estimates of the 20X6 gross expenses relating to each of the properties based on an historical analysis of expenses over the prior three years, plus the Advisor's knowledge of the industry and comparable operating results of similar properties.

These expenses are partly reimbursable by the tenants as described in note **c**. The expenses are escalated 4 percent and 6 percent annually.

Property Management Fees

The property management fees range from 2 percent to 5 percent of effective gross income as detailed in note **b**. All property management fees are grouped in expenses and will be passed through to tenants under the terms of the respective leases.

g. Mortgage Loans

Inverness Business Center and Inverness Plaza will be acquired subject to a 10.375 percent first mortgage loan of $5,970,466 as of the assumed date of purchase, requiring monthly payments of $56,213 including principal and interest.

The leasehold interest in the Bank of Toledo Building will be acquired subject to an 8.75 percent first mortgage loan of $3,412,689 as of the assumed date of purchase, requiring monthly payments of $32,681 including principal and interest.

h. Secured Notes

The secured notes will have a stated amount of $40,400,000 and a thirty-year maturity. The pay rate on these notes is assumed to be 9.5 percent with an assumed accrual rate assumed of 10.5 percent, which is compounded monthly.

i. Convertible Notes

The convertible notes of $6,475,000, under the terms of the notes, must be converted by October 1, 20X8. These notes will carry a coupon rate of 10 percent, simple interest. No interest is payable through the date of conversion. For purposes of these forecasts, the convertible notes, together with the accrued but unpaid interest, are expected to be converted to 647,500 shares of common stock on October 1, 20X8.

j. Acquisition Fee

The Advisor is to provide advice to the Company on the acquisition of the properties and to render other services. The Advisor is to receive an acquisition fee of 1 percent of the purchase price of the properties.

k. Base Advisory Fee

The Advisor will receive an annual base advisory fee calculated by determining the annual cash from operations from the properties or other investments held by the Company, capitalizing that amount at 10 percent and multiplying by .75 percent. The Advisor will defer payment of its base advisory fee for the first thirty months of the Company's operations, up to a maximum of $1,263,300 without interest, payable on liquidation of the Company. After the maximum base deferred amount has been reached, the base advisory fee will be payable only after stockholders have received cash distributions equivalent to a specified rate of return for the particular year, based on an initial price per share of $10.00. From inception through December 31, 20X7, no base advisory fee will be payable until stockholders have received an 11 percent rate of return and, from January 1, 20X8, through December 31, 20X9, no base advisory fee will be payable until stockholders have received an 11.5 percent rate of return. Any base advisory fee or portion that is deferred (other than the base deferred amount) will be accrued without interest and paid in succeeding periods after receipt by the stockholders of the then-current year's specified rate of return, receipt by stockholders of the cumulative rate of return for prior years to the extent previously unpaid, and payment of the base advisory fee for that year.

l. Administrative Expenses

Administrative expenses, including, but not limited to, directors' fees and expenses, professional fees, and printing, mailing, and transfer agent fees, are expected to increase in the range of 4 percent and 6 percent annually.

m. Interest Income

Interest income on average distributable cash and cash reserves is forecasted to be earned at an annual rate of 6.5 percent on short-term funds invested by the Company in real estate-related securities.

n. Distribution of Cash Flow

All available funds are assumed to be distributed to stockholders from January 1, 20X6, through October 1, 20X8. On October 1, 20X8, the convertible notes are assumed to be converted into common stock. All cash distributions will be distributed pro rata to all stockholders.

Pretax cash return per share represents forecasted distributable cash divided by the average number of shares outstanding for that given year.

o. Stipulated Cash Amount

The Advisor will provide to the Company up to an aggregate amount of $721,100 (the "stipulated cash amount") as required by the Company, to provide the holders of its common stock with distributions of up to an 11 percent annual return for the fiscal year ending December 31, 20X6.

p. Basic and Diluted Earnings Per Share

Basic earnings per share of common stock were computed by dividing income available to common stockholders by the weighted average number of common shares outstanding for the year. Diluted earnings per share of common stock gives effect to all dilutive potential common shares that were outstanding during the year. Diluted earnings per share were computed by dividing income available to common stockholders, adjusted for changes in income or loss that would result from the assumed conversion of potential common shares, by the weighted average number of common shares outstanding for the year, increased to include the number of additional common shares that would have been outstanding if the dilutive potential common shares had been issued.

q. Related Party Transactions

Six of the properties to be acquired will be purchased from limited partnerships of which the managing general partner is ABC. Two will be purchased from Capital Corporation, an Affiliate, and the remaining two properties will be purchased from ABC.

Each of the properties will be advised on behalf of the Company by ABC Investment Properties, Inc. (the Advisor), an affiliate, and will be managed by ABC Property Management Company, Inc. (the Property Manager), also an affiliate.

The Company has been organized by ABC and Affiliates, and the Advisor and Property Manager have been organized and are wholly owned by ABC.

Exhibit 9-6

ABC COMPANY, INC.

**Statement of Projected Results of Operations and Cash Flow
Assuming Construction of an Additional Plant
For Each of the Five Years Ending December 31, 20X7**

(in thousands except for per-share amounts)

	Year Ending December 31,				
	20X3	20X4	20X5	20X6	20X7
Net sales	$101,200	$112,300	$142,000	$156,200	$173,400
Cost of sales	77,500	86,100	109,300	120,100	133,300
Gross profit	23,700	26,200	32,700	36,100	40,100
Selling, general, and administrative expenses	15,100	16,500	19,500	21,400	23,400
Operating income	8,600	9,700	13,200	14,700	16,700
Other income (deductions):					
Miscellaneous	1,700	1,200	1,000	1,300	1,800
Interest expense	(2,400)	(3,500)	(3,400)	(3,200)	(3,000)
	(700)	(2,300)	(2,400)	(1,900)	(1,200)
Income before taxes	7,900	7,400	10,800	12,800	15,500
Income taxes	3,400	2,800	4,700	5,500	6,700
Net income	4,500	4,600	6,100	7,300	8,800
Add noncash expenses:					
Depreciation and amortization					
Deferred taxes	2,800	500	2,800	450	3,400
	500	2,750	1,150	3,650	750
	500	2750	1150	3650	750
Add (deduct)					
Loans proceeds for additional plant facility	8,500	1,500	—	—	—
Increase in excess of receivables and other assets over payables	(1,000)	(1,000)	(2,000)	(3,000)	(3,500)
Cash requirements for building costs	(8,200)	(1,800)	—	—	—
Other additions to plant and equipment	(3,400)	(2,200)	(2,200)	(2,200)	(2,200)
Cash requirements for repayment of debt	(2,600)	(2,600)	(3,700)	(3,500)	(3,500)
Dividends	(1,400)	(1,400)	(1,900)	(2,200)	(2,700)
Increase (decrease) in cash	(300)	350	250	500	1,050
Cash, beginning of year	3,300	3,000	3,350	3,600	4,100
Cash, end of year	$ 3,000	$ 3,350	$ 3,600	$ 4,100	$ 5,150
Earnings per share	$ 4.80	$ 4.92	$ 6.51	$ 7.79	$ 9.39
Dividends per share	$ 1.50	$ 1.50	$ 2.03	$ 2.35	$ 2.88

See accompanying Summary of Significant Forecast Assumptions and Accounting Policies.

ABC COMPANY, INC.

Summary of Significant Assumptions Employed in Preparation of the Statement of Projected Results of Operations and Cash Flow

Assuming Construction of an Additional Plant

For Each of the Five Years Ending December 31, 20X7

This financial projection of operations and cash flow assuming construction of an additional plant presents, to the best of management's knowledge and belief, the expected results of operations and cash flow for the projection period if a plant were constructed to increase production capacity by approximately 20 percent. Accordingly, the projection reflects management's judgment as of October 24, 20X2, the date of this projection, of the expected conditions and its expected course of action if such a plant were constructed. The presentation is designed to provide information for potential bank financing of the construction of the additional plant and cannot be considered to be a presentation of expected future results. Accordingly, this projection may not be useful for other purposes. The assumptions disclosed herein are those that management believes are significant to the projection; however, management has not decided that it will construct such a plant. Even if the plant were constructed, there will usually be differences between projected and actual results, because events and circumstances frequently do not occur as expected, and those differences may be material.

    a. **Summary of Significant Accounting Policies.** (not illustrated)

    b. **Hypothetical Assumption—Increase in Production Capacity by Construction of a New Plant.** The projection is based on the assumption that production capacity will be increased by approximately 20 percent by the construction of a 160,000 square foot production facility in Richmond, Virginia.

        Construction on the new plant is projected to begin in February, 20X3 and to be completed by June 30, 20X4, at a total cost of $10,000,000 including construction-period interest of $1,300,000. Production cost estimates and the projected completion date have been estimated based on competitive bids received.

        The decision to proceed with the project and the awarding of contracts will depend on the completion of financing arrangements.

    c. **Sales.** The overall market for the Company's products has grown over the past five years at an average rate of 2 percent above the actual increase in gross domestic product, and the Company's market share has remained steady at 14 percent to 16 percent. Based on a recent market study of demand for the Company's products, sales are projected to increase 11 percent per annum from 20X2 to 20X4 (which is consistent with a rate of 2 percent above the Department of Commerce Bureau of Economic Analysis' estimate of the rise in gross domestic product in the projection period), with a market share of 15 percent and unit prices increased to cover projected increases in cost of manufacturing. Based on the study, an additional 15 percent increase in sales is projected to occur beginning in 20X5 and will be met by the added capacity resulting from the plant expansion.

d. Cost of Sales

Materials. Materials used by the Company are expected to be readily available, and the Company has generally used producer associations' estimates of prices in the projection period to project material costs. The Company expects to be able to assure a sufficient supply of materials and estimates that the cost of materials will increase by 12 percent per annum.

Labor. The Company's labor union contract, which covers substantially all manufacturing personnel, will be subject to renegotiation in 20X6. Labor costs until that time are projected based on the existing contract. For 20X7, labor costs, including fringe benefits, are projected to increase 19 percent per year above the 20X6 level. The outcome of the projection is particularly sensitive to variances in such labor costs. For each percentage point variance from the projected increase, net income and cash will vary by approximately $380,000.

e. Plant and Equipment and Depreciation Expense.
Projected additions to plant and equipment, other than the assumed plant expansion, are principally the regular periodic replacement of manufacturing plant and vehicles at suppliers' quoted estimated prices and do not involve any significant changes in manufacturing capacity or processes. Depreciation is projected on an item-by-item basis. Depreciation on the new facility is projected on a straight-line basis over twenty years.

f. Selling, General, and Administrative Expense.
The principal types of expenses within this category are salaries, transportation costs, and sales promotion. Salaries are projected on an individual basis, using expected salary rates in the projection period. Transportation costs are principally for contract carriers; volume is projected based on sales and inventory projections, and rates are forecasted by 16 percent per year based on trucking industry forecasts. Sales promotion costs are expected to increase in line with the consumer price index, as is the level of other expenses.

g. Bank Borrowings and Interest Expense.
The projection assumes that the Company will obtain an extension of existing short-term lines of credit at terms comparable to those in effect in 20X2 (two percent over the prime rate). The Company used the arithmetic mean of [*three widely used estimates*] of bank prime rate during the projection period (ranging from 12 percent to 14 percent) to estimate prime rate at 13 percent. The Company projects additional long-term borrowing of $10 million to finance the planned plant expansion (including $1,300,000 of construction-period capitalized interest) and has entered into preliminary negotiations with its bankers for this financing. Based on the preliminary negotiations, the Company has assumed that the additional long-term financing will bear interest at 14 percent.

h. Miscellaneous Income.
The projection assumes that royalty income of $950,000 will be received annually based on an agreement under which the Company is to receive a minimum of $950,000 for the first 10,000,000 units produced under its patented die casting process and $.05 per unit above that level. Management believes it

is unlikely that production will exceed 10,000,000 units in any of the projection periods.

i. **Income Taxes.** The provision for income taxes is computed using the statutory rates in effect during 20X2, which are not expected to change. The Company anticipates that it will take investment tax credits on the machinery and equipment to be installed in the new plant when the plant is placed in service in 20X4.

j. **Dividend.** The Company's normal dividend policy is to pay out the previous year's dividend increased to the extent of at least one-third of any increase in profits over the previous year, provided the board of directors considers that the Company's cash and working-capital position will not be adversely affected.

_____

Part 3

Guidance for Practitioners Who Provide Services on Prospective Financial Statements

Chapter 10

Types of Practitioners' Services

> Because financial forecasts and projections are similar in many respects, separate guidance for projections is provided only to the extent that it differs from that for forecasts. *Italicized* paragraphs in this chapter that include a "P" in the paragraph number show how the guidance presented for forecasts should be modified for projections. Any plain-text paragraph not followed by an italicized paragraph applies to both forecasts and projections even though it uses only the term *forecast.*

10.01 The paragraphs that follow provide guidance to practitioners concerning performance and reporting for engagements in order to compile (paragraph 10.04), examine (paragraph 10.06), or apply agreed-upon procedures to (paragraph 10.08) financial forecasts. Chapter 23, "Partial Presentations of Prospective Financial Information," explains how this guidance applies to the unique aspects of partial presentations.

10.02 Whenever a practitioner (*a*) submits, to clients or others, a financial forecast that he or she has assembled, or assisted in assembling, that is or reasonably might be expected to be used by another (third) party[1] or (*b*) reports on a financial forecast that is, or reasonably might be, expected to be used by another (third) party[2] he should perform one of the engagements described in the preceding paragraph.[3] In deciding whether the financial forecast is, or reasonably might be, expected to be used by a third party, the practitioner may rely on either the written or oral representation of the responsible party, unless information comes to his or her attention that contradicts the responsible party's representation. If such third-party use of the financial forecast is not reasonably expected, the provisions of this chapter are not applicable unless the practitioner has been engaged to examine, compile, or apply agreed-upon procedures to the financial forecast (Chapter 22, "Guidance on the Practitioner's Services and Reports on Prospective Financial Statements for Internal Use Only," provides guidance on the types of services a practitioner may provide on prospective financial statements for internal use only).

10.03 This guide does not provide standards or procedures for engagements involving financial forecasts used solely in connection with litigation

---

[1] However, paragraph 10.20 permits an exception to this rule for certain types of budgets.

[2] In deciding whether a party that is or reasonably might be expected to use a practitioner's report is considered a third party, the practitioner may consider the degree of consistency of interest between the responsible party and the user regarding the forecast. If their interests are substantially consistent (for example, both the responsible party and the user are employees of the entity about which the forecast is made), the user would not be deemed a third party. On the other hand, if the interests of the responsible party and the user are potentially inconsistent (for example, the responsible party is a nonowner manager and the user is an absentee owner), the user would be deemed a third party. In some cases, this determination will require the exercise of considerable professional judgment.

[3] This requirement does not preclude limited distribution of a financial forecast that is clearly identified as a draft prior to the issuance of the practitioner's report. When a forecast is issued as a draft, it is not deemed to be submitted because the forecast may be relied on only when the final forecast and practitioner's report are submitted. A practitioner may not undertake an engagement to assist in assembling a financial forecast that is or reasonably might be expected to be used by another (third) party without intending to issue a final report.

support services. A practitioner may, however, look to this guide because it provides helpful guidance for many aspects of such engagements and may be referred to as useful guidance in such engagements. Litigation support services are engagements involving pending or potential formal legal proceedings before a trier of fact in connection with the resolution of a dispute between two or more parties, for example, when a practitioner acts as an expert witness. This exception is provided because, among other things, the practitioner's work in such proceedings is ordinarily subject to detailed analysis and challenge by each party to the dispute. This exception does not apply, however, if either of the following occurs:

　　a. The practitioner is specifically engaged to issue or does issue an examination, a compilation, or an agreed-upon procedures report on the financial forecast.

　　b. The financial forecast is for use by third parties who, under the rules of the proceedings, do not have the opportunity for analysis and challenge by each party to a dispute in a legal proceeding.

For example, creditors may not have such opportunities when the financial forecast is submitted to them to secure their agreement to a plan of reorganization.

10.04 A compilation of a financial forecast is a professional service that involves the following:

　　a. Assembling, to the extent necessary, the financial forecast based on the responsible party's assumptions

　　b. Performing the required compilation procedures,[4] including reading the financial forecast with its summaries of significant assumptions and accounting policies, and considering whether they appear to be presented in conformity with AICPA presentation guidelines[5] and not obviously inappropriate

　　c. Issuing a compilation report

10.05 A compilation is not intended to provide assurance on a financial forecast or the assumptions underlying it. Because of the limited nature of the practitioner's procedures, a compilation does not provide assurance that the practitioner will become aware of significant matters that might be disclosed by more extensive procedures, for example, those performed in an examination of a financial forecast. Chapters 12–14 provide guidance on engagements to compile a financial forecast.

10.06 An examination of a financial forecast is a professional service that involves

　　a. evaluating the preparation of the financial forecast.

　　b. evaluating the support underlying the assumptions.

　　c. evaluating the presentation of the financial forecast for conformity with AICPA presentation guidelines.[6]

　　d. issuing an examination report.

---

[4] See chapter 12, "Compilation Procedures," for the required procedures.
[5] AICPA presentation guidelines are detailed in chapter 8, "Presentation Guidelines."
[6] See footnote 5.

10.07 Chapters 15–17 provide guidance on engagements to examine a financial forecast.

10.08 An engagement to apply agreed-upon procedures to a financial forecast is a professional service that involves

    a. having the specified users agree upon the procedures performed or to be performed by the practitioner and take responsibility for the sufficiency of the procedures for their purposes.

    b. applying the agreed-upon procedures.

    c. issuing a report that indicates it is limited in use and intended solely for the specified users, enumerates the procedures performed, states the practitioner's findings, and refers to conformity with the arrangements made with the specified users.

10.09 Chapters 19–21 provide guidance on engagements to apply agreed-upon procedures to financial forecasts.

10.10 If a practitioner is not engaged to compile, examine, or apply agreed-upon procedures and the financial forecast is not reasonably expected to be used by third parties, he or she may provide other services, such as consulting or assembly services, with respect to that forecast without having to report on such statements. Chapter 22 provides guidance to a practitioner in such circumstances.

Reporting Considerations

10.11 The summary of significant assumptions is essential to the user's understanding of the financial forecast. Accordingly, the practitioner should not submit or report on financial forecasts that exclude disclosure of the summary of significant assumptions.

10.11P *In addition, the practitioner should not submit or report on a financial projection that excludes either the identification of the hypothetical assumptions or a description of the limitations on the usefulness of the presentation.*

10.12 If the practitioner considers the assumptions to be inappropriate, see the guidance in paragraph 12.11*j* if engaged to compile the financial forecast or paragraph 17.08 if engaged to examine the statements.

10.12P *Because a financial projection is not appropriate for general use, for example, in an offering statement of an entity's debt or equity interest, a practitioner also should not submit or report on or consent to the use of his or her name in conjunction with a financial projection that he or she believes will be distributed to those who will not be negotiating directly with the responsible party, unless the projection is used to supplement a financial forecast (see paragraph 4.05).*

10.13 In reporting on a financial forecast, the practitioner may be called on to assist the responsible party in identifying assumptions, gathering information, or assembling the statements.[7] The responsible party is nonetheless responsible for the preparation and presentation of the financial forecast

---

[7] Some of the services may not be appropriate if the accountant is to be named as the person reporting on an examination in a filing with the Securities and Exchange Commission.

because the financial forecast is dependent on the actions, plans, and assumptions of the responsible party, and only it can take responsibility for the assumptions. Accordingly, the practitioner's engagement should not be characterized in his or her report or in the document containing the report as including "preparation" of the financial forecast. A practitioner may be engaged to prepare a financial analysis of a potential project in which the engagement includes obtaining information, making appropriate assumptions, and assembling the presentation. Such an analysis is not, and should not be characterized as, a forecast (*or a projection*) and would not be appropriate for general use. However, if the responsible party reviewed and adopted the assumptions and presentation, or based its assumptions and presentation on the analysis, the practitioner could compile or examine the forecast and issue a report appropriate for general use. (Paragraph .06 of AT section 301, *Financial Forecasts and Projections* [AICPA, *Professional Standards*]).

Reasonably Objective Basis for Presentation

10.14 When the practitioner has been engaged to examine, compile, or apply agreed-upon procedures to a financial forecast, he or she should consider whether the responsible party has a reasonably objective basis for presenting a forecast (see chapter 7, "Reasonably Objective Basis"). In considering whether the responsible party has a reasonably objective basis, the practitioner should consider whether sufficiently objective assumptions can be developed for each key factor. If engaged to compile a forecast, the practitioner is not required to obtain or review documentation supporting the assumptions in order to determine whether the responsible party has a reasonably objective basis for the forecast. Rather, this consideration would be a factor in his or her considerations about whether the presentation would be misleading. Similarly, the practitioner would not need to obtain or review documentation supporting the assumptions in an engagement to apply agreed-upon procedures to a forecast unless obtaining or reviewing such documentation was among the procedures requested by the user.

10.14P *For a financial projection, there need not be a reasonably objective basis for the hypothetical assumptions as long as they are consistent with the expected purpose and use of the projection. However, the practitioner should consider that as the number or significance (or both) of hypothetical assumptions increases, it may be inappropriate for the responsible party to present a financial projection.*

10.15 When a forecast is presented in terms of a range, the presentation may become less meaningful as the size of the range increases. As a result, it may be inappropriate to examine, compile, or apply agreed-upon procedures to it.

Change in Engagement to a Lower Level of Service

10.16 A practitioner who has been engaged to perform a service on a forecast may, before the completion of his or her engagement, be requested to change the engagement to a lower level of service. A request to change the engagement may result from a change in circumstances affecting the entity's requirement for the service, a misunderstanding as to the nature of the service or the alternative services originally available, or a restriction on the scope of the service, whether imposed by the entity or caused by circumstances.

10.17 In complying with the request to change the nature of the engagement, the practitioner should evaluate the possibility that information affected by the scope restriction may be inappropriate, incomplete, or otherwise misleading. If the practitioner believes that the information so affected is misleading, he or she should try to obtain that information and consider whether a change to a lower level of service would be inappropriate and whether he or she should issue, for example, an adverse examination report or withdraw from the engagement. The practitioner should not change the engagement to a lower level of service if he or she concludes that the responsible party has no reasonably objective basis to present a forecast.

10.18 If the engagement is changed,[8] upon completion of the engagement the practitioner should issue an appropriate report. The report should not include reference to the original engagement or scope limitations that resulted in the changed engagement, or, in the case of a compilation, any examination procedures that may have been performed.

A Practitioner's Responsibility for a Financial Forecast That Contains Disclosures About Periods Beyond the Forecast Period

10.19 A responsible party may present a financial forecast that contains, in the notes to the forecast, disclosures about events and circumstances expected to occur in periods beyond the forecast period.[9] The nature and extent of the practitioner's procedures on such disclosures depend on whether he or she is engaged to compile or examine the forecast. In either case, however, the practitioner should consider whether such disclosures are required and, if so, whether they are made (see paragraphs 8.34 and 8.40). The practitioner is not required to design specific procedures solely to identify conditions and events that might occur beyond the forecast period. Rather, the practitioner's consideration is based on information about management's existing plans, future events, and circumstances obtained during the course of the engagement.[10] The practitioner also should consider whether the disclosures made are (a) consistent with management's existing plans and knowledge of future events and circumstances, and (b) presented in conformity with the guidelines in paragraph 8.42.

---

[8] If the engagement is changed, the practitioner may deem it appropriate to establish an understanding in writing with the client as to the new service to be performed.

[9] Because such disclosures are included in the notes to the financial forecast, they are covered by the practitioner's standard report. Paragraphs 14.17–.18 discuss reporting when a practitioner is engaged to compile a forecast containing such disclosures; paragraphs 17.21–.22 discuss reporting when the practitioner is engaged to examine a forecast containing such disclosures.

[10] The practitioner is not responsible for anticipating future events, circumstances, or management plans. Furthermore, the practitioner's report does not imply assurance that all such matters that might occur beyond the forecast have been disclosed.

A Practitioner's Responsibility If a Financial Forecast Is Included in a Document Containing Historical Financial Statements

Practitioner-Submitted Documents

10.20 According to paragraph .59 of AT section 301, when a practitioner's compilation, review, or audit report on historical financial statements is included in a practitioner-submitted document containing a financial forecast, the practitioner should either examine, compile, or apply agreed-upon procedures to the financial forecast and report accordingly, unless

　　a. the financial forecast is labeled as a "budget,"

　　b. the budget does not extend beyond the end of the current fiscal year, and

　　c. the budget is presented with interim historical financial statements for the current year.

In such circumstances, the practitioner need not examine, compile, or apply agreed-upon procedures to the budget; however, he or she should report on it and

　　a. indicate that he or she did not examine or compile the budget and

　　b. disclaim an opinion or any other form of assurance on the budget.

In addition, the budgeted information may omit the summaries of significant assumptions and accounting policies required by the guidelines for presentation of a financial forecast established by the AICPA, provided that such omission is not, to the practitioner's knowledge, undertaken with the intention of misleading those who might reasonably be expected to use such budgeted information, and is disclosed in the practitioner's report. The following is the form of the standard paragraphs to be added to the practitioner's report in this circumstance when the summaries of significant assumptions and policies have been omitted.

> The accompanying budgeted balance sheet, statements of income, retained earnings, and cash flows of XYZ Company as of December 31, 20XX, and for the six months then ending, have not been compiled or examined by us and, accordingly, we do not express an opinion or any other form of assurance on them.

> Management has elected to omit the summaries of significant assumptions and accounting policies required under established guidelines for presentation of prospective financial statements. If the omitted summaries were included in the budgeted information, they might influence the user's conclusions about the company's budgeted information. Accordingly, this budgeted information is not designed for those who are not informed about such matters.

Client-Prepared Documents

10.21 According to paragraph .60 of AT section 301, when the practitioner's compilation, review, or audit report on historical financial statements is included in a client-prepared document containing a financial forecast, the practitioner should not consent to the use of his or her name in the document unless

    a. he or she has examined, compiled, or applied agreed-upon procedures to the financial forecast and his or her report accompanies it,

    b. the financial forecast is accompanied by an indication by the responsible party or the practitioner that the practitioner has not performed such a service on the forecast and that the practitioner assumes no responsibility for it, or

    c. another practitioner has examined, compiled, or applied agreed-upon procedures to the forecast and his or her report is included in the document.

In addition, if the practitioner has audited the historical financial statements and they accompany a financial forecast that he or she did not examine, compile, or apply agreed-upon procedures to in certain[11] client-prepared documents, refer to AU-C section 720, *Other Information in Documents Containing Audited Financial Statements* (AICPA, *Professional Standards*).

10.22 If a practitioner consents to the use of his or her report on historical financial statements in a client-prepared, general-use document that contains a financial projection for a period not covered by the forecast, such projection should be accompanied by an indication by the responsible party or the practitioner that the practitioner provides no assurance on the financial projection. AU-C section 720 provides guidance when the practitioner has audited the historical financial statements. Although the practitioner may consider informing the responsible party that the presentation of a financial projection for a period not covered by the forecast in a general-use document is not in conformity with the provisions of this guide, the use of such a projection in a general-use document is not presumed to be a material misstatement of fact.

10.23 The practitioner whose report on a financial forecast is included in a client-prepared document containing historical financial statements should not consent to the use of his or her name in the document unless

    a. he or she has compiled, reviewed, or audited the historical financial statements and his or her report accompanies them,

    b. the historical financial statements are accompanied by an indication by the responsible party or the practitioner that the practitioner has not performed such a service on the historical financial statements and that he or she assumes no responsibility for them, or

---

[11] AU-C section 720, *Other Information in Documents Containing Audited Financial Statements* (AICPA, *Professional Standards*), applies only to such financial forecasts contained in annual reports (or similar documents) that are issued to owners (or similar stakeholders) and annual reports of governments and organizations for charitable or philanthropic purposes that are available to the public and may be applied to other documents to which the auditor, at the client's request, devotes attention. AU-C section 720 does not apply when the historical financial statements and report appear in a registration statement filed under the Securities Act of 1933 (in which case, see AU-C section 925, *Filings With the U.S. Securities and Exchange Commission Under the Securities Act of 1933* [AICPA, *Professional Standards*], and for auditors subject to Public Company Accounting Oversight Board requirements at AU section 711, *Filings Under Federal Securities Statutes* [AICPA, *PCAOB Standards and Related Rules*, Interim Standards]).

    c. another practitioner has compiled, reviewed or audited the historical
    financial statements and his or her report is included in the docu-
    ment.

Other Information in a Client-Prepared Document Containing a Financial Forecast

10.24 An entity may publish various documents that contain information other than historical financial statements in addition to the compiled or examined financial forecast and the practitioner's report thereon. The practitioner's responsibility with respect to information in such a document does not extend beyond the financial information identified in the report and he or she has no obligation to perform any procedures to corroborate other information contained in the document. However, the practitioner should read the other information and consider whether such information, or the manner of its presentation, is materially inconsistent with the information, or the manner of its presentation, appearing in the financial forecast. (Paragraph .62 of AT section 301).

10.25 Examples of information included in a document containing a financial forecast that would be considered materially inconsistent with the financial forecast include phrases relating to the forecasted amounts, such as the following:

- Cannot be predicted at this time
- Unlikely to occur
- No prediction can be made

These phrases are inconsistent with the definition of a financial forecast, which is based on the responsible party's assumptions reflecting conditions it expects to exist and the course of action it expects to take (paragraph 3.04). Therefore, prospective statements in a document containing such statements should not be characterized as a forecast (see paragraph 10.12).

10.25P *The examples given previously would not necessarily be inconsistent information in a document containing a financial projection (for example, a hypothetical assumption may be unlikely to occur). Although the examples may not apply, the practitioner should use his or her judgment in determining whether information in the document is inconsistent with the presentation (see paragraph 10.24).*

10.26 If the practitioner examines a financial forecast included in a document containing inconsistent information, he or she might not be able to conclude that there is adequate support for each significant assumption. The practitioner should consider whether the forecast, his or her report, or both require revision. Depending on the conclusion he or she reaches, the practitioner should consider other actions that may be appropriate, such as issuing an adverse opinion, disclaiming an opinion because of a scope limitation, withholding the use of his or her report in the document, or withdrawing from the engagement. (Paragraph .63 of AT section 301).

10.27 If the practitioner compiles a financial forecast included in the document containing inconsistent information, he or she should attempt to obtain additional or revised information. If he or she does not receive such information, the practitioner should withhold the use of his or her report or withdraw from the compilation engagement.

10.28 If, while reading the other information appearing in the document containing the examined or compiled financial forecast, as described in the preceding paragraphs, the practitioner becomes aware of information that he or she believes is a material misstatement of fact that is not an inconsistent statement, he or she should discuss the matter with the responsible party. In connection with this discussion, the practitioner should consider that he or she may not have the expertise to assess the validity of the statement made, that there may be no standards by which to assess its presentation, and that there may be valid differences of judgment or opinion. If the practitioner concludes that he or she has a valid basis for concern, he or she should propose that the responsible party consult with some other party whose advice might be useful, such as the entity's legal counsel.

10.29 If, after discussing the matter as described in paragraph 10.28, the practitioner concludes that a material misstatement of fact remains, the action he or she takes will depend on using judgment in the particular circumstances. The practitioner should consider steps such as notifying the responsible party in writing of his or her views concerning the information and consulting legal counsel about further appropriate action in the circumstances.

10.30 If certain other information has been subjected to the procedures applied to the financial forecast, the practitioner may report on the other information. In those circumstances, the practitioner's report on the information should describe clearly the character of the practitioner's work and the degree of responsibility the practitioner is taking.

10.31 If a practitioner consents to the use of his or her report on a financial forecast in a client-prepared, general-use document that also contains a financial projection for a period not covered by the forecast, such projection should be accompanied by an indication by the responsible party or the practitioner that the practitioner provides no assurance on the financial projection. In addition, the practitioner should refer to the guidance in paragraphs 10.24–.30 and consider informing the responsible party that the presentation, in a general-use document, of a projection for a period not covered by the forecast is not in conformity with this guide.

Materiality

10.32 The concept of materiality affects the application of this guide to a financial forecast, as materiality affects the application of generally accepted auditing standards to historical financial statements. Materiality is a concept that is judged in light of the expected range of reasonableness of the information; therefore, users should not expect prospective information (information about events that have not yet occurred) to be as precise as historical information. (Paragraph .07 of AT section 301).

Chapter 11

Tax Shelter Opinions

> Because a tax shelter offering document is a general use document, it would be inappropriate to include in it a projection unless the projection was used to supplement a forecast. Accordingly, the guidance in this chapter applies only to forecasts.

11.01 As of the time of printing, the Treasury Department regulations governing practice before the IRS include standards for providing tax opinions used in the promotion of tax shelter offerings (31 U.S. *Code of Federal Regulations* [CFR] Part 10, published in Treasury Department Circular No. 230 [Circular 230], *Regulations Governing Practice before the Internal Revenue Service* [see appendix C of this guide]).[1] Under these regulations, a practitioner's services with regard to a forecast on a tax shelter may be deemed to be a *covered opinion.*

11.02 If engaged to render services on a forecast and it is not clear whether the written advice is a covered opinion, the practitioner should refer to Circular 230, Section 10.35(b)(2) (see appendix C), which contains the definition of a covered opinion.

11.03 Under Circular 230, a practitioner may be deemed to be associated with tax shelter forecasts if that practitioner examines, compiles, assembles, or applies agreed-upon procedures to such forecasts, whether or not named in the offering materials or in connection with sales efforts, as long as such forecasts are disseminated or directed to persons other than the client who engaged the practitioner.

11.04 Although Circular 230 also refers to projections, as discussed in paragraph *10.12P* of this guide, a practitioner may not submit or report on a financial projection for general use (unless it supplements a forecast), for example, to solicit debt or equity financing. Also, if the practitioner's services are limited to the application of agreed-upon procedures to a financial forecast, the report on the results of applying such procedures should be restricted to specified parties (paragraph 19.01). Thus, under AICPA standards, a practitioner may accept an engagement on prospective financial statements for general use in connection with a tax shelter offering only for a financial forecast upon which a compilation or examination report will be issued.

11.05 A practitioner who compiles a forecast in connection with a tax shelter offering may rely on the opinion of another professional, that is, an attorney or another practitioner, concerning material tax issues, unless the practitioner knows or should know that the opinion of the other practitioner

---

[1] In September 2012, the IRS issued proposed regulations (REG-138367-06) that would eliminate the complex covered opinion rules of Treasury Department Circular No. 230, *Regulations Governing Practice before the Internal Revenue Service*, Section 10.35, and expand the requirements governing written tax advice in Section 10.37. Proposed Section 10.37 would require practitioners to base all written advice on reasonable factual and legal assumptions, exercise reasonable reliance, and consider all relevant facts that the practitioner knows or should know. The proposed changes would be effective when issued as final regulations.

should not be relied on. If the practitioner examines the forecast, the procedures in paragraph 15.34 should be applied.

11.06 Covered opinions must provide the practitioner's conclusion as to the likelihood that the taxpayer will prevail on the merits with respect to each significant Federal tax issue considered in the opinion. The opinion also must provide the practitioner's overall conclusion as to the likelihood that the Federal tax treatment of the transaction or matter that is the subject of the opinion is the proper treatment and the reasons for that conclusion. If the practitioner is unable to reach an overall conclusion, the opinion must state that the practitioner is unable to reach an overall conclusion and describe the reasons for the practitioner's inability to reach a conclusion.

11.07 Circular 230 requires that if the practitioner relies on the opinion of another practitioner, the relying practitioner's opinion must identify the other opinion and set forth the conclusions reached in the other opinion.

11.08 If the practitioner believes that the tax opinion rendered by another professional does not fully meet the Treasury standards for such opinions, the practitioner should request the responsible party to secure a revised tax opinion or revise the forecast and its underlying assumptions accordingly. Alternatively, the practitioner's engagement could be expanded to include rendering a tax opinion or a partial tax opinion that would remedy the deficiencies in the opinion rendered by the other professional.

11.09 If, in the course of an examination, the practitioner is not satisfied about the tax assumptions, an adverse opinion (paragraph 17.06*b*) or disclaimer of opinion (paragraph 17.06*c*) should be rendered. If, in a compilation, the practitioner believes the tax assumptions to be obviously inappropriate, incomplete, or otherwise misleading, the practitioner should withdraw from the engagement (paragraph 12.11*j*).

11.10 The practitioner's covered opinion may be presented in the compilation or examination report on the financial forecast or in a separate report. If the practitioner renders such an opinion, the requirements of Circular 230 (see appendix C) apply.

Chapter 12

Compilation Procedures

> Because financial forecasts and projections are similar in many respects, separate guidance for projections is provided only to the extent that it differs from that for forecasts. *Italicized* paragraphs in this chapter that include a "P" in the paragraph number show how the guidance presented for forecasts should be modified for projections. Any plain-text paragraph not followed by an italicized paragraph applies to both forecasts and projections even though it uses only the term *forecast.*

12.01 A compilation of a financial forecast is a professional service that involves the following:

    a. Assembling, to the extent necessary, the financial forecast based on the responsible party's assumptions

    b. Performing the required compilation procedures,[1] including reading the financial forecast with its summaries of significant assumptions and accounting policies and considering whether they appear to be presented in conformity with AICPA presentation guidelines[2] and not obviously inappropriate

    c. Issuing a compilation report.

A compilation is not intended to provide assurance on the financial forecast or the assumptions underlying it. Because of the limited nature of the practitioner's procedures, a compilation does not provide assurance that the practitioner will become aware of significant matters that might be disclosed by more extensive procedures, for example, those performed in an examination of a financial forecast

12.02 During the course of a compilation, the practitioner may assist the responsible party in identifying assumptions, gathering information, or assembling the financial forecast. In assisting the client, the practitioner is not required to perform those procedures contemplated by chapter 6, "Preparation Guidelines."

12.03 The summary of significant assumptions is essential to the reader's understanding of financial forecasts. Accordingly, the practitioner should not compile financial forecasts that exclude disclosure of the summary of significant assumptions (Paragraph .14 of AT section 301, *Financial Forecasts and Projections* [AICPA, *Professional Standards*]).

12.03P The practitioner should not compile a financial projection that excludes either (a) an identification of the hypothetical assumptions or (b) a description of the limitations on the usefulness of the presentation (Paragraph .14 of AT section 301).

12.04 According to paragraph .15 of AT section 301, the following standards apply to a compilation of a financial forecast and to the resulting report:

---

[1] See paragraph 12.11 for the required procedures.

[2] AICPA presentation guidelines are detailed in chapter 8, "Presentation Guidelines."

    a. The compilation should be performed by a person or persons having adequate technical training and proficiency to compile a financial forecast.

    b. Due professional care should be exercised in the performance of the compilation and the preparation of the report.

    c. The work should be adequately planned, and assistants, if any, should be properly supervised.

    d. Applicable compilation procedures should be performed as a basis for reporting on the compiled financial forecast. (See paragraph 12.11 for the procedures to be performed.)

    e. The report based on the practitioner's compilation of a financial forecast should conform to the applicable guidance in chapter 14, "The Practitioner's Compilation Report."

Materiality

12.05 Per paragraph .07 of AT section 301, the concept of materiality affects the application of this guide to a financial forecast, as materiality affects the application of generally accepted auditing standards to historical financial statements. Materiality is a concept that is judged in light of the expected range of reasonableness of the information, and therefore users should not expect prospective information (information about events that have not yet occurred) to be as precise as historical information. For example, procedures that might otherwise normally be performed need not be performed if the effect of the procedures on the forecasted item would not be material.

Training and Proficiency

12.06 The practitioner should be familiar with the guidelines for the preparation and presentation of a financial forecast. The guidelines are contained in chapters 6 and 8, "Presentation Guidelines," respectively, of this guide.

Planning a Compilation Engagement

12.07 The practitioner should possess or obtain a level of knowledge of the industry and the accounting principles and practices of the industry in which the entity operates, or will operate, that will enable the practitioner to compile a financial forecast that are appropriate form for an entity operating in that industry. If a practitioner has no previous experience in the industry, the level of knowledge can be obtained by consulting AICPA guides, industry publications, financial statements of other entities in the industry, textbooks, periodicals, or individuals knowledgeable about the industry.

12.08 To compile a financial forecast of an existing entity, the practitioner should obtain a general knowledge of the nature of the entity's business transactions and the key factors on which its future financial results appear to depend. He or she should also obtain an understanding of the accounting principles and practices of the entity to determine whether they are comparable to those used within the industry in which the entity operates.

12.09 If the practitioner has audited, reviewed, or compiled historical financial statements, or performed services on previous financial forecasts of the entity, the practitioner may already have attained familiarity with the items mentioned previously.

12.10 To compile a financial forecast of a proposed entity, the practitioner should obtain knowledge of the proposed operations and of the key factors upon which its future results appear to depend and that have affected the performance of entities in the same industry. The practitioner can obtain this knowledge in the same manner as described in paragraph 12.07.

Compilation Procedures

12.11 In performing a compilation of a financial forecast the practitioner should perform the following, where applicable:

a. Establish an understanding with the client, regarding the services to be performed. The understanding should include the objectives of the engagement, the client's responsibilities, the practitioner's responsibilities, and limitations of the engagement. The practitioner should document the understanding in the attest documentation, preferably through a written communication with the client. If the practitioner believes an understanding with the client has not been established, he or she should decline to accept or perform the engagement. (Excerpts from example engagement letters appear in chapter 13, "Illustrative Engagement and Representation Letters for a Compilation.")

b. Inquire about the accounting principles used in the preparation of the financial forecast.

(1) For existing entities, compare the accounting principles used to those used in the preparation of previous historical financial statements and inquire whether such principles are the same as those expected to be used in the historical financial statements covering the forecast period.

(2) For entities to be formed or entities already formed that have not commenced operations, compare specialized industry accounting principles used, if any, to those typically used in the industry. Inquire about whether the accounting principles used for the financial forecast are those that are expected to be used when or if the entity commences operations.

c. Ask how the responsible party identifies the key factors and develops its assumptions.

d. List, or obtain a list, of the responsible party's significant assumptions providing the basis for the financial forecast and consider whether there are any obvious omissions in light of the key factors upon which the prospective results of the entity appear to depend.

e. Consider whether there appear to be any obvious internal inconsistencies in the assumptions.

f. Perform, or test the mathematical accuracy of, the computations that translate the assumptions into the financial forecast.

g. Read the financial forecast, including the summary of significant assumptions, and consider whether

(1) the forecast, including the disclosures of assumptions and accounting policies, appears to be not presented in conformity with the AICPA presentation guidelines for a financial forecast, which appear in chapter 8.

(2) the forecast, including the summary of significant assumptions, appears to be not obviously inappropriate in relation to

    (*a*) the practitioner's knowledge of the entity and its industry.

    (*b*) the expected conditions and course of action in the forecast period.

12.11(g)(2)P *the practitioner should also consider whether the projection appears to be obviously inappropriate in relation to the purpose of the presentation.*

h. If a significant part of the prospective period has expired, inquire about the results of operations or significant portions of the operations (such as sales volume) and significant changes in financial position, and consider their effect in relation to the financial forecast. If historical financial statements have been prepared for the expired portion of the period, the practitioner should read such statements and consider those results in relation to the financial forecast.

i. Confirm his or her understanding of the forecast (including assumptions) by obtaining written representations from the responsible party. Because the amounts reflected in the forecast are not supported by historical books and records but rather by assumptions, the practitioner should obtain representations in which the responsible party indicates its responsibility for the assumptions. The representations should be signed by the responsible party at the highest level of authority who the practitioner believes is responsible for and knowledgeable, directly or through others, about matters covered by the representations. The representations should include the responsible party's assertion that the financial forecast presents, to the best of the responsible party's knowledge and belief, the expected financial position, results of operations, and cash flows for the forecast period, and that the forecast reflects the responsible party's judgment, based on present circumstances, of the expected conditions and its expected course of action. The representations should also include a statement that the forecast is presented in conformity with guidelines for presentation of a forecast established by the AICPA. The representations should also include a statement that the assumptions on which the forecast is based are reasonable. If the forecast contains a range, the representations should also include a statement that, to the best of the responsible party's knowledge and belief, the item or items subject to the assumption are expected to actually fall within the range, and that the range was not selected in a biased or misleading manner.

12.11(i)P *The practitioner should confirm his or her understanding of the projection (including assumptions) by obtaining written representations from the responsible party. Because the amounts reflected in the statements are not supported by historical books and records but rather by assumptions, the practitioner should obtain representations in which the responsible party indicates its responsibility for the* *assumptions. The representations should be signed by the responsible party at the highest level of authority who the practitioner believes is responsible for and knowledgeable, directly or through others, about matters covered by the representations. The representations should include the responsible party's assertion that the financial projection presents, to the best of the responsible party's knowledge and belief, the expected financial position, results of operations, and cash flows for the projection period given the hypothetical assumptions, and that the projection reflects its judgment, based on present circumstances, of expected conditions and its expected course of action given the occurrence of the hypothetical events. The representations should also (1) identify the hypothetical assumptions and describe the limitations on the usefulness of the presentation, (2) state that the assumptions are appropriate, (3) indicate if the hypothetical assumptions are improbable, and (4) if the projection contains a range, include a statement that, to the best of the responsible party's knowledge and belief, given the hypothetical assumptions, the item or items subject to the assumption are expected to actually fall within the range and that the range was not selected in a biased or misleading manner. The representations should also include a statement that the projection is presented in conformity with guidelines for presentation of a projection established by the AICPA.*

j. Consider, after applying the preceding procedures, whether he or she has received representations or other information received that appears to be obviously inappropriate, incomplete, or otherwise misleading.[3] If the practitioner believes the presentation is obviously inappropriate, incomplete or otherwise misleading, he or she should attempt to obtain additional or revised information. If such information is not received, the practitioner should ordinarily withdraw from the compilation engagement.[4] (Note that the omission of disclosures, other than those relating to significant assumptions, would not require the practitioner to withdraw; see paragraph 14.09.)

Documentation

12.12 Although it is not possible to specify the form or content of the working papers that an accountant should prepare in connection with a compilation of a financial forecast because of the different circumstances of individual engagements, the accountant's working papers ordinarily should indicate that

a. the work was adequately planned and supervised.

b. the required compilation procedures were performed as a basis for the compilation report.

12.13 Some accountants use a checklist or work program similar to that shown in paragraph 12.11 to document the items discussed in paragraph 12.12. The inclusion of the checklist would frequently be sufficient documentation of

---

[3] The practitioner's compilation procedures do not contemplate an evaluation of the support for underlying assumptions, which is required in an examination of prospective information. Because of the limited nature of the procedures, a compilation does not provide assurance that the practitioner will become aware of significant matters that might be disclosed by more extensive procedures.

[4] The practitioner need not withdraw from the engagement if the effect of such information on the financial forecast does not appear to be material.

planning, and signing off after completion of procedures would ordinarily be sufficient documentation of performance.

Chapter 13

Illustrative Engagement and Representation Letters for a Compilation

Because financial forecasts and projections are similar in many respects, separate guidance for projections is provided only to the extent that it differs from that for forecasts. *Italicized* paragraphs in this chapter that include a "P" in the paragraph number show how the guidance presented for forecasts should be modified for projections. Any plain-text paragraph not followed by an italicized paragraph applies to both forecasts and projections even though it uses only the term *forecast.*

Engagement Letter

13.01 The following is an excerpt from a sample engagement letter for a compilation of a financial forecast:[1]

> This letter sets forth our understanding of the terms and objectives of our engagement and the nature and limitations of the services we will provide.
>
> We will compile, in accordance with attestation standards established by the American Institute of Certified Public Accountants, from information management[2] provides, the forecasted balance sheet, statements of income, retained earnings, and cash flows, and summaries of significant assumptions and accounting policies of XYZ Company as of December 31, 20XX, and for the year then ending. A compilation is limited to presenting, in the form of a financial forecast, information that is the representation of management. We will not examine the financial forecast and therefore, will not express any form of assurance on the achievability of the forecast or the reasonableness of the underlying assumptions.
>
> A compilation of a financial forecast involves assembling the forecast based on management's assumptions and performing certain other procedures with respect to the forecast without evaluating the support for, or expressing an opinion or any other form of assurance on, the assumptions underlying it.
>
> If for any reason we are unable to complete our compilation of your financial forecast, we will not issue a report on it as a result of this engagement.

---

[1] If the assumptions regarding income taxes are sensitive (for example, in a tax shelter offering), the practitioner may want his or her engagement letter to provide that the client will obtain a tax opinion from its counsel, or that the practitioner will undertake to apply those procedures necessary to obtain satisfaction about the tax assumptions. Treasury Department Circular No. 230 establishes certain requirements regarding such opinions. See appendix C, "IRS Regulations Regarding Tax Shelter Opinions (Circular 230)."

[2] If the responsible party is other than management, the references to management should generally be replaced with the name of the party who assumes responsibility for the assumptions.

A financial forecast presents, to the best of management's knowledge and belief, the Company's expected financial position, results of operations, and cash flows for the forecast period. It is based on management's assumptions, reflecting conditions it expects to exist and the course of action it expects to take during the forecast period.

Management is responsible for representations about its plans and expectations and for disclosure of significant information that might affect the ultimate realization of the forecasted results.

There will usually be differences between the forecasted and actual results, because events and circumstances frequently do not occur as expected, and those differences may be material. Our report will contain a statement to that effect.

We have no responsibility to update our report for events and circumstances occurring after the date of such report.

At the conclusion of the engagement, management agrees to supply us with a representation letter that, among other things, will confirm management's responsibility for the underlying assumptions and the appropriateness of the financial forecast and its presentation.

In order for us to complete this engagement, management must provide assumptions that are appropriate for the forecast. If the assumptions provided are inappropriate and have not been revised to our satisfaction, we will be unable to complete the engagement, and, accordingly, we will not issue a report on the forecast.

If management intends to reproduce and publish the forecast and our report thereon, they must be reproduced in their entirety, and both the first and subsequent, corrected drafts of the document containing the forecast and any accompanying material must be submitted to us for approval.

13.01P *The following is an excerpt from a sample engagement letter on a compilation of a financial projection:*

This letter sets forth our understanding of the terms and objectives of our engagement and the nature and limitations of the services we will provide.

We will compile, in accordance with attestation standards established by the American Institute of Certified Public Accountants, from information management[3] provides, the projected balance sheet, statements of income, retained earnings, and cash flows, and summaries of significant assumptions and accounting policies of XYZ Company as of December 31, 20XX, and for the year then ending. A compilation is limited to presenting, in the form of projected financial statements, information that is the representation of management. We will not examine the projected financial statements and therefore, will not express any form of assurance on the achievability of the projection or the reasonableness of the underlying assumptions.

A compilation of a financial projection involves assembling the projection based on management's assumptions and performing certain other procedures with respect to the projection without evaluating the support for, or expressing an opinion or any other form of assurance on, the assumptions underlying it.

---

[3] *If the responsible party is other than management, the references to management should generally be replaced with the name of the party who assumes responsibility for the assumptions.*

If for any reason we are unable to complete our compilation of your financial projection, we will not issue a report on it as a result of this engagement.

The financial projection presents, to the best of management's knowledge and belief, the Company's expected financial position, results of operations, and cash flows for the projection period assuming [describe hypothetical assumptions]. It is based on management's assumptions reflecting conditions it expects would exist and courses of action it expects would be taken during the projection period assuming [describe hypothetical assumptions].

Management is responsible for representations about its plans and expectations and for disclosure of significant information that might affect the ultimate realization of the projected results.

Even if [describe hypothetical assumptions] were to occur, there will usually be differences between projected and actual results, because events and circumstances frequently do not occur as expected, and those differences may be material. Our report will contain a statement to that effect.

We have no responsibility to update our report for events and circumstances occurring after the date of such report.

At the conclusion of the engagement, management agrees to supply us with a representation letter that, among other things, will confirm management's responsibility for the underlying assumptions and the appropriateness of the financial projection and its presentation.

In order for us to complete this engagement, management must provide assumptions that are appropriate for the projection. If the assumptions provided are inappropriate and have not been revised to our satisfaction, we will be unable to complete the engagement and, accordingly, we will not issue a report on the projection.

We understand that the projection and our report thereon will be used only for [state intended limited use]. If management intends to reproduce the projection and our report thereon, they must be reproduced in their entirety, and both the first and subsequent corrected drafts of the document containing the projection and any accompanying material must be submitted to us for approval.

Representation Letter

13.02 The following is an illustrative representation letter for an engagement to compile a financial forecast. The written representations to be obtained should be based on the circumstances.

[Date of Practitioner's report]

[Practitioner's name]

In connection with your compilation of the forecasted balance sheet, statements of income, retained earnings, and cash flows and summaries of significant assumptions and accounting policies of XYZ Company as of December 31, 20XX, and for the year then ending, we make the following representations:

1. The financial forecast presents our assumptions and, to the best of our knowledge and belief, the Company's expected financial position,

results of operations, and cash flows for the period[4] in conformity with the generally accepted accounting principles expected to be used by the Company during the forecast period, which are consistent with the principles XYZ Company uses in preparing its historical financial statements.

2. The financial forecast reflects our judgment based on present circumstances of the expected conditions and our expected course of action.

3. The financial forecast is presented in conformity with the guidelines for presentation of a financial forecast established by the American Institute of Certified Public Accountants.

4. We believe that the assumptions underlying the forecast are reasonable and appropriate.

5. We have made available to you all significant information that we believe is relevant to the forecast.

6. To the best of our knowledge and belief, the documents and records supporting the assumptions are appropriate.

[*Signatures*]

13.02P   *The following is an illustrative representation letter for an engagement to compile a financial projection. The written representations to be obtained should be based on the circumstances.*

[Date of Practitioner's report]

[Practitioner's name]

In connection with your compilation of the projected balance sheet, statements of income, retained earnings, and cash flows and summaries of significant assumptions assuming [describe hypothetical assumptions] and accounting policies of XYZ Company as of December 31, 20XX, and for the year then ending, we make the following representations:

1. *The financial projection presents our assumptions and, to the best of our knowledge and belief, the Company's expected financial position, results of operations, and cash flows for the projection period assuming [describe the hypothetical assumptions].*[5]

2. *The accounting principles used in the financial projection are in conformity with the generally accepted accounting principles expected to be used by the Company during the projection period, which are consistent with the principles XYZ Company uses in preparing its historical financial statements.*[6]

---

[4] If the forecast is presented as a range, the description of the forecast would refer to the range, for example, ". . . at occupancy rates of 75 percent and 95 percent." See also paragraph 13.03.

[5] *If the projection is presented as a range, the description of the projection would refer to the range, for example, ". . . at occupancy rates of 75 percent and 95 percent." See also paragraph 13.03P.*

[6] *If the projection is not presented on the basis of the accounting principles used for the historical financial statements, this sentence might read, "The accounting principles used in the financial projection are consistent with [the special purpose of the projection]."*

3. *The financial projection reflects our judgment, based on present circumstances, of the expected conditions and our expected course of action assuming [*describe hypothetical assumptions*].*[7]

4. *The financial projection is presented in conformity with presentation guidelines established by the American Institute of Certified Public Accountants.*

5. *We believe that the assumptions underlying the projection are appropriate and reasonable assuming [*describe hypothetical assumptions*].*

6. *We have made available to you all significant information that we believe is relevant to the financial projection.*

7. *To the best of our knowledge and belief, the documents and records supporting the assumptions are appropriate.*

8. *We intend to use this projection only for [*describe intended limited use*].*

[Signatures]

13.03 If the forecast is presented as a range, the following representation would be added:

We reasonably expect, to the best of our knowledge and belief, that the actual [*describe items presented as a range*] achieved will be within the range shown; however, there can be no assurances that it will. The range shown was not selected in a biased or misleading manner.

13.03P *If the presentation is presented as a range, the following representation would be added:*

*We reasonably expect, to the best of our knowledge and belief, that the actual [*describe items presented as a range*] achieved will be within the range shown assuming [*describe hypothetical assumptions*]; however, there can be no assurance that it will. The range shown was not selected in a biased or misleading manner.*

13.04 If the date of the signed representations is later than the date of the preparation of the forecast (see paragraph 8.11), the following representation would be added:

We are not aware of any material changes in the information or circumstances from [*date*], the date of the forecast, to the present.

---

[7] *If the hypothetical assumption is considered improbable the representations should generally say so, for example, ". . . assuming [*describe hypothetical assumptions*], which we consider to be highly unlikely."*

Chapter 14

The Practitioner's Compilation Report

> Because financial forecasts and projections are similar in many respects, separate guidance for projections is provided only to the extent that it differs from that for forecasts. *Italicized* paragraphs in this chapter show how the guidance presented for forecasts should be modified for projections. Any plain-text paragraph not followed by an italicized paragraph applies to both forecasts and projections even though it uses only the term *forecast*.

14.01 According to paragraph .18 of AT section 301, *Financial Forecasts and Projections* (AICPA, *Professional Standards*), the practitioner's standard report on a compilation of a financial forecast should include

    a. an identification of the financial forecast presented by the responsible party.

    b. a statement that the practitioner has compiled the financial forecast in accordance with attestation standards established by the AICPA.

    c. a statement that a compilation is limited in scope and does not enable the practitioner to express an opinion or any other form of assurance on the financial forecast or the assumptions.

    d. a caveat that the forecasted results may not be achieved.

    e. a statement that the practitioner assumes no responsibility to update the report for events and circumstances occurring after the date of the report.

    f. the manual or printed signature of the practitioner's firm or practitioner, as appropriate.

    g. the date of the compilation report.

14.01P   When reporting on a compiled financial projection, the practitioner should add to the items discussed in paragraph 14.01 a statement describing the special purpose for which the projection was prepared as well as a separate paragraph that restricts the use of the report because it is intended to be used solely by the specified parties.

14.02 The following is the form of the practitioner's standard report on the compilation of a forecast that does not contain a range:[1]

> We have compiled the accompanying forecasted balance sheet, statements of income, retained earnings, and cash flows of XYZ Company as of December 31, 20XX, and for the year then ending, in accordance with attestation standards established by the American Institute of Certified Public Accountants.[2]

---

[1] The forms of reports provided in this guide are appropriate whether the presentation is based on generally accepted accounting principles or on another financial reporting framework.

[2] When the presentation is summarized as discussed in paragraph 8.06, this sentence might read "We have compiled the accompanying summarized forecast of XYZ Company as of December 31, 20XX, and for the year then ending, in accordance with attestation standards established by the American Institute of Certified Public Accountants."

A compilation is limited to presenting in the form of a forecast information that is the representation of management[3] and does not include evaluation of the support for the assumptions underlying the forecast. We have not examined the forecast and, accordingly do not express an opinion or any other form of assurance, on the accompanying statements or assumptions. Furthermore, there will usually be differences between the forecasted and actual results, because events and circumstances frequently do not occur as expected, and those differences may be material. We have no responsibility to update this report for events and circumstances occurring after the date of this report.

[*Signature*]

[*Date*]

14.02P *The following is the form of the practitioner's standard report on a compilation of a projection that does not contain a range:*

> *We have compiled the accompanying projected balance sheet, statements of income, retained earnings, and cash flows of XYZ Company as of December 31, 20XX, and for the year then ending, in accordance with attestation standards established by the American Institute of Certified Public Accountants.[4] The accompanying projection was prepared for* [state special purpose, for example, "the purpose of negotiating a loan to expand XYZ Company's plant"].

> *A compilation is limited to presenting, in the form of a projection information that is the representation of management and does not include evaluation of the support for the assumptions underlying the projection. We have not examined the projection and, accordingly do not express an opinion or any other form of assurance on the accompanying statements or assumptions. Furthermore, even if* [describe hypothetical assumption, for example, "the loan is granted and the plant is expanded"] *there will usually be differences between the projected and the actual results, because events and circumstances frequently do not occur as expected, and those differences may be material. We have no responsibility to update this report for events and circumstances occurring after the date of this report.*

> *The accompanying projection and this report are intended solely for the information and use of* [identify specified parties, for example, "Company and DEF Bank"] *and are not intended to be and should not be used by anyone other than these specified parties.*

> [Signature]

> [Date]

14.03 When the financial forecast contains a range, the practitioner's standard report should also include a separate paragraph that states that the responsible party has elected to portray the expected results of one or more assumptions as a range. The following is an example of the separate paragraph

---

[3] If the responsible party is other than management, the references to management should generally be replaced with the name of the party who assumes responsibility for the assumptions.

[4] *When the presentation is summarized as discussed in paragraph 8.06, this sentence might read, "We have compiled the accompanying summarized projection of XYZ Company as of December 31, 20XX, and for the year then ending, in accordance with attestation standards established by the American Institute of Certified Public Accountants."*

to be added to the practitioner's report when he or she compiles a forecast that contains a range:

> As described in the summary of significant assumptions, management of XYZ Company has elected to portray forecasted [*describe financial statement element or elements for which the expected results of one or more assumptions fall within a range, and identify the assumptions expected to fall within a range, for example, "revenue at the amounts of $X,XXX and $Y,YYY, which is predicated on occupancy rates of XX percent and YY percent of available apartments"*] rather than as a single-point estimate. Accordingly, the accompanying forecast presents forecasted financial position, results of operations, and cash flows [*describe one or more assumptions expected to fall within a range, for example, "at such occupancy rates"*]. However, there is no assurance that the actual results will fall within the range of [*describe one or more of the assumptions expected to fall within a range, for example, "occupancy rates"*] presented.

14.04 The date of completion of the practitioner's compilation procedures should be used as the date of the report (paragraph .22 of AT section 301).

14.05 A practitioner may compile a financial forecast for an entity with respect to which he or she is not independent.[5] In such circumstances, the practitioner's report should be modified to indicate his or her lack of independence in a separate paragraph of the practioner's report. An example of such disclosure would be as follows:

We are not independent with respect to XYZ Company.

The practitioner is not precluded from disclosing a description about the reason(s) that his or her independence is impaired. The following are examples of descriptions the practitioner may use:

a. We are not independent with respect to XYZ Company as of and for the year ended [or ending, as applicable] December 31, 20XX, because a member of the engagement team had a direct financial interest in XYZ Company.

b. We are not independent with respect to XYZ Company as of and for the year ended [or ending, as applicable] December 31, 20XX, because an immediate family member of one of the members of the engagement team was employed by XYZ Company.

c. We are not independent with respect to XYZ Company as of and for the year ended [or ending, as applicable] December 31, 20XX, because we performed certain accounting services (the practitioner may include a specific description of those services) that impaired our independence.

If the accountant elects to disclose a description about the reasons his or her independence is impaired, the accountant should ensure that all reasons are included in the description.

14.06 A financial forecast may be included in a document that also contains historical financial statements and the practitioner's report thereon. In addition, the historical financial statements that appear in the document may be summarized and presented with the financial forecast for comparative

---

[5] In making a judgment about whether he or she is independent, AICPA members should be guided by the AICPA Code of Professional Conduct.

purposes.[6] An example of the reference to the practitioner's report on the historical financial statements when he or she audited, reviewed, or compiled those statements is presented as follows:

(concluding sentence of last paragraph)

The historical financial statements for the year ended December 31, 20XX (from which the historical data are derived) and our report thereon are set forth on pages xx–yy of this document.

14.07   In some circumstances, a practitioner may want to expand his or her report to emphasize a matter regarding the financial forecast. Such information may be presented in a separate paragraph of the practitioner's report. However, the practitioner should exercise care that emphasizing such a matter does not give the impression that he or she is expressing assurance or expanding the degree of responsibility he or she is taking with respect to such information.[7] For example, the practitioner should not include statements in his or her compilation report about the mathematical accuracy of the statements or their conformity with presentation guidelines (paragraph .25 of AT section 301).

14.08   If the practitioner compiles a financial forecast in conjunction with an examination of the forecast, he or she need only report on the examination.

Modifications of the Standard Compilation Report

Presentation Deficiencies or Omitted Disclosures

14.09   An entity may request a practitioner to compile a financial forecast that contains presentation deficiencies or omits disclosures other than those relating to significant assumptions. The practitioner may compile such a financial forecast provided the deficiency or omission is clearly indicated in his or her report and is not, to his or her knowledge, undertaken with the intention of misleading those who might reasonably be expected to use the forecast.

14.10   The following is an example of a paragraph that should be added to a report on a compiled financial forecast in which the summary of significant accounting policies has been omitted:

Management has elected to omit the summary of significant accounting policies required by the guidelines for presentation of a forecast established by the American Institute of Certified Public Accountants. If the omitted disclosures were included in the forecast, they might influence the user's conclusions about the Company's financial position, results of operations, and cash flows for the forecast period. Accordingly, this forecast is not designed for those who are not informed about such matters (paragraph .28 of AT section 301).

14.11   Notwithstanding the preceding, if the compiled financial forecast is presented on a comprehensive basis of accounting other than generally accepted accounting principles and does not include disclosure of the basis of accounting used, the basis should be disclosed in the practitioner's report.

---

[6] AU-C section 810, *Engagements to Report on Summary Financial Statements* (AICPA, *Professional Standards*), discusses the practitioner's report where summarized financial statements are derived from audited statements that are not included in the same document.

[7] However, the practitioner may provide assurance on tax matters in order to comply with the requirements of regulations governing practice before the IRS contained in 31 U.S. *Code of Federal Regulations* Part 10 (Treasury Department Circular No. 230, *Regulations Governing Practice before the Internal Revenue Service*).

Reporting on Information Accompanying a Financial Forecast in a Practitioner-Submitted Document

14.12 An entity may request that additional details or explanations of items included in a financial forecast (for example, details of sales or forecasted product line information) be included in a practitioner-submitted document that contains a financial forecast and the practitioner's report thereon. An entity also may request that certain nonaccounting information or other information not directly related to the basic forecast be included in such a document. The accompanying information is presented outside the basic financial forecast and is not considered necessary in order for the presentation of the forecast to be in conformity with guidelines for presentation of a financial forecast established by the AICPA.

14.13 If the practitioner compiles such information and includes it in a document that includes the financial forecast and the practitioner's compilation report thereon, the practitioner's compilation report should refer to the accompanying information or the practitioner can issue a separate report on the accompanying information. If a separate report is issued, the report should state that the information accompanying the financial forecast is presented only for supplementary analysis purposes and that the information has been compiled from information that is the representation of management, without audit or review, and the accountant does not express an opinion or any other form of assurance on such information. The following is an example of a paragraph that may be added to the standard compilation report if the practitioner compiled the accompanying information:

> We also compiled [*identify accompanying information*] and, accordingly, do not express an opinion, or any other form of assurance, on such information.

Other Reporting Examples

14.14 The following is an example of a report on a compilation of a financial forecast shown as a single-point estimate for one period and a forecast that contains a range for a later period:

> We have compiled the accompanying forecasted balance sheets, statements of income, retained earnings, and cash flows of XYZ Company as of December 31, 20X1 and 20X2, and for the years then ending, in accordance with attestation standards established by the American Institute of Certified Public Accountants.
>
> A compilation is limited to presenting, in the form of a forecast, information that is the representation of management and does not include evaluation of the support for the assumptions underlying the forecasts. We have not examined the forecasts and, accordingly, do not express an opinion or any other form of assurance on the accompanying statements or assumptions. Furthermore, there will usually be differences between the forecasted and actual results, because events and circumstances frequently do not occur as expected, and those differences may be material. We have no responsibility to update this report for events and circumstances occurring after the date of this report.

As described in the summary of significant assumptions, management of XYZ Company has, for 20X2, elected to portray forecasted [*describe financial statement element or elements for which the expected results of one or more assumptions fall within a range, and identify the assumptions expected to fall within the range, for example, "revenue at amounts of $X,XXX and $Y,YYY which is predicated on occupancy rates of XX percent and YY percent of available apartments"*] rather than as a single-point estimate. Accordingly, the 20X2 forecast presents forecasted financial position, results of operations and cash flows [*describe one or more assumptions expected to fall within a range, for example, "at such occupancy rates"*]. However, there is no assurance that the actual results will fall within the range of [*describe one or more assumptions expected to fall within a range, for example, "occupancy rates"*] presented.

[*Signature*]

[*Date*]

14.15 The following is an example of a practitioner's report when he or she is engaged to examine[8] a forecast for one period and to compile a forecast for a later period:

Independent Accountant's Report

We have examined the accompanying forecasted balance sheet, statements of income, retained earnings, and cash flows of XYZ Company as of December 31, 20X1, and for the year then ending. XYZ Company's management is responsible for the forecast. Our responsibility is to express an opinion on the forecast based on our examination.

Our examination was conducted in accordance with attestation standards established by the American Institute of Certified Public Accountants and, accordingly, included such procedures as we considered necessary to evaluate both the assumptions used by management and the preparation and presentation of the forecast. We believe that our examination provides a reasonable basis for our opinion.

In our opinion the accompanying forecast is presented in conformity with guidelines for presentation of a forecast established by the American Institute of Certified Public Accountants, and the underlying assumptions provide a reasonable basis for management's forecast.

We have compiled the accompanying forecasted balance sheet, statements of income, retained earnings, and cash flows of XYZ Company as of December 31, 20X2, and for the year then ending, in accordance with attestation standards established by the American Institute of Certified Public Accountants. A compilation is limited to presenting, in the form of a forecast, information that is the representation of management and does not include evaluation of the support for the assumptions underlying the forecast. We have not examined the forecast as of December 31, 20X2, and for the period then ending and, accordingly, do not express an opinion or any other form of assurance on the forecast or assumptions.

---

[8] See chapter 17, "The Practitioner's Examination Report."

For both years presented there will usually be differences between the forecasted and actual results, because events and circumstances frequently do not occur as expected, and those differences may be material. We have no responsibility to update this report for events and circumstances occurring after the date of this report.

[*Signature*]

[*Date*]

Reporting on a Financial Forecast That Includes a Projected Sale of an Entity's Real Estate Investment at the End of the Forecast Period

14.16 If a hypothetical sale of an entity's real estate is presented as a separate statement (that is, as a financial projection) within a financial forecast, the practitioner's report should be modified to report specifically on the statement.[9] The following is an example of a practitioner's report on a financial forecast supplemented by a financial projection[10] of the effect on limited partners of a hypothetical sale of the entity's properties on the last day of the forecast period:[11]

> We have compiled the accompanying forecasted balance sheet, statements of income, retained earnings, and cash flows of XYZ Company as of December 31, 20X8, and for the year then ending (the forecast), and the accompanying statement of the effect on limited partners of the projected sale of property at December 31, 20X8 (the projection) in accordance with attestation standards established by the American Institute of Certified Public Accountants.
>
> The accompanying projection was prepared by management to provide potential investors with information about the effect of a hypothetical sale of the properties as of December 31, 20X8, and should not be considered a presentation of expected future results.
>
> A compilation is limited to presenting, in the form of prospective financial statements, information that is the representation of management, and does not include an evaluation of the support for the assumptions underlying the forecast or projection. We have not examined the forecast or projection and, accordingly, do not express an opinion or any other form of assurance on the accompanying statements or assumptions. Furthermore, because events and circumstances frequently do not occur as expected, there will usually be differences between the forecasted and actual results, and even if the properties are sold on the date and for the prices indicated, there will usually be differences between projected and actual results, and those differences may be material. We have no responsibility to

---

[9] When the effects of a hypothetical sale of an entity's real estate investment are included in a note to the financial forecast, the disclosure is considered part of the forecast and is covered by the practitioner's standard report.

[10] As stated in paragraph 4.05, a financial projection is not appropriate for general use and should not be used by those who will not be negotiating directly with the responsible party unless the projection is used to supplement a financial forecast and is for a period covered by the forecast. Because in this example the projection supplements a forecast covering the same period, it is appropriate for general use and the report need not include a use-restriction paragraph.

[11] In rare cases, management may forecast the sale of its real estate investment during the forecast period. In such circumstances, the sale is not hypothetical and should be included in the financial forecast with other operating results and cash flows. Furthermore, the sale would be covered by the practitioner's standard report.

update this report for events and circumstances occurring after the date of this report.

[*Signature*]

[*Date*]

Reporting If the Financial Forecast Includes Disclosures About Periods Beyond the Forecast Period

14.17 If a practitioner is engaged to compile a financial forecast that contains disclosures about plans, events, or circumstances beyond the forecast period,[12] the practitioner's standard report covers such disclosures because they are included in the notes to the financial forecast.

14.18 If the practitioner concludes, on the basis of known facts, that the disclosures are obviously inappropriate, incomplete, or misleading given their purpose, or the disclosures are not presented in conformity with the guidelines in paragraph 8.42, the practitioner should discuss the matter with the responsible party and propose appropriate revision of the disclosures. If the responsible party will not agree to revision of the disclosures, the practitioner should either modify the report on the financial forecast or withdraw from the engagement (see paragraphs 12.11*j* and 14.09).

---

[12] Paragraph 10.19 discusses the practitioner's responsibility for such disclosures when he or she is engaged to compile the forecast.

Chapter 15

Examination Procedures

> Because financial forecasts and projections are similar in many respects, separate guidance for projections is provided only to the extent that it differs from that for forecasts. *Italicized* paragraphs in this chapter that include a "P" in the paragraph number show how the guidance presented for forecasts should be modified for projections. Any plain-text paragraph not followed by an italicized paragraph applies to both forecasts and projections even though it uses only the term *forecast.*

15.01 An examination of a financial forecast is a professional service that involves

a. evaluating the preparation of the financial forecast.

b. evaluating the support underlying the assumptions.

c. evaluating the presentation of the financial forecast for conformity with AICPA presentation guidelines.[1]

d. issuing an examination report.

15.02 As a result of the examination, the practitioner has a basis for reporting on whether, in his or her opinion

a. the financial forecast is presented in conformity with AICPA guidelines.

b. the assumptions provide a reasonable basis for the responsible party's forecast.

15.02P As a result of the examination, the practitioner has a basis for reporting on whether a financial projection is presented in conformity with AICPA guidelines and whether the assumptions provide a reasonable basis for the responsible party's presentation, given the hypothetical assumptions.

15.03 During the course of the examination, the practitioner may assist the responsible party in identifying assumptions, gathering information, or assembling the financial forecast. In assisting the client, the practitioner is not required to perform those procedures contemplated by chapter 6, "Preparation Guidelines."

15.04 The practitioner should follow the general, fieldwork, and reporting standards for attestation engagements established in AT section 50, *SSAE Hierarchy* (AICPA, *Professional Standards*), and further explained in AT section 101, *Attest Engagements* (AICPA, *Professional Standards*), in performing an examination of a financial forecast and reporting thereon. This chapter describes standards concerning such technical training and proficiency (paragraph 15.06), planning an examination engagement (paragraphs 15.08–.11), and the types of procedures a practitioner should perform to obtain sufficient evidence for the examination report (paragraphs 15.12–.40).

---

[1] AICPA presentation guidelines are detailed in chapter 8, "Presentation Guidelines."

Materiality

15.05 The concept of materiality affects the application of this guide to a financial forecast as materiality affects the application of generally accepted auditing standards to historical financial statements. Materiality is a concept that is judged in light of the expected range of reasonableness of the information, and therefore users should not expect prospective information (information about events that have not yet occurred) to be as precise as historical information. For example, procedures that might otherwise normally be performed need not be performed if the effect of the procedures on the forecasted item would not be material (paragraph .07 of AT section 301, *Financial Forecasts and Projections* [AICPA, *Professional Standards*]).

Training and Proficiency

15.06 The practitioner should be familiar with the guidelines for the preparation and presentation of a financial forecast (appendix C of AT section 301). The guidelines are contained in chapters 6 and 8, "Presentation Guidelines," respectively, of this guide.

15.07 The practitioner should possess or obtain a level of knowledge of the industry and of the accounting principles and practices of the industry in which the entity operates, or will operate, that will enable him or her to examine a financial forecast that is in appropriate form for an entity operating in that industry.

Planning an Examination Engagement

15.08 Planning the examination engagement involves developing an overall strategy for the expected scope and conduct of the engagement. To develop such a strategy, the practitioner needs to have sufficient knowledge to enable him or her to adequately understand the events, transactions, and practices that, in his or her judgment, may have a significant effect on the financial forecast.

15.09 Factors to be considered by the practitioner in planning the examination include

    a. the accounting principles to be used and the type of presentation,

    b. the anticipated level of attestation risk[2] related to the financial forecast,

    c. preliminary judgments about materiality levels,

    d. items within the financial forecast that are likely to require revision or adjustment,

    e. conditions that may require extension or modification of the practitioner's examination procedures,

---

[2] Attestation risk is the risk that the practitioner may unknowingly fail to appropriately modify his or her examination report on a financial forecast that is materially misstated; that is, a financial forecast that is not presented in conformity with AICPA presentation guidelines or that has assumptions that do not provide a reasonable basis for management's forecast (*or do not provide a reasonable basis for management's projection, given the hypothetical assumptions*). It consists of (*a*) the risk (consisting of inherent risk and control risk) that the financial forecast contains errors that could be material, and (*b*) the risk (detection risk) that the practitioner will not detect such errors.

f. knowledge of the entity's business and its industry,

g. the responsible party's experience in preparing financial forecasts,

h. the length of the period covered by the financial forecast, and

i. the process by which the responsible party develops its financial forecast.

15.10 The practitioner should obtain knowledge of the entity's business, accounting principles, and the key factors on which its future financial results appear to depend, in a manner similar to that described in paragraphs 12.07–.10. The practitioner should focus on such areas as the following:

a. The availability and cost of resources needed in order to operate (principal items usually include raw materials, labor, short-term and long-term financing, and plant and equipment)

b. The nature and condition of markets in which the entity sells its goods or services, including final consumer markets if the entity sells to intermediate markets

c. Factors specific to the industry, including competitive conditions, sensitivity to economic conditions, accounting policies, specific regulatory requirements, and technology

d. Patterns of past performance for the entity or comparable entities, including trends in revenue and costs, turnover of assets, uses and capacities of physical facilities, and management policies

15.11 If the practitioner has reviewed or audited the entity's historical financial statements or performed services on previous financial forecasts, he or she may be generally familiar with certain of these areas.[3] However, the practitioner may acquire or augment this knowledge in other ways, such as by inquiry of entity personnel, experience with other similar entities in the industry, consultation with individuals knowledgeable about the industry, or use of industry publications, financial statements of other entities in the industry, textbooks, or periodicals.

Examination Procedures

15.12 The practitioner should establish an understanding with the responsible party regarding the services to be performed. The understanding should include the objectives of the engagement, the responsible party's responsibilities, the practitioner's responsibilities, and limitations of the engagement. The practitioner should document the understanding in the attest documentation, preferably through a written communication with the responsible party. If the practitioner believes an understanding with the responsible party has not been established, he or she should decline to accept or perform the engagement. If the responsible party is different than the client, the practitioner should establish the understanding with both the client and the responsible party, and the understanding also should include the client's responsibilities. (An excerpt from an illustrative engagement letter is presented in chapter 16, "Illustrative Engagement and Representation Letters for an Examination.")

---

[3] See AU-C section 300, *Planning an Audit*; AU-C section 315, *Understanding the Entity and Its Environment and Assessing the Risks of Material Misstatement*; and AR section 90, *Review of Financial Statements* (AICPA, *Professional Standards*).

15.13 The practitioner's objective in an examination of a financial forecast is to accumulate sufficient evidence to limit attestation risk to a level that is, in his or her professional judgment, appropriate for the level of assurance that may be imparted by the examination report. In a report on an examination of a financial forecast, the practitioner provides assurance only about whether the forecast is presented in conformity with AICPA presentation guidelines and whether the assumptions provide a reasonable basis for management's forecast. He or she does not provide assurance about the achievability of the prospective results, because events and circumstances frequently do not occur as expected, and achievement of the prospective results is dependent on the actions, plans, and assumptions of the responsible party.

15.13P   In a report on an examination of a projection, the practitioner provides assurance on whether the assumptions provide a reasonable basis for the projection, given the hypothetical assumptions.

15.14 In his or her examination of a financial forecast, the practitioner should select from all available procedures—that is, procedures that assess inherent and control risk and restrict detection risk—any combination that can restrict attestation risk to such an appropriate level. The extent to which examination procedures will be performed should be based on the practitioner's consideration of the following:

a. The nature and materiality of the information to the financial forecast taken as a whole

b. The likelihood of misstatements

c. Knowledge obtained during current and previous engagements

d. The responsible party's competence with respect to financial forecasts

e. The extent to which the financial forecast is affected by the responsible party's judgment, for example, its judgment in selecting the assumptions used to prepare the financial forecast

f. The adequacy of the responsible party's underlying data

The Responsible Party's Experience in Preparing Financial Forecasts

15.15 Analysis of any financial forecasts developed for past periods compared to the historical results for those periods may indicate the effectiveness of the process to prepare financial forecasts. However, the responsible party's previous experience is not necessarily indicative of the reliability of the forecast under examination.

Prospective Period

15.16 The practitioner should consider the length of the prospective period[4] and the extent to which historical results for part of the prospective period are included in the forecast. These two factors may affect the amount and reliability of support for the assumptions underlying the financial forecast.

15.17 When examining a financial forecast that presents individual discrete periods, a practitioner should evaluate the support for the underlying assumptions used in the preparation of the forecast for each period presented.

---

[4] See paragraphs 8.32–.34.

Process by Which the Responsible Party Develops Its Financial Forecasts

15.18 The practitioner's understanding of the process helps determine the scope of the examination. The practitioner's initial understanding usually is obtained in discussions with personnel responsible for the presentation. More detailed understanding, including the process by which the key factors are identified and the assumptions are developed, reviewed, and approved, is generally obtained through inquiry; observation; review of manuals, memoranda, instructions, and forms used (if any); analysis of models and statistical techniques (if used); and review of documentation. The extent to which the practitioner obtains or develops documentation in support of the assumptions will depend upon the complexity of the process.

15.19 In determining the scope of the examination, the practitioner may consider the process in relation to the guidance in chapter 6.[5]

Procedures to Evaluate Assumptions

15.20 The practitioner should perform those procedures he or she considers necessary in the circumstances to report on whether the assumptions provide a reasonable basis for the financial forecast. The practitioner can form an opinion that the assumptions provide a reasonable basis for the forecast if the responsible party represents that the presentation reflects, to the best of its knowledge and belief, its estimate of expected financial position, results of operations, and cash flows for the forecast period,[6] and the practitioner concludes, based on his or her examination, (a) that the responsible party has explicitly identified all factors expected to materially affect the operations of the entity during the forecast period and has developed appropriate assumptions for such factors[7] and (b) that the assumptions are suitably supported (see paragraph 15.23).

15.20P *In an examination of a financial projection, the practitioner should perform those procedures that he or she considers necessary in the circumstances to report on whether the assumptions provide a reasonable basis for the financial projection given the hypothetical assumptions. The practitioner can form an opinion that the assumptions provide a reasonable basis for the financial projection given the hypothetical assumptions if the responsible party represents that the presentation reflects, to the best of its knowledge and belief, expected financial position, results of operations, and cash flows for the prospective period given the hypothetical assumptions[8] and the practitioner concludes, based on the examination, (a) that the responsible party has explicitly identified all factors that would materially affect the operations of the entity during the prospective*

---

[5] The practitioner's consideration of the process may also provide a basis for constructive suggestions concerning improvements in the process used to develop financial forecasts.

[6] If the forecast contains a range, the representation should also generally include a statement that, to the best of the responsible party's knowledge and belief, the item or items subject to the assumption are expected to actually fall within the range and that the range was not selected in a biased or misleading manner.

[7] An attempt to list all assumptions is inherently not feasible. Frequently, basic assumptions that have enormous potential impact are considered to be implicit, such as conditions of peace and the absence of natural disasters.

[8] *If the projection contains a range, the representation should also generally include a statement that, to the best of the responsible party's knowledge and belief, given the hypothetical assumptions, the item or items subject to the assumptions are expected to actually fall within the range, and that the range was not selected in a biased or misleading manner.*

period if the hypothetical assumptions were to materialize, and has developed appropriate assumptions with respect to such factors and (b) that the other assumptions are suitably supported given the hypothetical assumptions. However, as the number and significance of the hypothetical assumptions increase, the practitioner may not be able to satisfy himself or herself about the presentation as a whole by obtaining support for the remaining assumptions.

Development of Assumptions

15.21 Using his or her knowledge of the business, the practitioner should evaluate whether assumptions have been developed for all key factors on which the entity's financial results appear to depend. In evaluating the assumptions, the practitioner should consider the relevance and overall completeness of the factors identified, as well as the risks inherent in the business and the sensitivity of the financial forecast to variations in particular assumptions.

15.22 Analyzing prior-period financial statements may help identify the principal factors that influence financial results. The practitioner should consider whether any significant deviations from historical trends exist, including deviations from historical results included for part of the prospective period. The deviations might highlight significant factors that previously were not deemed important to the business.

Support for Assumptions

15.23 Having obtained satisfaction that all key factors have been identified and assumptions have been developed for each key factor, the practitioner should evaluate support for the assumptions.

15.24 The practitioner can conclude that the assumptions are suitably supported if the preponderance of information supports each significant assumption.

15.24P *For a financial projection, in evaluating support for assumptions other than hypothetical assumptions, the practitioner can conclude that they are suitably supported if the preponderance of information supports each significant assumption given the hypothetical assumptions. The practitioner need not obtain support for the hypothetical assumptions, although he or she should consider whether they are consistent with the purpose of the presentation.*

15.25 As used here, *preponderance* is not meant to imply that a statistical majority of available information points to a specific assumption. Rather, a preponderance of information exists for an assumption if the weight of available information tends to support that assumption. Furthermore, because of the judgments involved in developing assumptions, different people may arrive at somewhat different but equally reasonable assumptions based on the same information.

15.26 In an evaluation of whether the assumptions provide a reasonable basis for the forecast, the practitioner should consider the assumptions in the aggregate. If certain assumptions do not have a material impact on the presentation, they may not have to be individually evaluated. Nonetheless, the practitioner should consider the aggregate impact of individually insignificant assumptions in making his or her overall evaluation.

15.27 The financial forecast that the practitioner is engaged to examine is defined in terms of the responsible party's estimate, to the best of its knowledge and belief, of expected future results based on expected conditions and courses of action. Although the practitioner can reach a conclusion that the assumptions provide a reasonable basis for the presentation, he or she cannot conclude that any outcome is expected because (*a*) realization of the financial forecast may depend on the responsible party's intentions, which cannot be examined, (*b*) there is substantial inherent uncertainty in the assumptions, (*c*) some of the information accumulated about an assumption may appear contradictory, and (*d*) different but similarly reasonable assumptions concerning a particular matter might be derived from common information.

15.28 Specific assumptions that ordinarily require the most scrutiny are those that are

    a. material to the prospective amounts.

    b. especially sensitive to variations.

    c. deviations from historical trends.

    d. especially uncertain.

15.29 In evaluating the support for assumptions, the practitioner should consider

    a. whether sufficient pertinent sources of information about the assumptions have been considered. Examples of external sources the practitioner might consider are government publications, industry publications, economic forecasts, existing or proposed legislation, and reports of changing technology. Examples of internal sources are budgets, labor agreements, patents, royalty agreements and records, sales backlog records, debt agreements, and actions of the board of directors involving entity plans.

    b. whether the assumptions are consistent with the sources from which they are derived.

    c. whether the assumptions are consistent with each other.

    d. whether the historical financial information and other data used in developing the assumptions are sufficiently reliable for that purpose. Reliability can be assessed by inquiry and analytical or other procedures, some of which may have been completed in past audits or reviews of the historical financial statements. If historical financial statements have been prepared for an expired part of the prospective period, the practitioner should consider the historical data in relation to the prospective results for the same period, when applicable. If the financial forecast incorporates such historical financial results and that period is significant to the presentation, the practitioner should make a review of the historical information in conformity with the applicable standards for a review.[9]

    e. whether the historical financial information and other data used in developing the assumptions are comparable over the periods specified or whether the effects of any lack of comparability were considered in developing the assumptions.

---

[9] If the entity is a public company and has audited financial statements, refer to the procedures in AU section 722, *Interim Financial Information* (AICPA, *PCAOB Standards and Related Rules*, Interim Standards). If the entity is nonpublic, refer to the procedures in paragraphs .16–.26 of AR section 90 and AU-C section 930, *Interim Financial Information* (AICPA, *Professional Standards*).

f. whether the logical arguments or theory, considered with the data supporting the assumptions, are reasonable.

15.30 Support for assumptions may include market surveys, engineering studies, general economic indicators, industry statistics, trends and patterns developed from an entity's operating history, and internal data and analyses, accompanied by their supporting logical argument or theory. The practitioner may also obtain support during the evaluation of the process by which the responsible party develops its financial forecasts. Support can range from information based on informed opinion (such as economists' estimates of the inflation rate) to data that can be tested in traditional ways (such as completed transactions).

15.31 In addition to evaluating the assumptions and the sources of information used to develop them, the practitioner might use alternative approaches to the development of assumptions in evaluating forecasted amounts. For example, to test a forecast of aggregate sales developed from individual salesmen's estimates the practitioner may employ a historical trend estimate.

Support for Tax Assumptions

15.32 Sometimes, one of the most sensitive assumptions underlying a financial forecast relates to the income tax treatment of prospective transactions. This is usually the case for financial forecasts used for tax shelter offerings.[10] If this is the case, the practitioner should obtain satisfaction as to the appropriateness of the tax assumptions either (*a*) through inquiry and analysis or (*b*) by obtaining an opinion about those tax consequences (a *tax opinion*) rendered by the entity's tax counsel or another practitioner and applying the procedures described in paragraph 15.34.

15.33 Technical training and experience, as well as knowledge of the client and its industry, enable the practitioner to be knowledgeable about income tax matters and competent in assessing their presentation in prospective financial statements. Therefore, when carrying out procedures to determine whether another professional's tax opinion provides suitable support for tax assumptions, the practitioner is viewed as being one who is knowledgeable in income tax matters related to the entity's forecast.[11]

15.34 When determining whether another professional's tax opinion provides suitable support for tax assumptions underlying a financial forecast, the practitioner should

a. obtain a copy of the tax opinion expected to be issued.

b. apply the following procedures from AU-C section 620, *Using the Work of an Auditor's Specialist* (AICPA, *Professional Standards*):

---

[10] The practitioner might consider Treasury Department Circular No. 230, *Regulations Governing Practice before the Internal Revenue Service*, involving tax shelter opinions (see appendix C, "IRS Regulations Regarding Tax Shelter Opinions (Circular 230)"), which establishes certain requirements regarding the practitioner's consideration of tax assumptions in tax shelter offering materials. Also see chapter 11, "Tax Shelter Opinions," in this guide.

[11] The tax opinion provided by the other professional may address matters of a legal nature that are not directly related to amounts included in the forecast—for example, matters related to the legal form of the entity. Practitioners are not expected to have the technical training and experience necessary to form an opinion on legal matters.

- Evaluate whether the auditor's specialist has the necessary competence, capabilities, and objectivity for the practioner's purposes.

- Agree with the practitioner's specialist regarding (1) the nature, scope, and objectives of the work of the auditor's specialist; (2) the respective roles and responsibilities of the practitioner and the practitioner's specialists; (3) the nature, timing, and extent of communication; and (4) the need for the practitioner's specialist to observe confidentiality requirements.

- Evaluate the relevance, completeness, and accuracy of source data used that is significant to the auditor's specialist work.

- Evaluate whether the other professional's findings support the related representations in the prospective financial statements. In doing this, the practitioner should read the tax opinion and consider whether (1) the facts used in the tax opinion are consistent with the information obtained during the examination of the forecast; (2) the assumptions and arguments used in the tax opinion are reasonable;[12] and (3) the assumptions, facts, and arguments used in the tax opinion support the conclusions reached.

The tax assumptions would be appropriate only in those situations in which the practitioner is satisfied about each material issue, both individually and in the aggregate, that the tax consequences are more likely than not the proper tax treatment.

Evaluating Preparation and Presentation

15.35 In evaluating the preparation and presentation of the financial forecast, the practitioner should perform procedures that will provide reasonable assurance as to the following:

a. The presentation reflects the identified assumptions.

b. The computations made to translate the assumptions into prospective amounts are mathematically accurate.

c. The assumptions are internally consistent.

d. The accounting principles used in the financial forecast are consistent with the accounting principles expected to be used in the historical financial statements covering the prospective period and with those used in the most recent historical financial statements, if any.

15.35(d)P *The accounting principles used in the financial projection are consistent with the accounting principles expected to be used in the prospective period and with those used in the most recent historical financial statements, if any, or they are consistent with the purpose of the presentation.*[13]

---

[12] See footnote 16.

[13] *The accounting principles used in a financial projection need not be those expected to be used in the historical financial statements for the prospective period if use of different principles is consistent with the purpose of the presentation (for example, an entity that reports its inventory on a first-in, first-out basis for its historical financial statements might present a projection using a last-in, first-out inventory basis to analyze the effects of a change in inventory method).*

    e. The presentation of the financial forecast follows the AICPA guidelines applicable for such statements.[14]

    f. The assumptions have been adequately disclosed based on AICPA presentation guidelines in chapter 8.

15.36 The practitioner should consider whether the financial forecast, including related disclosures, should be revised because of any of the following: (*a*) mathematical errors, (*b*) unreasonable or internally inconsistent assumptions, (*c*) inappropriate or incomplete presentation, or (*d*) inadequate disclosure.

15.37 The practitioner should obtain written representations from the responsible party acknowledging its responsibility for the assumptions. The representations should be signed by the responsible party at the highest level of authority who the practitioner believes is responsible for and knowledgeable, directly or through others in the organization, about the matters covered by the representations.

15.38 The representations should include the responsible party's assertion that the financial forecast presents, to the best of the responsible party's knowledge and belief, the expected financial position, results of operations, and cash flows for the forecast period and that the forecast reflects the responsible party's judgment, based on present circumstances, of the expected conditions and its expected course of action. The representations should also include a statement that the forecast is presented in conformity with guidelines for the presentation of a forecast established by the American Institute of Certified Public Accountants. The representations should also include a statement that the assumptions on which the forecast is based are reasonable. If the forecast contains a range, the representation should also include a statement that, to the best of the responsible party's knowledge and belief, the item or items subject to the assumption are expected to actually fall within the range, and that the range was not selected in a biased or misleading manner.

15.38P The representations should include the responsible party's assertion that the financial projection presents, to the best of the responsible party's knowledge and belief, the expected financial position, results of operations, and cash flows for the projection period, given the hypothetical assumptions, and that the projection reflects its judgment, based on present circumstances, of expected conditions and its expected course of action given the occurrence of the hypothetical events. The representations should also (a) identify the hypothetical assumptions and describe the limitations on the usefulness of the presentation, (b) state that the assumptions are appropriate, (c) indicate if the hypothetical assumptions are improbable, and (d) include, if the projection contains a range, include a statement that, to the best of the responsible party's knowledge and belief, given the hypothetical assumptions, the item or items subject to the assumption are expected to actually fall within the range, and that the range was not selected in a biased or misleading manner. The representations should also include a statement that the projection is presented in conformity with guidelines for the presentation of a projection established by the American Institute of Certified Public Accountants.

---

[14] Presentation guidelines for entities that issue financial forecasts are set forth in chapter 8.

Using the Work of a Specialist

15.39 During the examination, the practitioner may encounter matters that, in his or her judgment, require using the work of a specialist; for example, an engineer, economist, investment banker, or architect. Although the guidance provided in AU-C section 620 is intended for the auditor of historical financial statements, it is generally applicable if the practitioner examining a financial forecast uses the work of a specialist.

Assumptions Dependent on the Actions of Users

15.40 Occasionally, a forecast is predicated on a significant assumption that relates directly to a user's prospective action. For example, an assumption may relate to obtaining debt or equity when the forecast is to be used to solicit that debt or equity, or an assumption may relate to the passage of a referendum when the forecast is to be used by voters deciding on the referendum. In such a case, the practitioner may have difficulty in obtaining support for the assumption. If the assumption is subject to many possible outcomes (for example, if the entity would be willing to issue debt or equity in an amount less than that reflected in the forecast), the practitioner would need to obtain support for the assumption in order to issue an unqualified examination report. If, on the other hand, the assumption is subject to only two possible outcomes (that is, an either/or situation), for example, if an entity will not issue the debt or equity unless it places the *entire* debt or equity reflected in the forecast, the practitioner may issue an examination report without obtaining support for that assumption as long as the assumption is not unreasonable on its face. In such a case, users would not be expected to rely on the forecast once the prospective action does not take place and the assumption does not materialize. Accordingly, the practitioner's report would be unaffected by the lack of support for the assumption, provided that the forecast discloses the limitations on the usefulness of the presentation.[15] That is, the forecast should disclose that the responsible party believes that the forecast represents the entity's expected financial position, results of operations, and cash flows, only if the prospective action of users takes place.

Documentation[16]

15.41 The practitioner should prepare and maintain attest documentation, the form and content of which should be designed to meet the circumstances of the particular attest engagement. Attest documentation is the principal record of attest procedures applied, information obtained, and conclusions or findings reached by the practitioner in the engagement. The quantity, type, and content of attest documentation are matters of the practitioner's professional judgment.

---

[15] In such circumstances the representations the practitioner receives from the responsible party may be modified to state that the forecast presents, to the best of the responsible party's knowledge and belief, expected financial position, results of operations, and cash flows, based on the assumed prospective action of the users.

[16] Attest documentation also may be referred to as *working papers.*

15.42 Attest documentation serves mainly to

a. provide the principal support for the practitioner's report, including the representation regarding observance of the standards of fieldwork, which is implicit in the reference in the report to the attestation standards.[17]

b. aid the practitioner in the conduct and supervision of the attest engagement.

The attest documentation in an examination ordinarily should indicate that the process by which the entity develops its financial forecast was considered in determining the scope of the examination.

15.43 Examples of attest documentation are work programs, analyses, memoranda, letters of confirmation and representation, abstracts or copies of entity documents, and schedules or commentaries prepared or obtained by the practitioner. Attest documentation may be in paper form, electronic form, or other media.

15.44 Attest documentation should be sufficient to (a) enable members of the engagement team with supervision and review responsibilities to understand the nature, timing, extent, and results of attest procedures performed, and the information obtained[18] and (b) indicate the engagement team member(s) who performed and reviewed the work.

15.45 Attest documentation is the property of the practitioner and some states recognize this right of ownership in the statutes. The practitioner should adopt reasonable procedures to retain attest documentation for a period of time sufficient to meet the needs of his or her practice and to satisfy any applicable legal or regulatory requirements of records retention.[19]

15.46 The practitioner has an ethical, and in some situations a legal, obligation to maintain the confidentiality of client information or information of the responsible party.[20] Because attest documentation often contains confidential information, the practitioner should adopt reasonable procedures to maintain the confidentiality of that information.

15.47 The practitioner should also adopt reasonable procedures to prevent unauthorized access to attest documentation.

15.48 Certain attest documentation may sometimes serve as a useful reference source for the client, but it should not be regarded as a part of, or a substitute for, the client's records.

---

[17] However, there is no intention to imply that the practitioner would be precluded from supporting his or her report by other means in addition to attest documentation.

[18] A firm of practitioners has a responsibility to adopt a system of quality control policies and procedures to provide the firm with reasonable assurance that its personnel comply with applicable professional standards, including attestation standards, and the firm's standards of quality in conducting individual attest engagements. Review of attest documentation and discussions with attest team members are among the procedures a firm performs when monitoring compliance with the quality control policies and procedures that it has established.

[19] The procedures should generally enable the practitioner to access electronic attest documentation throughout the retention period.

[20] Also, see Rule 301, *Confidential Client Information* (AICPA, *Professional Standards*, ET sec. 301 par. .01), of the AICPA's Code of Professional Conduct.

Illustrative Examination Procedures

15.49 The following procedures are listed to assist the practitioner in planning examinations of financial forecasts. The list is neither a complete summary of all possible procedures nor an outline of minimum procedures, but it might aid in the development and selection of procedures for a particular engagement. The practitioner may be able to achieve the same objectives by procedures other than those illustrated.

15.50 Although the responsible party may call upon the practitioner to assist in identifying and formulating assumptions, as well as translating those assumptions into dollar estimates for inclusion in the financial forecast, the practitioner is responsible for performing examination procedures to obtain appropriate support in order to afford a reasonable basis for his or her report.

15.51 The procedures are divided into three categories:

a. Procedures to determine the scope of the examination

b. Procedures to evaluate assumptions

c. Procedures to evaluate the preparation and presentation of the financial forecast

15.52 Procedures to Determine the Scope of the Examination

a. Obtain knowledge of the entity's business by

(1) interviewing entity personnel and other individuals knowledgeable about the industry.

(2) consulting AICPA guides, industry publications, textbooks, and periodicals.

(3) analyzing financial statements of the entity and of other entities in the industry.

The practitioner may have obtained previously some or all of this knowledge through experience with the entity or its industry.

b. In obtaining knowledge of the entity's business, consider

(1) resources needed by the company (availability and cost):
- Material
- Labor
- Capital
- Fixed assets (for example, capacity of plant and equipment)

(2) markets served by the company (nature and condition):
- Intermediate market
- Final consumer markets
- Entity's market share
- Advertising and marketing plans

    (3) factors specific to the industry:

- Competitive conditions
- Sensitivity to economic conditions
- Accounting policies
- Specific regulatory requirements
- Technology

    (4) patterns of past performance for the entity or comparable entities:

- Trends in revenue and costs
- Turnover of assets
- Uses and capabilities of physical facilities
- Management policies

  c. Obtain or assemble the financial forecast together with a list of the significant assumptions and their descriptions.

  d. Review the process used in preparing the financial forecast to obtain an understanding of the rationale by which key factors are identified and assumptions are developed and of the process by which assumptions are translated into prospective data. The practitioner would look for answers to such questions as these:

    (1) Is preparation of the financial forecast adequately documented to permit tracing through the process? The practitioner may decide to prepare a brief outline of the process used to develop financial forecast.

    (2) Has the process been used in the past to generate financial forecasts, and, if so, was it effective?

    (3) What procedures provide reasonable assurance that all significant factors are included in the assumptions?

    (4) What procedures provide reasonable assurance that the financial forecast is based on assumptions approved by the responsible party?

    (5) What are the methods for collecting, calculating, and aggregating prospective data?

    (6) What methods identify and quantify the impact of variations in assumptions?

    (7) What are the procedures to effect changes in accounting principles and reflect them in the financial forecast?

    (8) If the process used to develop financial forecasts has been in operation or used in the past, are there procedures to compare prior prospective amounts with the historical results for the same period and to analyze the differences where applicable? (For example, differences in forecasted amounts and actual results would be analyzed to ascertain that identified causes are considered.) Are the procedures used to adjust the process, if applicable, as a result of such analysis?

(9) What are the responsible party's review and approval procedures?

(10) How are errors prevented or detected?

e. Identify any models and techniques that are used. If possible, obtain a description of them.

f. Having reviewed the process by which the responsible party develops its financial forecasts, analyze its strengths and weaknesses by comparing it with the guidelines outlined in chapter 6.

g. Consider the competence of the entity's personnel involved in the process, including their degree of authority, prior experience with the entity and industry, and understanding of both the entity's plans and the process, in relation to their functions in the process and in entity operations.

h. Review documentation of both the financial forecasts and process to develop them or otherwise to investigate whether there is

(1) review and approval by the responsible party.

(2) determination of the relative effect of variations in major underlying assumptions.

(3) use of appropriate accounting principles and practices.

i. Test significant elements of the process designed to prevent or detect errors, including clerical errors.

j. If applicable, review the entity's documentation of the comparison of actual results with amounts contained in previous financial forecasts (if any) for that period and consider (a) whether the comparison was performed using correct, comparable data and whether analyzed differences were documented and appropriately supported, (b) whether the process was adjusted where appropriate, (c) whether the procedures to develop financial forecasts in the past have reflected the entity's plans properly, and (d) whether any consistent biases have been observed.

k. Based on the knowledge obtained in the foregoing procedures, design the examination procedures for evaluating the assumptions and the preparation and presentation of the financial forecast.

15.53 Procedures to Evaluate Assumptions

a. Identify key factors on which the financial results of the entity appear to depend.

(1) Evaluate both the assumptions listed in the financial forecast and the more detailed data included in the underlying documentation to determine the completeness of the list. Factors to consider include

- risks inherent in the business.

- sensitivity to variations.

- pervasiveness of the impact of particular factors on the various assumptions.

(2) Obtain financial forecasts of similar entities, if available, and consider whether the key factors covered by the assumptions therein are covered in the client's statements.

(3) Analyze prior-period financial results to help identify the principal factors that influenced the results. If any interim historical results are available, consider any significant deviations from historical patterns and investigate the causes.

(4) Review any public statements, formal plans, and the minutes of board of directors' meetings, noting any significant decisions regarding plans, contracts, or legal agreements.

(5) Question the responsible party regarding possible additional factors or changes in assumptions about factors.

(6) Using the knowledge of the entity and its industry, investigate any particularly risky or sensitive aspects of the business—market trends, competitive conditions, pending laws and regulations, social, economic, political and technological influences, and dependence on major customers and suppliers.

b. Evaluate whether the assumptions are suitably supported.

(1) Evaluate the support for the assumptions, giving special attention to specific assumptions that are

- material to the prospective amounts.
- especially sensitive to variations.
- deviations from historical patterns.
- especially uncertain.

(2) For key assumptions, obtain a list of internal and external sources of information that the entity used in formulating the assumptions. On a test basis, evaluate whether the information was considered in formulating the assumptions.

(3) Trace assumptions about selected key factors to the support for the assumptions to determine whether the indicated sources of information were actually used and to evaluate the suitability of existing support. If the information is taken from internal analyses, consider the need for testing the supporting information.

(4) Review any available documentation of the responsible party's plans, such as budgets, spending estimates, policy statements, or contractual agreements, and inquire about those plans, goals, and objectives and consider their relationship to the assumptions.

(5) Investigate alternative sources of support for the assumptions and evaluate whether the preponderance of available information supports each significant assumption.[21]

(6) Inquire about and analyze the historical data used in developing prospective amounts to assess

---

[21] The cost to acquire the additional information should generally be commensurate with anticipated benefits. See paragraph 6.21.

- whether it is comparable and consistent with the forecast period.

- whether it is sufficiently reliable for the purpose.

(7) If historical financial statements have been prepared for an expired part of the prospective period, read the historical data and consider them in relation to the prospective results for the same period.

(8) If the financial forecast is based on the historical financial results for part of the forecast period, and that part is significant to the presentation, make a review of the historical information in conformity with applicable standards for a review.

(9) Consider alternative approaches to the development of the assumptions. For example, if the sales assumption was developed by aggregating individual salesperson's estimates, consider comparing the assumptions to historical patterns. Also consider trying other models and techniques.

(10) Evaluate whether the presentation extends to time periods for which suitable support for assumptions is not available, considering

- the nature of the entity's industry.

- patterns of past performance for the entity or comparable entities.

(11) If appropriate, consider confirming with external sources information supporting the assumptions. (For example, if the backlog of sales orders is significant to the financial forecast and is not adequately supported, consider sending written confirmation requests to customers.)

(12) If the support for key assumptions comes from experts, such as lawyers, engineers, economists, investment bankers, and architects

- consider their professional standing.

- consider using the work of another expert in the field.

- review the data and plans the entity submitted to the expert for consistency with the financial forecast and supporting data.

(13) If the assumptions about the tax treatment of prospective transactions are sensitive, obtain support for their appropriateness by (a) analyzing prospective transactions in the context of applicable tax laws or (b) obtaining an opinion as to such matters from the entity's tax counsel or another practitioner and applying the procedures in paragraph 15.34.

(14) Obtain a representation letter from the responsible party.

(15) Consider obtaining a letter from the client's legal counsel, as of the report date, covering

- litigation, claims, and assessments.

- legality of any major changes planned (such as marketing considerations, environmental impact, or patents) and other matters (such as the impact of new laws affecting the industry).

15.53(b)P *For a financial projection, the procedures shown in paragraph 15.53b would be applicable only to assumptions other than hypothetical ones. In addition, the practitioner should determine if the hypothetical assumptions are consistent with the purpose of the presentation.*

15.54 Procedures to Evaluate the Preparation and Presentation of the Financial Forecast

a. Test the mathematical accuracy of, or perform, the computations made in translating the assumptions into prospective amounts.

b. Evaluate whether data have been appropriately aggregated by

(1) evaluating the appropriateness of mathematical equations, statistical techniques, or modeling procedures.

(2) recomputing on a test basis.

(3) tracing aggregate amounts to the financial forecast.

c. Determine whether the listed assumptions are those used in preparing the financial forecast.

d. Determine whether the effects of each assumption on all of the related prospective amounts have been reflected in the presentation.

e. Determine whether any assumption contradicts, or is inconsistent with, another.

f. Review the relationship between financial and other relevant data by using appropriate mathematical or judgmental methods.

g. Review adjustments made in the data, considering whether they are justified and reasonable in relation to other information and whether their impact has been properly reflected in the financial forecast.

h. If historical data for part of the forecast period are included in the financial forecast, trace the amounts from the books, records, and other indicated sources to the financial forecast.

i. Determine whether the presentation is in conformity with the presentation guidelines in chapter 8, considering the following:

(1) Is the financial forecast presented in the format of the historical financial statements expected to be issued? If not, are the required items presented?

(2) Are the accounting principles used

- consistent with those used in the historical financial statements, if any?

- consistent with those expected to be used in future financial statements (including expected changes in accounting principles)?

- generally accepted accounting principles or based on another comprehensive basis of accounting?

(3) Is the basis of accounting used

- consistent with that used in historical financial statements, if any?
- reconciled with the historical methods where different, or are the differences described?

(4) Are the assumptions adequately disclosed?

(5) Are particularly sensitive assumptions identified?

(6) If the impact of a variation in an assumption is disclosed, is it appropriately stated?

(7) Is the financial forecast appropriately distinguished from historical financial statements?

15.54P *For a financial projection, the procedures in paragraph 15.54 should be supplemented by the following considerations:*

a. *Are the purpose and limitations on the usefulness of the presentation disclosed?*

b. *Are the accounting principles used consistent with the purpose of the presentation?*

c. *Is there an excessive number of hypothetical assumptions?*

d. *Are the hypothetical assumptions identified as such?*

Chapter 16

Illustrative Engagement and Representation Letters for an Examination

> Because financial forecasts and projections are similar in many respects, separate guidance for projections is provided only to the extent that it differs from that for forecasts. *Italicized* paragraphs in this chapter that include a "P" in the paragraph number show how the guidance presented for forecasts should be modified for projections. Any plain-text paragraph not followed by an italicized paragraph applies to both forecasts and projections even though it uses only the term *forecast*.

Engagement Letter

16.01 The following is an excerpt from a sample engagement letter for an examination of a financial forecast:[1]

> This letter sets forth our understanding of the terms and objectives of our engagement and the nature and limitations of the services we will provide.
>
> We will examine, in accordance with attestation standards established by the American Institute of Certified Public Accountants, from information management[2] provides, the forecasted balance sheet, statements of income, retained earnings, and cash flows, and summaries of significant assumptions and accounting policies of XYZ Company as of December 31, 20XX, and the year then ending. We will examine the financial forecast for the purpose of issuing a report stating whether, in our opinion, (*a*) management's financial forecast is presented in conformity with applicable guidelines established by the American Institute of Certified Public Accountants and (*b*) management's assumptions provide a reasonable basis for its forecast.
>
> Our examination of the financial forecast will include procedures we consider necessary to evaluate (*a*) the assumptions used by management as a basis for the financial forecast, (*b*) the preparation of the financial forecast, and (*c*) the presentation of the financial forecast.
>
> Our report will detail the nature of reservations (if any) we have about the forecast. Should any such reservations develop, we will discuss them with you before the report is issued.
>
> A financial forecast presents, to the best of management's knowledge and belief, the Company's expected financial position, results of operations, and cash flows for the forecast period. It is based on management's assumptions reflecting conditions it expects to exist and the course of action it expects to take during the forecast period.

---

[1] If the assumptions regarding income taxes are sensitive (for example, in a tax shelter offering), the practitioner may want his or her engagement letter to provide that the client will obtain a tax opinion from its counsel, or that the practitioner will undertake to apply those procedures necessary to obtain satisfaction about the tax assumptions.

[2] If the responsible party is other than management, the references to management should generally be replaced with the name of the party who assumes responsibility for the assumptions.

Management is responsible for representations about its plans and expectations and for disclosure of significant information that might affect the ultimate realization of the forecasted results.

There will usually be differences between the forecasted and actual results, because events and circumstances frequently do not occur as expected, and those differences may be material. Our report will contain a statement to that effect.

We have no responsibility to update our report for events and circumstances occurring after the date of our report.

At the conclusion of the engagement, management agrees to supply us with a representation letter that, among other things, will confirm management's responsibility for the underlying assumptions and the appropriateness of the financial forecast and its presentation.

If management intends to reproduce and publish the forecast and our report thereon, they must be reproduced in their entirety, and both the first and subsequent corrected drafts of the document containing the forecast and any accompanying material must be submitted to us for approval.

16.01P *The following is an excerpt from a sample engagement letter for an examination of a financial projection. The letter would be modified as appropriate.*[3]

This letter sets forth our understanding of the terms and objectives of our engagement and the nature and limitations of the services we will provide.

We will examine, in accordance with attestation standards established by the American Institute of Certified Public Accountants, from information management[4] provides, the projected balance sheet, statements of income, retained earnings, and cash flows, and summaries of significant assumptions and accounting policies of XYZ Company as of December 31, 20XX, and the year then ending. We will examine the financial projection for the purpose of issuing a report stating whether, in our opinion, (a) management's financial projection is presented in conformity with applicable guidelines established by the American Institute of Certified Public Accountants and (b) management's assumptions provide a reasonable basis for its projection given the hypothetical assumptions.

Our examination of the financial projection will include procedures we consider necessary to evaluate (a) the assumptions used by management as a basis for the financial projection, (b) the preparation of the financial projection, and (c) the presentation of the financial projection.

Our report will detail the nature of reservations (if any) we have about the projection. Should any such reservations develop, we will discuss them with you before the report is issued.

---

[3] *If the assumptions regarding income taxes are sensitive, the practitioner may want the engagement letter to provide that the client will obtain a tax opinion from its counsel, or that the practitioner will undertake to apply those procedures necessary to obtain satisfaction about the tax assumptions.*

[4] *If the responsible party is other than management, the references to management should generally be replaced with the name of the party who assumes responsibility for the assumptions.*

The financial projection presents, to the best of management's knowledge and belief, the Company's expected financial position, results of operations, and cash flows for the projection period assuming [describe hypothetical assumptions]. It is based on management's assumptions reflecting conditions it expects would exist and courses of action it expects would be taken, assuming [describe hypothetical assumptions].

Management is responsible for representations about its plans and expectations and for disclosure of significant information that might affect the ultimate realization of the projected results.

Even if [state hypothetical assumptions] were to occur, there will usually be differences between the projected and actual results, because events and circumstances frequently do not occur as expected, and the differences may be material. Our report will contain a statement to that effect.

We have no responsibility to update our report for events and circumstances occurring after the date of our report.

At the conclusion of the engagement, management agrees to supply us with a representation letter that, among other things, will confirm management's responsibility for the underlying assumptions and the appropriateness of the financial projection and its presentation.

We understand that the projection and our report thereon will be used only for [state intended limited use]. If management intends to reproduce the projection and our report thereon, they must be reproduced in their entirety, and both the first and subsequent corrected drafts of the document containing the projection and any accompanying material must be submitted to us for approval.

Representation Letter

16.02 The following is a sample representation letter for an examination of a financial forecast. The written representations to be obtained should be based on the circumstances of the engagement.

[*Date of Practitioner's report*]

[*Practitioner's name*]

In connection with your examination of the forecasted balance sheet, statements of income, retained earnings, and cash flows and summaries of significant assumptions and accounting policies of XYZ Company as of December 31, 20XX, and for the year then ending, we make the following representations:

1. The financial forecast presents our assumptions and, to the best of our knowledge and belief, the Company's expected financial position, results of operations, and cash flows for the period[5] in conformity with the generally accepted accounting principles expected to be used by the Company during the forecast period, which are consistent with the principles that XYZ Company uses in preparing its historical financial statements.

---

[5] If the forecast is presented as a range, the description of the forecast would refer to the range (for example, ". . . at occupancy rates of 75 percent and 95 percent"). See also paragraph 16.03.

2. The financial forecast reflects our judgment based on present circumstances of the expected conditions and our expected course of action.

3. The financial forecast is presented in conformity with presentation guidelines established by the American Institute of Certified Public Accountants.

4. We believe that the assumptions underlying the forecast are reasonable and appropriate.

5. We have made available to you all significant information that we believe is relevant to the forecast.

6. To the best of our knowledge and belief, the documents and records supporting the assumptions are appropriate.

[*Signatures*]

16.02P *The following is a sample representation letter for an examination of a financial projection. The written representations to be obtained should be based on the circumstances of the engagement.*

[Date of Practitioner's report]

[Practitioner's name]

*In connection with your examination of the projected balance sheet, statements of income, retained earnings, and cash flows and summaries of significant assumptions assuming [*describe hypothetical assumptions*] and accounting policies of XYZ Company as of December 31, 20XX, and for the year then ending, we make the following representations*:

1. *The financial projection presents our assumptions and, to the best of our knowledge and belief, the Company's expected financial position, results of operations, and cash flows for the projection period assuming [*describe hypothetical assumptions*].[6]*

2. *The accounting principles used in the financial projection are in conformity with the generally accepted accounting principles expected to be used by the Company during the projection period, which are consistent with the principles that XYZ Company uses in preparing its historical financial statements.[7]*

3. *The financial projection reflects our judgment, based on present circumstances, of the expected conditions and our expected course of action assuming [*describe hypothetical assumptions*].[8]*

4. *The financial projection is presented in conformity with presentation guidelines established by the American Institute of Certified Public Accountants.*

---

[6] *If the projection is presented as a range, the description of the projection would refer to the range (for example, ". . . at occupancy rates of 75 percent and 95 percent"). See also paragraph 16.03P.*

[7] *If the projection is not presented on the basis of the accounting principles used for the historical financial statements, this sentence might read "The accounting principles used in the financial projection are consistent with [*the special purpose for the projection*]."*

[8] *If the hypothetical assumption is considered improbable the representation should generally say so, for example, ". . . assuming [*describe hypothetical assumption*], which we consider to be highly unlikely."*

5. *We believe that the assumptions underlying the projection are appropriate and reasonable assuming [describe hypothetical assumptions].*

6. *We have made available to you all significant information that we believe is relevant to the financial projection.*

7. *To the best of our knowledge and belief, the documents and records supporting the assumptions are appropriate.*

8. *We intend to use this projection only for [describe intended limited use].*

[Signatures]

16.03 If the forecast is presented as a range, the following representation would be added:

> We reasonably expect that the actual [*described items presented as a range*] achieved will be within the range shown; however, there can be no assurance that it will. The range shown was not selected in a biased or misleading manner.

16.03P *For a financial projection, if the presentation is presented as a range, the following representation would be added:*

> *We reasonably expect that the actual [describe items presented as a range] achieved will be within the range shown assuming [describe hypothetical assumption]; however, there can be no assurance that it will. The range shown was not selected in a biased or misleading manner.*

16.04 If the date of the signed representations is later than the date of the preparation of the forecast (see paragraph 8.11), the following representation would be added:

> We are not aware of any material changes in the information or circumstances from [*date*], the date of the forecast, to the present.

Chapter 17

The Practitioner's Examination Report

Because financial forecasts and projections are similar in many respects, separate guidance for projections is provided only to the extent that it differs from that for forecasts. *Italicized* paragraphs in this chapter show how the guidance presented for forecasts should be modified for projections. Any plain-text paragraph not followed by an italicized paragraph applies to both forecasts and projections even though it uses only the term *forecast*.

17.01 Per paragraph .33 of AT section 301, *Financial Forecasts and Projections* (AICPA, *Professional Standards*), the practitioner's standard report on an examination of a financial forecast should include the following:

a. A title that includes the word *independent*

b. An identification of the financial forecast presented

c. An identification of the responsible party and a statement that the financial forecast is the responsibility of the responsible party

d. A statement that the practitioner's responsibility is to express an opinion on the financial forecast based on his or her examination

e. A statement that the examination of the financial forecast was conducted in accordance with attestation standards established by the AICPA[1] and accordingly included such procedures as the practitioner considered necessary in the circumstances

f. A statement that the practitioner believes the examination provides a reasonable basis for his or her opinion

g. The practitioner's opinion that the financial forecast is presented in conformity with AICPA presentation guidelines[2,3] and that the underlying assumptions provide a reasonable basis for the forecast

17.01(g)P *The practitioner's opinion that the financial projection is presented in conformity with AICPA presentation guidelines[4,5] and that the underlying assumptions provide a reasonable basis for the projection given the hypothetical assumptions*

h. A caveat that the forecasted results may not be achieved

---

[1] Public Company Accounting Oversight Board (PCAOB) Auditing Standard No. 1, *References in Auditors' Reports to the Standards of the Public Company Accounting Oversight Board* (AICPA, *PCAOB Standards and Related Rules*, Auditing Standards), requires registered public accounting firms to make reference in his or her report to the "standards of the Public Company Oversight Board (United States)." The PCAOB standards are to be used by registered public accounting firms in the preparation and issuance of audit (or attestation) reports, as required by the Sarbanes Oxley Act of 2002 or the rules of the Securities and Exchange Commission (SEC).

[2] The practitioner's report need not comment on the consistency of the application of accounting principles as long as the presentation of any change in accounting principles is in conformity with AICPA presentation guidelines as detailed in chapter 8, "Presentation Guidelines."

[3] See footnote 1.

[4] *See footnote 2.*

[5] *See footnote 1.*

i. A statement that the practitioner assumes no responsibility to update the report for events and circumstances occurring after the date of the report

j. The manual or printed signature of the practitioner's firm

k. The date of the examination report

17.01P *In addition, the practitioner's report on an examination of a financial projection should include a statement describing the special purpose for which the projection was prepared as well as a separate paragraph that restricts the use of the report because it is intended to be used solely by specified parties.*

17.02 The following is the form of the practitioner's standard report on an examination of a forecast that does not contain a range:

Independent Accountant's Report

We have examined the accompanying forecasted balance sheet, statements of income, retained earnings, and cash flows of XYZ Company as of December 31, 20XX, and for the year then ending.[6] XYZ Company's management is responsible for the forecast. Our responsibility is to express an opinion on the forecast based on our examination.

Our examination was conducted in accordance with attestation standards established by the American Institute of Certified Public Accountants[7] and, accordingly, included such procedures as we considered necessary to evaluate both the assumptions used by management and the preparation and presentation of the forecast. We believe that our examination provides a reasonable basis for our opinion.

In our opinion, the accompanying forecast is presented in conformity with guidelines for presentation of a forecast established by the American Institute of Certified Public Accountants,[8] and the underlying assumptions provide a reasonable basis for management's forecast. However, there will usually be differences between the forecasted and actual results, because events and circumstances frequently do not occur as expected, and those differences may be material. We have no responsibility to update this report for events and circumstances occurring after the date of this report.

[*Signature*]

[*Date*]

17.02P *The following is the form of the practitioner's standard report on an examination of a projection that does not contain a range:*

Independent Accountant's Report

We have examined the accompanying projected balance sheet, statements of income, retained earnings, and cash flows of XYZ Company

---

[6] When the presentation is summarized as discussed in paragraph 8.06, this sentence might read "We have examined the accompanying summarized forecast of XYZ Company as of December 31, 20XX, and for the year then ending."

[7] See footnote 1.

[8] See footnote 1.

as of December 31, 20XX, and for the year then ending.[9] *XYZ Company's management is responsible for the projection, which was prepared for [*state special purpose, for example, "the purpose of negotiating a loan to expand XYZ Company's plant"*]. Our responsibility is to express an opinion on the projection based on our examination.*

Our examination was conducted in accordance with attestation standards established by the American Institute of Certified Public Accountants[10] *and, accordingly, included such procedures as we considered necessary to evaluate both the assumptions used by management and the preparation and presentation of the projection. We believe our examination provides a reasonable basis for our opinion.*

In our opinion, the accompanying projection is presented in conformity with guidelines for presentation of a projection established by the American Institute of Certified Public Accountants,[11] *and the underlying assumptions provide a reasonable basis for management's projection [*describe the hypothetical assumption, for example, "assuming the granting of the requested loan for the purpose of expanding XYZ Company's plant as described in the summary of significant assumptions"*]. However, even if [*describe hypothetical assumption, for example, "the loan is granted and the plant is expanded"*] , there will usually be differences between the projected and actual results, because events and circumstances frequently do not occur as expected, and those differences may be material. We have no responsibility to update this report for events and circumstances occurring after the date of this report.*

*The accompanying projection and this report are intended solely for the information and use of [*identify specified parties, for example, "XYZ Company and DEF National Bank"*] and are not intended to be and should not be used by anyone other than these specified parties.*

[Signature]

[Date]

17.03 When the financial forecast contains a range, the practitioner's standard report should also include a separate paragraph that states that the responsible party has elected to portray the expected results of one or more assumptions as a range. The following is an example of the separate paragraph to be added to the practitioner's report if he or she examines a forecast that contains a range:

As described in the summary of significant assumptions, management of XYZ Company has elected to portray forecasted [*describe financial statement element or elements for which the expected results of one or more assumptions fall within a range, and identify assumptions expected to fall within a range, for example, "revenue at the amounts of $X,XXX and $Y,YYY, which is predicated upon occupancy rates of XX percent and YY percent of available apartments"*] rather than as a single-point estimate. Accordingly, the accompanying forecast presents forecasted financial position, results of operations, and

---

[9] *If the presentation is summarized as discussed in paragraph 8.06, this sentence might read "We have examined the accompanying summarized projection of XYZ Company as of December 31, 20XX, and for the year then ending."*

[10] *See footnote 1.*

[11] *See footnote 1.*

cash flows [*describe one or more assumptions expected to fall within a range, for example, "at such occupancy rates"*]. However, there is no assurance that the actual results will fall within the range of [*describe one or more assumptions expected to fall within a range, for example, "occupancy rates"*] presented.

17.04 The practitioner's report on a financial forecast should correspond to the form of the forecast. Accordingly, if the forecast is presented in a columnar format in which each column represents a specific period, the practitioner's report on the forecast applies to each period presented in the forecast. Conversely, a practitioner's report would pertain to the entire period covered by the forecast (taken as a whole) if the presentation included a single column labeled "for the five years ending December 31, 20X6."

17.05 The date of completion of the practitioner's examination procedures should be used as the date of the report.

Modifications to the Practitioner's Opinion

17.06 The following circumstances result in the following types of modified practitioner's report involving the practitioner's opinion:

　　a. If, in the practitioner's opinion, the prospective financial statements depart from AICPA presentation guidelines,[12] he or she should express a qualified opinion (see paragraph 17.07) or an adverse opinion (see paragraph 17.09).[13] However, if the presentation departs from the presentation guidelines because it fails to disclose assumptions that appear to be significant, the practitioner should issue an adverse opinion (see paragraphs 17.09–.10).

　　b. If the practitioner believes that one or more significant assumptions do not provide a reasonable basis for the forecast, he or she should issue an adverse opinion (see paragraph 17.09).

　　c. If the practitioner's examination is affected by conditions that preclude application of one or more procedures he or she considers necessary in the circumstances, he or she should disclaim an opinion and describe the scope limitation in the report (see paragraph 17.11).

17.06P *Because of the nature of financial projections, a hypothetical assumption is not intended to provide a reasonable basis for the presentation. Thus, the practitioner's standard report on a financial projection would not be affected by the reasonableness of the hypothetical assumption. If, however, one or more of the other significant assumptions do not provide a reasonable basis for the presentation given the hypothetical assumption, the practitioner should give an adverse report. Paragraph 17.09 illustrates the form of adverse report, which should be adapted for a financial projection.*

17.07 *Qualified opinion.* In a qualified opinion, the practitioner should state, in a separate paragraph, all of the substantive reasons for modifying his or her opinion and describe the departure from AICPA presentation guidelines.[14] His or her opinion should include the words "except" or "exception" as

---

　　[12] See footnote 1.

　　[13] However, the practitioner may issue the standard examination report on a financial forecast filed with the SEC that meets the presentation requirements of Article XI of Regulation S-X.

　　[14] See footnote 1.

the qualifying language and should refer to the separate explanatory paragraph. The following is an example of an examination report on a forecast that is at variance with AICPA guidelines[15] for presentation of a financial forecast:

Independent Accountant's Report

We have examined the accompanying forecasted balance sheet, statements of income, retained earnings, and cash flows of XYZ Company as of December 31, 20XX, and for the year then ending. XYZ Company's management is responsible for the forecast. Our responsibility is to express an opinion on the forecast based on our examination.

Our examination was conducted in accordance with attestation standards established by the American Institute of Certified Public Accountants[16] and, accordingly, included such procedures as we considered necessary to evaluate both the assumptions used by management and the preparation and presentation of the forecast. We believe our examination provides a reasonable basis for our opinion.

The forecast does not disclose significant accounting policies. Disclosure of such policies is required by guidelines for presentation of a forecast established by the American Institute of Certified Public Accountants.[17]

In our opinion, except for the omission of the disclosure of the significant accounting policies as discussed in the preceding paragraph, the accompanying forecast is presented in conformity with guidelines for presentation of a forecast established by the American Institute of Certified Public Accountants,[18] and the underlying assumptions provide a reasonable basis for management's forecast. However, there will usually be differences between the forecasted and actual results, because events and circumstances frequently do not occur as expected, and those differences may be material. We have no responsibility to update this report for events and circumstances occurring after the date of this report.

[*Signature*]

[*Date*]

17.08 Because of the nature, sensitivity, and interrelationship of prospective information, a reader would find a practitioner's report qualified for a measurement departure,[19] the reasonableness of the underlying assumptions, or a scope limitation difficult to interpret. Accordingly, the practitioner should not express his or her opinion about these items with language such as "except for . . ." or "subject to the effects of . . . ." Rather, if a measurement departure, an unreasonable assumption, or a limitation on the scope of the practitioner's examination has led him or her to conclude that he or she cannot issue an unqualified opinion, he or she should issue the appropriate type of modified opinion described in paragraphs 17.09–.15.

---

[15] See footnote 1.

[16] See footnote 1.

[17] See footnote 1.

[18] See footnote 1.

[19] An example of a measurement departure is the failure to capitalize a capital lease in a forecast where the historical financial statements for the prospective period are expected to be presented in conformity with generally accepted accounting principles.

17.09 *Adverse opinion.* In an adverse opinion the practitioner should state, in a separate paragraph, all of the substantive reasons for his or her adverse opinion. His or her opinion should state that the presentation is not in conformity with presentation guidelines and should refer to the explanatory paragraph. When applicable, his or her opinion paragraph should also state that, in the practitioner's opinion, the assumptions do not provide a reasonable basis for the prospective financial statements. Set forth as follows is an example of an adverse opinion on an examination of a financial forecast which, in the practitioner's opinion, contains a significant assumption that was unreasonable. The example should be revised as appropriate if the adverse opinion is issued because the statements do not conform to the presentation guidelines.

Independent Accountant's Report

We have examined the accompanying forecasted balance sheet, statements of income, retained earnings, and cash flows of XYZ Company as of December 31, 20XX, and for the year then ending. XYZ Company's management is responsible for the forecast. Our responsibility is to express an opinion on the forecast based on our examination.

Our examination was conducted in accordance with attestation standards established by the American Institute of Certified Public Accountants[20] and, accordingly, included such procedures as we considered necessary to evaluate both the assumptions used by management and the preparation and presentation of the forecast. We believe our examination provides a reasonable basis for our opinion.

As discussed under the caption "Sales" in the summary of significant forecast assumptions, the forecasted sales include, among other things, revenue from the Company's federal defense contracts continuing at the current level. The Company's present federal defense contracts will expire in March, 20XX. No new contracts have been signed and no negotiations are underway for new federal defense contracts. Furthermore, the federal government has entered into contracts with another company to supply the items being manufactured under the Company's present contracts.

In our opinion, the accompanying forecast is not presented in conformity with guidelines for presentation of a financial forecast established by the American Institute of Certified Public Accountants[21] because management's assumptions, as discussed in the preceding paragraph, do not provide a reasonable basis for management's forecast. We have no responsibility to update this report for events and circumstances occurring after the date of this report.

[*Signature*]

[*Date*]

17.10 If the presentation, including the summary of significant assumptions, fails to disclose assumptions that, at the time, appear to be significant, the practitioner should describe the assumptions in his or her report and express an adverse opinion. The practitioner should not examine a presentation that omits all disclosures of assumptions.

---

[20] See footnote 1.
[21] See footnote 1.

17.10P *In addition, the practitioner should not examine a financial projection that omits (a) an identification of the hypothetical assumptions or (b) a description on the limitations of the usefulness of the presentation.*

17.11 *Disclaimer of opinion.* The practitioner can issue the standard report only if the examination has been conducted in accordance with AICPA standards[22] and he or she has been able to apply all the procedures considered necessary in the circumstances. The scope of the practitioner's examination might be limited either (*a*) by client-imposed conditions that preclude the application of one or more procedures that the practitioner considers necessary in the circumstances to comply with the standards or (*b*) by circumstances, such as the practitioner's inability to evaluate one or more significant assumptions because they are not suitably supported. In the case where there are limitations on the scope of the examination, whether imposed by the client or by other circumstances, the practitioner should state in the report that the scope of the examination was not sufficient to enable him or her to express an opinion with respect to the presentation or the underlying assumptions, and his or her disclaimer of opinion should include a direct reference to the explanatory paragraph.

17.12 If the practitioner does not believe an assumption to be suitably supported, he or she should assess its effect on the interrelationships of assumptions and on the financial forecast taken as a whole.

17.13 If the responsible party restricts the scope of the practitioner's procedures or declines to develop the information the practitioner considers necessary to evaluate one or more significant assumptions, the practitioner generally should issue a report describing a scope limitation.

17.14 In a disclaimer of opinion, the practitioner's report should indicate, in a separate paragraph, the respects in which the examination did not comply with standards for an examination. The practitioner should state that the scope of the examination was not sufficient to enable him or her to express an opinion with respect to the presentation or the underlying assumptions, and his or her disclaimer of opinion should include a direct reference to the explanatory paragraph. The following is an example of a report on an examination of a financial forecast for which a significant assumption could not be evaluated:

Independent Accountant's Report

We were engaged to examine the accompanying forecasted balance sheet, statements of income, retained earnings, and cash flows of XYZ Company as of December 31, 20XX, and for the year then ending. XYZ Company's management is responsible for the forecast.

As discussed under the caption "Income From Investee" in the summary of significant forecast assumptions, the forecast includes income from an equity investee constituting 23 percent of forecasted net income, which is management's estimate of the Company's share of the investee's income to be accrued for 20XX. The investee has not prepared a forecast for the year ending December 31, 20XX, and we were therefore unable to obtain suitable support for this assumption.

Because, as described in the preceding paragraph, we are unable to evaluate management's assumption regarding income from an equity investee and other assumptions that depend thereon, the scope of our work was not sufficient to express, and we do not express, an opinion

---

[22] See footnote 1.

with respect to the presentation of, or the assumptions underlying, the accompanying forecast. We have no responsibility to update this report for events and circumstances occurring after the date of this report.

[*Signature*]

[*Date*]

17.15 When there is a scope limitation and the practitioner also believes there are material departures from the presentation guidelines, those departures should be described in the practitioner's report.

Other Modifications to the Standard Examination Report

17.16 The circumstances described in subsequent paragraphs, although not necessarily resulting in modifications to the practitioner's opinion, would result in the following types of modifications to the standard examination report.

17.17 *Emphasis of a matter.* In some circumstances, the practitioner may emphasize a matter regarding the financial forecast but nevertheless intends to express an unqualified opinion. The practitioner may present other information and comments he or she wants to include, such as explanatory comments or other informative material, in a separate paragraph of the report.

17.18 *Evaluation based in part on a report of another practitioner.* When more than one practitioner is involved in the examination, the guidance provided for that situation in connection with audits of historical financial statements is generally applicable. When the principal practitioner decides to refer to the report of another practitioner as a basis, in part, for his or her own opinion, he or she should disclose that fact in stating the scope of the examination and should refer to the report of the other practitioner in expressing his or her opinion. Such reference indicates the division of responsibility for the performance of the examination, not a qualification of opinion.

17.19 *Comparative historical financial information.* Prospective financial statements may be included in a document that also contains historical financial statements and a practitioner's report thereon.[23] In addition, the historical financial statements that appear in the document may be summarized and presented with the prospective financial statements for comparative purposes.[24] An example of the reference to the practitioner's report on the historical financial statements when he or she audited, reviewed, or compiled those statements is presented as follows:

(Concluding sentence of the last paragraph)

The historical financial statements for the year ended December 31, 20XX (from which the historical data are derived) and our report thereon are set forth on pages xx–yy of this document.

---

[23] The practitioner's responsibility for those historical financial statements upon which he or she is not engaged to perform a professional service is described in paragraph .59 of AT section 301, *Financial Forecasts and Projections* (AICPA, *Professional Standards*), and AR section 400, *Communications Between Predecessor and Successor Accountants* (AICPA, *Professional Standards*), in the case of nonpublic entities.

[24] AU-C section 810, *Engagements to Report on Summary Financial Statements* (AICPA, *Professional Standards*), discusses the practitioner's report for summarized financial statements derived from audited financial statements that are not included in the same document.

Reporting on a Financial Forecast That Includes a Projected Sale of an Entity's Real Estate Investment at the End of the Forecast Period

17.20 If a hypothetical sale of an entity's real estate investment is presented as a separate statement (that is, as a financial projection) within a financial forecast,[25] the practitioner's report should be modified to report specifically on the statement.[26] An example of an appropriate form of report follows:[27]

Independent Accountant's Report

We have examined the accompanying forecasted balance sheet, statements of income, retained earnings, and cash flows of XYZ Company as of December 31, 20X8, and for the year then ending (the forecast), and the accompanying statement of the effect on limited partners of the projected sale of property at December 31, 20X8 (the projection). XYZ Company's management is responsible for the forecast and for the projection, which was prepared by management to provide potential investors with information about the effect of a hypothetical sale of the properties as of December 31, 20X8, and should not be considered a presentation of expected future results. Our responsibility is to express an opinion on the forecast and on the projection based on our examinations.

Our examination was conducted in accordance with attestation standards established by the American Institute of Certified Public Accountants[28] and, accordingly, included such procedures as we considered necessary to evaluate both the assumptions used by management and the preparation and presentation of the statements. We believe our examinations provide a reasonable basis for our opinions.

In our opinion, the accompanying forecast is presented in conformity with guidelines for presentation of a forecast established by the American Institute of Certified Public Accountants,[29] and the underlying assumptions provide a reasonable basis for management's forecast. Also, in our opinion, the accompanying projection is presented in conformity with guidelines for presentation of a projection established by the American Institute of Certified Public Accountants,[30] and the underlying assumptions provide a reasonable basis for management's projection, assuming the hypothetical sale of properties on the date and for the sales prices indicated. However, because

---

[25] In rare cases, management may forecast the sale of its investment in real estate during the forecast period. In such circumstances, the sale would not be hypothetical and should be included in the financial forecast with other operating results and significant changes in financial position. When examining the forecast, the practitioner should treat the sale as any other significant assumption and consider, among other things, whether the assumptions related to the sale (*a*) are appropriate and suitably supported (for example, for the timing and the sales price) and (*b*) should be identified by the responsible party as being particularly sensitive as discussed in paragraph 8.24. Furthermore, the sale would be covered by the practitioner's standard examination report.

[26] When the effects of a hypothetical sale of an entity's real estate investment are included in a note to the financial forecast, the disclosure is considered part of the forecast and is covered by the practitioner's standard report.

[27] Because in this example the projection supplements a forecast for the same period, it is appropriate for general use and the report need not include a use-restriction paragraph.

[28] See footnote 1.

[29] See footnote 1.

[30] See footnote 1.

events and circumstances frequently do not occur as expected, there will usually be differences between the forecasted and actual results, and even if the properties are sold on the date and for the prices indicated, there will usually be differences between the projected and actual results, and those differences may be material. We have no responsibility to update this report for events and circumstances occurring after the date of this report.

[*Signature*]

[*Date*]

Reporting If the Financial Forecast Includes Disclosures About Periods Beyond the Forecast Period

17.21 If a practitioner is engaged to examine a financial forecast that contains disclosures about plans, events, or circumstances beyond the forecast period,[31] the practitioner's standard report covers such disclosures because they are included in the notes to the financial forecast.

17.22 While performing an examination engagement, if the practitioner has reservations about the disclosures or if he or she is unable to apply procedures to such disclosures considered necessary in the circumstances, the practitioner should discuss such matters with the responsible party and propose appropriate revision of the disclosures. If the responsible party will not agree to revision of the disclosures, the practitioner should either modify the report on the financial forecast or withdraw from the engagement.

Reporting on Information Accompanying a Financial Forecast in a Practitioner-Submitted Document

17.23 An entity may request that additional details or explanations of items in a financial forecast (for example, details of sales or forecasted product line information) be included in a practitioner-submitted document that contains a financial forecast and the practitioner's report thereon. An entity also may request that certain nonaccounting information or other information not directly related to the basic forecast be included in such a document. The accompanying information is presented outside the basic financial forecast, and is not considered necessary for the presentation of the forecast to be in conformity with guidelines for presentation of a financial forecast established by the American Institute of Certified Public Accountants.[32]

17.24 A practitioner's report on information accompanying a financial forecast in a practitioner-submitted document has the same objective as a practitioner's report on the financial forecast: to describe clearly the character of the practitioner's work and the degree of responsibility taken.

If a practitioner has examined a financial forecast included in a practitioner-submitted document, the practitioner's report on the accompanying information would ordinarily include the following:

- A statement that the examination has been made for the purpose of forming an opinion on whether (1) the financial forecast is presented

---

[31] Paragraph 10.19 discusses the practitioner's responsibility for such disclosures when engaged to examine the forecast.

[32] See footnote 1.

in conformity with AICPA guidelines[33] for the presentation of a forecast and (2) the underlying assumptions provide a reasonable basis for the forecast

• Identification of the accompanying information

• A statement that the accompanying information is presented for purposes of additional analysis and is not a required part of the financial forecast

• An opinion on whether the accompanying information is fairly stated in all material respects in relation to the financial forecast taken as a whole, or a disclaimer of opinion, depending on whether the information has been subjected to procedures applied in the examination of the financial forecast. The practitioner may express an opinion on a portion of the accompanying information and disclaim an opinion on the remainder[34]

• A caveat that the prospective results may not be achieved

17.25 Following are examples of reports that may be issued:

Accompanying information has been subjected to procedures applied in the examination

Our examination of the financial forecast presented in the preceding section of this document was made for the purpose of forming an opinion on whether the financial forecast is presented in conformity with AICPA guidelines[35] for the presentation of a forecast and the underlying assumptions provide a reasonable basis for the forecast. The [identify accompanying information] is presented for purposes of additional analysis and is not a required part of the financial forecast. Such information has been subjected to procedures applied in the examination of the financial forecast and, in our opinion, is fairly stated in all material respects in relation to the forecast taken as a whole. However, there will usually be differences between the forecasted and actual results, because events and circumstances frequently do not occur as expected, and those differences may be material. We have no responsibility to update this report for events and circumstances occurring after the date of this report.

Accompanying information has not been subjected to procedures applied in the examination

Our examination of the financial forecast presented in the preceding section of this document was made for the purpose of forming an opinion on whether the financial forecast is presented in conformity with AICPA guidelines[36] for the presentation of a forecast and whether the underlying assumptions provide a reasonable basis for the forecast. The [identify accompanying information] is presented for purposes of additional analysis and is not a required part of the

---

[33] See footnote 1.

[34] If the practitioner concludes, on the basis of known facts, that any accompanying information is materially misstated in relation to the financial forecast taken as a whole, he or she should discuss the matter with the responsible party and propose appropriate revision of the accompanying information or related disclosures. If the responsible party will not agree to revision of the accompanying information, the practitioner should either modify the report on the accompanying information and describe the reservations regarding the information or refuse to include the information in the document.

[35] See footnote 1.

[36] See footnote 1.

financial forecast. Such information has not been subjected to procedures applied in the examination of the financial forecast and, accordingly, we express no opinion or any other form of assurance on it. Furthermore, there will usually be differences between the forecasted and actual results, because events and circumstances frequently do not occur as expected, and those differences may be material. We have no responsibility to update this report for events and circumstances occurring after the date of this report.

Reporting If the Examination Is Part of a Larger Engagement

17.26 When the practitioner's examination of prospective financial statements is part of a larger engagement, for example, a financial feasibility or business acquisition study, it is appropriate to expand the report on the examination of the prospective financial statements to describe the entire engagement.

17.27 The following is a report that might be issued when a practitioner chooses to expand his or her report on a financial feasibility study:[37]

    a. The Board of Directors

        Example Hospital

        Example, Texas

    b. We have prepared a financial feasibility study of Example Hospital's (the hospital's) plans to expand and renovate its facilities. The study was undertaken to evaluate the ability of the hospital to meet its operating expenses, working capital needs, and other financial requirements, including the debt service requirements associated with the proposed $25,000,000 [*legal title of bonds*] issue, at an assumed average annual interest rate of 10.0 percent during the five years ending December 31, 20X6.

    c. The proposed capital improvements program (the Program) consists of a new two-level addition, which is to provide fifty additional medical-surgical beds, increasing the complement to 275 beds. In addition, various administrative and support service areas in the present facilities are to be remodeled. The hospital administration anticipates that construction will begin June 30, 20X2, and will be completed by December 31, 20X3.

    d. The estimated total cost of the Program is approximately $30,000,000. It is assumed that the $25,000,000 of revenue bonds that the Example Hospital Finance Authority proposes to issue would be the primary source of funds for the Program. The responsibility for payment of debt service on the bonds is solely that of the hospital. Other funds necessary to finance the Program are assumed to be provided from the hospital's funds, from a local fund drive, and from

---

[37] Although the entity referred to in the report is a hospital, the form of report is also applicable to other entities, such as hotels or stadiums. Also, although the illustrated report format and language should not be departed from in any significant way, the language used should be tailored to fit the circumstances that are unique to a particular engagement (for example, the description of the proposed capital improvement program, paragraph [c]; the proposed financing of the program, paragraphs [b] and [d]; the specific procedures applied by the practitioner, paragraph [e]; and any explanatory comments included in emphasis-of-a-matter paragraphs, paragraph [i], which deals with a general matter, and paragraph [j], which deals with specific matters).

interest earned on funds held by the bond trustee during the construction period.

e. Our procedures included analysis of the following:

- Program history, objectives, timing, and financing
- The future demand for the hospital's services, including consideration of the following:
  - Economic and demographic characteristics of the hospital's defined service area
  - Locations, capacities, and competitive information pertaining to other existing and planned area hospitals
  - Physician support for the hospital and its programs
  - Historical utilization levels
- Planning agency applications and approvals
- Construction and equipment costs, debt service requirements, and estimated financing costs
- Staffing patterns and other operating considerations
- Third-party reimbursement policy and history
- Revenue/expense/volume relationships

f. We also participated in gathering other information, assisted management in identifying and formulating its assumptions, and assembled the accompanying financial forecast based upon those assumptions.

g. The accompanying financial forecast for the annual periods ending December 31, 20X2 through 20X6, is based on assumptions that were provided by, or reviewed with and approved by, management. The financial forecast includes the following:

- Balance sheets
- Statements of operations
- Statements of cash flows
- Statements of changes in net assets

h. We have examined the financial forecast. Example Hospital's management is responsible for the forecast. Our responsibility is to express an opinion on the forecast based on our examination.

Our examination was conducted in accordance with attestation standards established by the American Institute of Certified Public Accountants[38] and, accordingly, included such procedures as we considered necessary to evaluate both the assumptions used by management and the preparation and presentation of the forecast. We believe our examination provides a reasonable basis for our opinion.

i. Legislation and regulations at all levels of government have affected and may continue to affect revenues and expenses of hospitals. The financial forecast is based on legislation and regulations currently in

---

[38] See footnote 1.

effect. If future legislation or regulations related to hospital operations are enacted, such legislation or regulations could have a material effect on future operations.

j. The interest rate, principal payments, Program costs, and other financing assumptions are described in the section entitled "Summary of Significant Forecast Assumptions and Rationale." If actual interest rates, principal payments, and funding requirements are different from those assumed, the amount of the bond issue and debt service requirements would need to be adjusted accordingly from those indicated in the forecast. If such interest rates, principal payments, and funding requirements are lower than those assumed, such adjustments would not adversely affect the forecast.

k. Our conclusions are presented as follows:

- In our opinion, the accompanying financial forecast is presented in conformity with guidelines for presentation of a financial forecast established by the American Institute of Certified Public Accountants.[39]

- In our opinion, the underlying assumptions provide a reasonable basis for management's forecast. However, there will usually be differences between the forecasted and actual results, because events and circumstances frequently do not occur as expected, and those differences may be material.

- The accompanying financial forecast indicates that sufficient funds could be generated to meet the hospital's operating expenses, working capital needs, and other financial requirements, including the debt service requirements associated with the proposed $25,000,000 bond issue, during the forecast periods. However, the achievement of any financial forecast is dependent on future events, the occurrence of which cannot be assured.

l. We have no responsibility to update this report for events and circumstances occurring after the date of this report.

Lack of Independence

17.28 Whether or not the practitioner is independent is something he or she must decide as a matter of professional judgment.[40] If the practitioner is not independent, he or she cannot perform an examination in accordance with AICPA standards. In that case, the practitioner may perform a compilation of the prospective financial statements and report accordingly (see paragraph 14.05).

---

[39] See footnote 1.

[40] In making a judgment about whether he or she is independent, an AICPA member should be guided by the AICPA Code of Professional Conduct. The SEC and PCAOB have different independence rules. Therefore, when providing services for public companies and other issuers, the practitioner should be aware of those rules.

Chapter 18

Considerations for the Practitioner Reporting on an Examination of a Financial Forecast Contained in a Public Offering Statement[1]

Because a public offering statement is a general-use document, it would be inappropriate to include in it a projection unless the projection was used to supplement a forecast. Accordingly, the guidance in this chapter applies only to forecasts.

18.01 This chapter discusses some aspects of the practitioner's services on financial forecasts when the forecast is included in a public offering statement. Public offering statements include registrations under the Securities Act of 1933 as well as certain non-Securities and Exchange Commission (SEC) offerings such as private placement memorandums and tax-exempt bond offerings.[2]

Procedures Between the Date of the Practitioner's Report and Effective Date in 1933 Act Filings

18.02 A registration statement filed under the Securities Act of 1933 speaks as of its effective date, and the statutory responsibility of a practitioner whose report is included in such a registration statement may be determined in the light of the circumstances as of such date. This aspect of an independent practitioner's responsibility is peculiar to registration statements filed with the SEC.

18.03 Unlike audited historical financial statements, financial forecasts, if prepared even a few weeks later, may well vary from earlier versions. Therefore, as provided in chapter 17, "The Practitioner's Examination Report," the report on an examination of a financial forecast should indicate that the practitioner has no responsibility to update the report for events and circumstances occurring after the date of the report. Nevertheless, the practitioner should have a reasonable basis to consent to the use of the report in a Securities Act of 1933 registration statement as of the consent date.[3]

---

[1] Public Company Accounting Oversight Board (PCAOB) Auditing Standard No. 1, *References in Auditors' Reports to the Standards of the Public Company Accounting Oversight Board* (AICPA, *PCAOB Standards and Related Rules,* Auditing Standards), requires registered public accounting firms to make reference in his or her report to the "standards of the Public Company Oversight Board (United States)." The PCAOB standards are to be used by registered public accounting firms in the preparation and issuance of audit (or attestation) reports, as required by the Sarbanes Oxley Act of 2002 or the rules of the Securities and Exchange Commission (SEC).

[2] These are categorized in chapter 4, "Types of Prospective Financial Information and Their Uses," as general uses of financial forecasts.

[3] Regulation S-K (Section 229.10[b][1]) states that in the case of a registration statement under the Securities Act of 1933 a "reviewer (of a financial forecast) would be deemed an expert and an appropriate consent must be filed with the registration statement." (This regulation was issued before AICPA standards for services on prospective financial information, which define the three levels of service described in this guide. Thus, the SEC's terminology does not correspond to that used in this guide.)

18.04   To have a reasonable basis to consent to the use of the report on the examination of a financial forecast in the registration statement, the practitioner should perform procedures with respect to the period from the date of the examination report up to the consent date or shortly before the effective date of the registration statement. Illustrative procedures the practitioner may perform include the following:

  a. Read the latest available interim financial statements, operating reports, and any relevant prospective information such as budgets; consider the prospective results in relation to the actual results achieved in the interim period; and inquire whether the accounting principles used in the preparation of such information are consistent with the principles used in preparing the forecast.

  b. Read the entire prospectus and other pertinent portions of the registration statement and consider that information in relation to the prospective results and the summary of significant assumptions.

  c. Inquire of and obtain written representations from the responsible party, including those individuals responsible for matters significant to the financial forecasts, as to whether there are any events, plans, or expectations (whether or not reflected or disclosed in the registration statement) that, in its opinion, may require the financial forecast to be modified, or that should be disclosed, in order that the forecast reflect the responsible party's judgment based on present circumstances of the expected conditions and its expected course of action. In lieu of obtaining an additional representation letter at the consent date, the practitioner may have the responsible party update the representation letter originally signed at the report date.

  d. Read the available minutes of meetings of the board of directors and related committees. Regarding meetings for which minutes are not available, inquire about matters dealt with at such meetings.

  e. Make such additional inquiries or perform such procedures as considered necessary and appropriate to dispose of questions that arise in carrying out the foregoing procedures.

18.05   If, as a result of the preceding procedures, the practitioner believes that the forecast, including the summary of significant assumptions, should be revised, he or she should request the client to revise its forecast and, if engaged to do so, examine the revised forecast. If the client does not make appropriate revision to the forecast, the practitioner should not consent to the use of the report in the registration statement.

The Practitioner's Consent

18.06   In registration statements filed with the SEC under the Securities Act of 1933, as in other types of offering materials, the practitioner's consent to the use of the report and to references to the practitioner in the offering materials should be in writing. In addition, the practitioner's consent for a 1933 Act filing should be manually signed and dated.

18.07   Because a registration statement under the Securities Act of 1933 speaks as of its effective date, the practitioner's consent should be dated at or near the effective date of such a registration statement. The dating of the consent at the effective date, however, as discussed in paragraph 18.03, does not constitute an update of the practitioner's report.

18.08 The following is an example of the practitioner's consent to the use of the report in an offering statement:[4]

> We hereby consent to the use of our report dated November 17, 20X3, on our examination of the financial forecast of XYZ Company and the use of our name, and the references to our firm appearing under the headings [*appropriate headings*] in the registration statement. It should be noted that, as indicated in our report, we have no responsibility, under the attestation standards established by the Public Company Accounting Oversight Board (United States),[5] to update our report for events and circumstances occurring after the date of the report, and consequently we have not updated our report.

Experts Section of 1933 Act Filings

18.09 The experts section of the registration statement should be so worded that there is no implication that the forecast has been prepared by the practitioner or that the forecast is not the direct responsibility of the responsible party. The following is an example of a reference to the practitioner in the experts section:[6]

> The financial forecast on pages xx–yy of this prospectus has been included in reliance on the report of [*name of practitioner*], independent public accountants, given on the authority of that firm as experts in reporting on examinations of financial forecasts.

Description of Additional Procedures and Comfort Letters

18.10 No description of the additional procedures (see paragraph 18.04) or any form of assurance based on those procedures should be included in the report on the forecast or in any document that includes the report. Furthermore, no such description or assurance should be contained in a letter to underwriters ("comfort letter") or others.

---

[4] This report consent example can also be used for non-SEC offerings if modified to not refer to the PCAOB.

[5] See footnote 1.

[6] The designation of the practitioner as an "expert" is a concept that appears in Section 11 of the Securities Act of 1933. Therefore, the term as defined is generally applicable only to filings under the Securities Act of 1933 and is not applicable to filings not made under that act.

Chapter 19

Application of Agreed-Upon Procedures

> Because financial forecasts and projections are similar in many respects, separate guidance for projections is provided only to the extent that it differs from that for forecasts. *Italicized* paragraphs in this chapter that include a "P" in the paragraph number show how the guidance presented for forecasts should be modified for projections. Any plain-text paragraph not followed by an italicized paragraph applies to both forecasts and projections even though it uses only the term *forecast*.

19.01 A practitioner may perform an agreed-upon procedures attest engagement on a financial forecast[1] provided that the following conditions are met:

a. The practitioner is independent.

b. The practitioner and the specified parties agree upon the procedures performed or to be performed by the practitioner.

c. The specified parties take responsibility for the sufficiency of the agreed-upon procedures for their purposes.

d. The financial forecast includes a summary of significant assumptions.

e. The financial forecast to which the procedures are to be applied is subject to reasonably consistent evaluation against criteria that are suitable and available to the specified parties.

f. Criteria[2] to be used in the determination of findings are agreed upon between the practitioner and the specified parties.

g. The procedures to be applied to the financial forecast are expected to result in reasonably consistent findings using the criteria.

h. Evidential matter related to the financial forecast to which the procedures are applied is expected to exist to provide a reasonable basis for expressing the findings in the practitioner's report.

i. Where applicable, the practitioner and the specified users agree on any agreed-upon materiality limits for reporting purposes (see paragraph .25 of AT section 201, *Agreed-Upon Procedures Engagements* [AICPA, *Professional Standards*]).

j. Use of the report is to be restricted to the specified parties.[3]

---

[1] See AU-C section 920, *Letters for Underwriters and Certain Other Requesting Parties* (AICPA, *Professional Standards*), when requested to perform agreed-upon procedures on a forecast and report thereon in a letter for an underwriter.

[2] For example, accounting principles and other presentation criteria as discussed in chapter 8, "Presentation Guidelines."

[3] In some cases, restricted-use reports filed with regulatory agencies are required by law or regulation to be made available to the public as a matter of public record. Also, a regulatory agency as part of its oversight responsibility may require access to restricted-use reports in which they are not named as a specified party. See paragraph .79 of AT section 101, *Attest Engagements* (AICPA, *Professional Standards*).

19.02 The practitioner who accepts an engagement to apply agreed-upon procedures to a financial forecast should follow the general, fieldwork, and reporting standards for attest engagements established in AT section 50, *SSAE Hierarchy* (AICPA, *Professional Standards*), and the guidance set forth in AT section 201 and AT section 301, *Financial Forecasts and Projections* (AICPA, *Professional Standards*).

19.03 Generally, the practitioner's procedures may be as limited or as extensive as the specified parties desire, as long as the specified parties take responsibility for their sufficiency. However, mere reading of a financial forecast does not constitute a procedure sufficient to permit a practitioner to report on the results of applying agreed-upon procedures to such a forecast.

19.04 To satisfy the requirements that the practitioner and the specified parties agree upon the procedures performed or to be performed and that the specified parties take responsibility for the sufficiency of the agreed-upon procedures for their purposes, ordinarily the practitioner should communicate directly with and obtain affirmative acknowledgment from each of the specified parties. For example, this may be accomplished by meeting with the specified parties or by distributing a draft of the anticipated report or a copy of an engagement letter to the specified parties and obtaining their agreement. If the practitioner is not able to communicate directly with all of the specified parties, the practitioner may satisfy these requirements by applying any one or more of the following or similar procedures:

- Compare the procedures to be applied to written requirements of the specified parties.

- Discuss the procedures to be applied with appropriate representatives of the specified parties involved.

- Review relevant contracts with or correspondence from the specified parties.

The practitioner should not report on an engagement when specified parties do not agree upon the procedures performed or to be performed and do not take responsibility for the sufficiency of the procedures for their purposes. (See paragraph 19.24 for guidance on satisfying these requirements when the practitioner is requested to add other parties as specified parties after the date of completion of the agreed-upon procedures.)

Engagement Letter

19.05 The practitioner should establish an understanding with the client regarding the services to be performed. When the practitioner documents the understanding through a written communication with the client (an engagement letter), such communication should be addressed to the client, and in some circumstances also to all specified parties. Matters that might be included in such an understanding include the following:

- The nature of the engagement

- Identification of the financial forecast the responsible party, and the criteria used

- Identification of specified parties

- Specified parties' acknowledgment of their responsibility for the sufficiency of the procedures

- Responsibilities of the practitioner

- Reference to attestation standards established by the AICPA
- Agreement on procedures by enumerating (or referring to) the procedures
- Disclaimers expected to be included in the practitioner's report
- Use restrictions
- Assistance to be provided to the practitioner
- Involvement of a specialist
- Agreed-upon materiality limits

Procedures to Be Performed

19.06 The procedures that the practitioner and specified users agree upon may be as limited or as extensive as the specified users desire. However, mere reading of the financial forecast or assumptions does not constitute a procedure sufficient to permit a practitioner to report on the results of applying agreed-upon procedures. In some circumstances, the procedures agreed upon evolve or are modified over the course of the engagement. In general, there is flexibility in determining the procedures as long as the specified parties acknowledge responsibility for the sufficiency of such procedures for their purposes. Matters that should be agreed upon include the nature, timing, and extent of the procedures.

19.07 The practitioner should not agree to perform procedures that are overly subjective and thus possibly open to varying interpretations. Terms of uncertain meaning (such as general review, limited review, reconcile, check, or test) should not be used in describing the procedures unless such terms are defined within the agreed-upon procedures. The practitioner should obtain evidential matter from applying the agreed-upon procedures to provide a reasonable basis for the finding or findings expressed in his or her report, but need not perform additional procedures outside the scope of the engagement to gather additional evidential matter.

19.08 Examples of appropriate procedures include

- inspection of specified documents evidencing certain types of transactions or detailed attributes thereof.
- confirmation of specific information with third parties.
- performance of mathematical computations.

19.09 Examples of inappropriate procedures include

- merely reading the work performed by others solely to describe their findings.
- evaluating the competency or objectivity of another party.
- obtaining an understanding about a particular subject.
- interpreting documents outside the scope of the practitioner's professional expertise.

19.10 The agreed-upon procedures to be enumerated or referred to in the practitioner's report are to be performed entirely by the practitioner except as discussed in paragraphs 19.21–.23.

Documentation

19.11 The practitioner should prepare and maintain attest documentation, the form and content of which should be designed to meet the circumstances of the particular attest engagement. Attest documentation is the principal record of attest procedures applied, information obtained, and conclusions or findings reached by the practitioner in the engagement. The quantity, type, and content of attest documentation are matters of the practitioner's professional judgment.

19.12 Attest documentation serves mainly to

a. provide the principal support for the practitioner's report, including the representation regarding observance of the standards of fieldwork, which is implicit in the reference in the report to the attestation standards.[4]

b. aid the practitioner in the conduct and supervision of the attest engagement.

19.13 Examples of attest documentation are work programs, analyses, memoranda, letters of confirmation and representation, abstracts or copies of entity documents, and schedules or commentaries prepared or obtained by the practitioner. Attest documentation may in paper form, electronic form, or other media.

19.14 Attest documentation should be sufficient to (a) enable members of the engagement team with supervision and review responsibilities to understand the nature, timing, extent, and results of attest procedures performed, and the information obtained[5] and (b) indicate the engagement team member(s) who performed and reviewed the work.

19.15 Attest documentation is the property of the practitioner and some states recognize this right of ownership in the statutes. The practitioner should adopt reasonable procedures to retain attest documentation for a period of time sufficient to meet the needs of his or her practice and to satisfy any applicable legal or regulatory requirements for records retention.[6]

19.16 The practitioner has an ethical, and in some situations a legal, obligation to maintain the confidentiality of client information or information of the responsible party.[7] Because attest documentation often contains confidential information, the practitioner should adopt reasonable procedures to maintain the confidentiality of that information.

19.17 The practitioner should also adopt reasonable procedures to prevent unauthorized access to attest documentation.

---

[4] However, there is no intention to imply that the practitioner would be precluded from supporting his or her report by other means in addition to attest documentation.

[5] A firm of practitioners has a responsibility to adopt a system of quality control policies and procedures to provide the firm with reasonable assurance that its personnel comply with applicable professional standards, including attestation standards, and the firm's standards of quality in conducting individual attest engagements. Review of attest documentation and discussions with attest team members are among the procedures a firm performs when monitoring compliance with the quality control policies and procedures that it has established.

[6] The procedures should enable the practitioner to access electronic attest documentation throughout the retention period.

[7] Also, see Rule 301, *Confidential Client Information* (AICPA, *Professional Standards*, ET sec. 301), of the AICPA's Code of Professional Conduct.

19.18 Certain attest documentation may sometimes serve as a useful reference source for the client, but it should not be regarded as a part of, or a substitute for, the client's records.

Representation Letter

19.19 A practitioner may find a representation letter to be a useful and practical means of obtaining representations from the responsible party. The need for such a letter may depend on the nature of the engagement and the specified parties. Examples of matters that might appear in a representation letter include

- the responsible party's responsibility for the assumptions.

- the responsible party's assertion that the financial forecast presents, to the best of the responsible party's knowledge and belief, the expected financial position, results of operations, and cash flows for the forecast period, and that the forecast reflects the responsible party's judgment, based on present circumstances, of the expected conditions and its expected course of action.

- a statement that the forecast is presented in conformity with guidelines for presentation of a forecast established by the American Institute of Certified Public Accountants.

- a statement that the assumptions on which the forecast is based are reasonable.

- if the forecast contains a range, a statement that, to the best of the responsible party's knowledge and belief, the item or items subject to the assumption are expected to actually fall within the range, and that the range was not selected in a biased or misleading manner.

19.19P *Examples of matters that might appear in a representation letter in connection with agreed-upon procedures applied to a projection include*

- *the responsible party's assertion that the financial projection presents, to the best of the responsible party's knowledge and belief, the expected financial position, results of operations, and cash flows for the projection period given the hypothetical assumptions, and that the projection reflects its judgment, based on present circumstances, of expected conditions and its expected course of action given the occurrence of the hypothetical events. An identification of the hypothetical assumptions and description of the limitations on the usefulness of the presentation.*

- *a statement that the assumptions are appropriate.*

- *an indication if the hypothetical assumptions are improbable.*

- *if the projection contains a range, a statement that, to the best of the responsible party's knowledge and belief, given the hypothetical assumptions, the item or items subject to the assumption are expected to actually fall within the range and that the range was not selected in a biased or misleading manner.*

- *a statement that the projection is presented in conformity with guidelines for presentation of a projection established by the American Institute of Certified Public Accountants.*

19.20 The responsible party's refusal to furnish written representations determined by the practitioner to be appropriate for the engagement constitutes a limitation on the performance of the engagement. In such circumstances, the practitioner should do one of the following:

a. Disclose in his or her report the inability to obtain representations from the responsible party.

b. Withdraw from the engagement.

c. Change the engagement to another form of engagement.

Involvement of a Specialist[8]

19.21 The practitioner's education and experience enable him or her to be knowledgeable about business matters in general, but he or she is not expected to have the expertise of a person trained for or qualified to engage in the practice of another profession or occupation. In certain circumstances, it may be appropriate to involve a specialist to assist the practitioner in the performance of one or more procedures. For example, a medical specialist might provide assistance in understanding the nature of special equipment needed in the expansion of a medical facility.

19.22 The practitioner and the specified users should explicitly agree to the involvement of the specialist in assisting a practitioner in the performance of an engagement to apply agreed-upon procedures. This agreement may be reached when obtaining agreement on the procedures performed or to be performed and acknowledgment of responsibility for the sufficiency of the procedures, as discussed in paragraph 19.04. The practitioner's report should describe the nature of the assistance provided by the specialist.

19.23 A practitioner may agree to apply procedures to the report or work product of a specialist that does not constitute assistance by the specialist to the practitioner in an agreed-upon procedures engagement. For example, the practitioner may make reference to information contained in a report of a specialist in describing an agreed-upon procedure. However, it is inappropriate for the practitioner to agree to merely read the specialist's report solely to describe or repeat the findings, or to take responsibility for all or a portion of any procedures performed by a specialist or the specialist's work product.

Adding Parties as Specified Parties (Nonparticipant Parties)

19.24 Subsequent to the completion of the agreed-upon procedures engagement, a practitioner may be requested to consider the addition of another party as a specified party (a nonparticipant party). The practitioner may agree to add a nonparticipant party as a specified party, based on consideration of factors such as the identity of the nonparticipant party and the intended use of the report.[9] If the practitioner does agree to add the nonparticipant party, he or she should obtain affirmative acknowledgment, normally in writing, from the

---

[8] A *specialist* is a person (or firm) possessing skill or knowledge in a particular field other than the attest function. As used herein, a specialist does not include a person employed by the practitioner's firm who participates in the attest engagement.

[9] When considering whether to add a nonparticipant party, the guidance in AU section 530, *Dating of the Independent Auditor's Report* (AICPA, *Professional Standards*), as amended, may be helpful.

nonparticipant party agreeing to the procedures performed and of its taking responsibility for the sufficiency of the procedures. If the nonparticipant party is added after the practitioner has issued his or her report, the report may be reissued or the practitioner may provide other written acknowledgment that the nonparticipant party has been added as a specified user. If the report is reissued, the report date should not be changed. If the practitioner provides written acknowledgment that the nonparticipant party has been added as a specified party, such written acknowledgment ordinarily should state that no procedures have been performed subsequent to the date of the report.

Change to an Agreed-Upon Procedures Engagement From Another Form of Engagement

19.25 A practitioner who has been engaged to perform another form of attest engagement or nonattest service may, before the engagement's completion, be requested to change the engagement to an agreed-upon procedures engagement. A request to change the engagement may result from a change in circumstances affecting the client's requirements, a misunderstanding about the nature of the original services or the alternative services originally available, or a restriction on the performance of the original engagement, whether imposed by the client or caused by circumstances.

19.26 Before a practitioner who was engaged to perform another form of engagement agrees to change the engagement to an agreed-upon procedures engagement, he or she should consider the following:

a. The possibility that certain procedures performed as part of another type of engagement are not appropriate for inclusion in an agreed-upon procedures engagement

b. The reason given for the request, particularly the implications of a restriction on the scope of the original engagement or the matters to be reported

c. The additional effort required to complete the original engagement

d. If applicable, the reasons for changing from a general-use report to a restricted-use report

19.27 If the specified parties acknowledge agreement to the procedures performed or to be performed and assume responsibility for the sufficiency of the procedures to be included in the agreed-upon procedures engagement, either of the following would be considered a reasonable basis for requesting a change in the engagement:

a. A change in circumstances that requires another form of engagement

b. A misunderstanding concerning the nature of the original engagement or the available alternatives

19.28 In all circumstances, if the original engagement procedures are substantially complete or the effort to complete such procedures is relatively insignificant, the practitioner should consider the propriety of accepting a change in the engagement.

19.29 If the practitioner concludes, based on his or her professional judgment, that there is reasonable justification to change the engagement, and provided he or she complies with the standards applicable to agreed-upon procedures engagements, the practitioner should issue an appropriate agreed-upon procedures report. The report should not include reference to either the original engagement or performance limitations that resulted in the changed engagement. (See paragraph 21.09.)

———————————

Chapter 20

Illustrative Engagement and Representation Letters for Agreed-Upon Procedures Engagements

Because financial forecasts and projections are similar in many respects, separate guidance for projections is provided only to the extent that it differs from that for forecasts. *Italicized* paragraphs in this chapter that include a "P" in the paragraph number show how the guidance presented for forecasts should be modified for projections. Any plain-text paragraph not followed by an italicized paragraph applies to both forecasts and projections even though it uses only the term *forecast*.

Engagement Letter

20.01 The following is an excerpt from a sample engagement letter for an engagement to apply agreed-upon procedures to a financial forecast:

> This letter sets forth our understanding for applying agreed-upon procedures to the financial forecast of XYZ Company as of December 31, 20XX, and the year then ending.
>
> A financial forecast presents, to the best of management's[1] knowledge and belief, the Company's expected financial position, results of operations, and cash flows for the forecast period. It is based on management's assumptions reflecting conditions it expects to exist and the course of action it expects to take during the forecast period.
>
> Management is responsible for representations about its plans and expectations and for disclosure of significant information that might affect the ultimate realization of the forecasted results.
>
> This engagement is solely to assist [*specified party(ies)*] in [*describe purpose of engagement—for example, evaluating the forecast in connection with XYZ's working capital loan with ABC Bank*]. We will apply the following procedures, which [*state name of specified party(ies)*] has specified.[2] [*List procedures to be applied.*]
>
> This agreed-upon procedures engagement will be performed in accordance with attestation standards established by the American Institute of Certified Public Accountants. The sufficiency of these procedures is solely the responsibility of the specified parties. Consequently, we make no representation as to the sufficiency of the procedures for [*state name of specified party(ies)*]'s purposes or for any other purpose.

---

[1] If the responsible party is other than management, the references to management should be replaced with the name of the party who assumes responsibility for the assumptions.

[2] If, at the time the engagement letter is prepared, the specified party has not established the necessary procedures, this paragraph might be replaced with (1) a list of procedures suggested by the practitioner or those often done in the circumstances, and (2) a statement that the engagement will not be completed until the specified party agrees that the procedures are sufficient for the intended purposes.

The agreed-upon procedures to be performed do not constitute an examination. Accordingly, we will not express an opinion on whether the forecast is in conformity with AICPA presentation guidelines or whether the assumptions provide a reasonable basis for the forecast. If we did perform additional procedures, other matters might come to our attention that would be reported to you.

There will usually be differences between the forecasted and actual results, because events and circumstances frequently do not occur as expected, and those differences may be material. Our report will contain a statement to that effect.

Our report will list the procedures performed and our findings.[3] Should we have any reservations with respect to the forecast, we will discuss them with you before the report is issued.

We have no responsibility to update our report for events and circumstances occurring after the date of our report.

Our report is intended solely for the use of [*name specified party(ies)*]. The report should not be used by anyone other than these specified parties.

At the conclusion of the engagement, management agrees to supply us with a representation letter that, among other things, will confirm management's responsibility for the underlying assumptions and the appropriateness of the financial forecast and its presentation.[4]

20.01P *The following is an excerpt from a sample engagement letter for an engagement to apply agreed-upon procedures to a financial projection:*

> *This letter sets forth our understanding for applying agreed-upon procedures to the financial projection of XYZ Company as of December 31, 20XX, and the year then ending.*
>
> *The financial projection presents, to the best of management's[5] knowledge and belief, the Company's expected financial position, results of operations, and cash flows for the projection period assuming [* describe hypothetical assumptions*]. It is based on management's assumptions reflecting conditions it expects would exist and the course of action it expects would be taken during the projection period, assuming [*describe hypothetical assumptions*].*
>
> *Management is responsible for representations about its plans and expectations and for disclosure of significant information that might affect the ultimate realization of the projected results.*
>
> *This engagement is solely to assist [*specified party(ies)*] in [*describe purpose of engagement*]. We will apply the following procedures,*

---

[3] The concept of materiality does not apply to findings to be reported in an agreed-upon procedures engagement unless the definition of materiality is agreed to by the specified parties. Any agreed-upon materiality limits should ordinarily be described in the practitioner's report.

[4] This paragraph would be included if the practitioner chooses to obtain a representation letter.

[5] *If the responsible party is other than management, the references to management should be replaced with the name of the party who assumes responsibility for the assumptions.*

*which [*state name of specified party(ies)*] has specified.*[6] *[*List procedures to be applied.*]*

*This agreed-upon procedures engagement will be performed in accordance with attestation standards established by the American Institute of Certified Public Accountants. The sufficiency of these procedures is solely the responsibility of the specified users of the report. Consequently, we make no representation as to the sufficiency of the procedures for [*state name of specified party(ies)*]'s purposes or for any other purpose.*

*The agreed-upon procedures to be performed do not constitute an examination. Accordingly, we will not express an opinion on whether the financial projection is in conformity with AICPA presentation guidelines or whether the assumptions provide a reasonable basis for the financial projection based on [*describe hypothetical assumptions*]. If we did perform additional procedures, other matters might come to our attention that would be reported to you.*

*Even if [*describe hypothetical assumptions*] were to occur, there will usually be differences between the projected and actual results, because events and circumstances frequently do not occur as expected, and those differences may be material. Our report will contain a statement to that effect.*

Our report will list the procedures performed and our findings.[7] *Should we have any reservations with respect to the projection, we will discuss them with you before the report is issued.*

We have no responsibility to update our report for events and circumstances occurring after the date of our report.

*Our report is intended solely for the use of [*name specified party(ies)*]. The report should not be used by anyone other than these specified parties.*

At the conclusion of the engagement, management agrees to supply us with a representation letter that, among other things, will confirm management's responsibility for the underlying assumptions and the appropriateness of the financial projection and its presentation.[8]

Representation Letter

20.02 The following is a sample representation letter for an engagement to apply agreed-upon procedures to a financial forecast. The written representations to be obtained should be based on the circumstances of the engagement.

[Date of Practitioner's report]

[Practitioner's name]

---

[6] *If, at the time the engagement letter is prepared the specified party has not established the necessary procedures, this paragraph might be replaced with (1) a list of procedures suggested by the practitioner or those often done in the circumstances and (2) a statement that the engagement will not be completed until the specified party agrees that the procedures are sufficient for the intended purposes.*

[7] *The concept of materiality does not apply to findings to be reported in an agreed-upon procedures engagement unless the definition of materiality is agreed to by the specified parties. Any agreed-upon materiality limits should ordinarily be described in the practitioner's report.*

[8] *This paragraph would be included if the practitioner chooses to obtain a representation letter.*

In connection with your engagement to apply agreed-upon procedures to the forecasted balance sheet, statements of income, retained earnings, and cash flows and summaries of significant assumptions and accounting policies of XYZ Company as of December 31, 20XX, and for the year then ending, we make the following representations:

1. The financial forecast presents our assumptions and, to the best of our knowledge and belief, the Company's expected financial position, results of operations, and cash flows for the period,[9] in conformity with the generally accepted accounting principles expected to be used by the Company during the forecast period, which are consistent with the principles that XYZ Company uses in preparing its historical financial statements.

2. The financial forecast reflects our judgment based on present circumstances of the expected conditions and our expected course of action.

3. The financial forecast is presented in conformity with presentation guidelines established by the American Institute of Certified Public Accountants.

4. We believe that the assumptions underlying the forecast are reasonable and appropriate.

5. We have made available to you all significant information that we believe is relevant to the forecast.

6. To the best of our knowledge and belief, the documents and records supporting the assumptions are appropriate.

7. Your report is intended solely for the use of [*name specified party(ies)*], and should not be used by anyone other than these specified parties.

[*Signatures*]

20.02P *The following is a sample representation letter for an engagement to apply agreed-upon procedures to a financial projection. The written representations to be obtained should be based on the circumstances of the engagement.*

[*Date of Practitioner's report*]

[*Practitioner's name*]

In connection with your engagement to apply agreed-upon procedures to the projected balance sheet, statements of income, retained earnings, and cash flows and summaries of significant assumptions assuming [describe hypothetical assumptions] and accounting policies of XYZ Company as of December 31, 20XX, and for the year then ending, we make the following representations:

1. *The financial projection presents our assumptions and, to the best of our knowledge and belief, the Company's expected financial position,*

---

[9] If the forecast is presented as a range, the description of the forecast would refer to the range (for example, "... at occupancy rates of 75 percent and 95 percent"). See also paragraph 20.03.

results of operations, and cash flows for the projection period assuming [describe hypothetical assumptions].[10]

2. *The accounting principles used in the financial projection are in conformity with the generally accepted accounting principles expected to be used by the Company during the projection period, which are consistent with the principles that XYZ Company uses in preparing its historical financial statements.*[11]

3. *The financial projection reflects our judgment based on present circumstances of the expected conditions and our expected course of action assuming [describe hypothetical assumptions].*[12]

4. *The financial projection is presented in conformity with presentation guidelines established by the American Institute of Certified Public Accountants.*

5. *We believe that the assumptions underlying the projection are appropriate and reasonable assuming [describe hypothetical assumptions].*

6. *We have made available to you all significant information that we believe is relevant to the financial projection.*

7. *To the best of our knowledge and belief, the documents and records supporting the assumptions are appropriate.*

8. *Your report and the accompanying projection are intended solely for the use of [name specified party(ies)] and should not be used by anyone other than these specified parties.*

20.03 If the forecast is presented as a range, the following representation would be added:

> We reasonably expect that the actual [*describe items presented in a range*] achieved will be within the range shown; however, there can be no assurance that it will. The range shown was not selected in a biased or misleading manner.

20.03P *For a financial projection, if the presentation is presented as a range, the following representation would be included:*

> *We reasonably expect that the actual [*describe items presented in a range*] achieved will be within the range shown assuming [*describe hypothetical assumption*]; however, there can be no assurance that it will. The range shown was not selected in a biased or misleading manner.*

---

[10] *If the projection is presented as a range, the description of the projection would refer to the range (for example, "... at occupancy rates of 75 percent and 95 percent"). See also paragraph 20.03P.*

[11] *If the projection is not presented on the basis of the accounting principles used for the historical financial statements, this sentence might read, "The accounting principles used in the financial projection are consistent with [the special purpose of the projection]."*

[12] *If the hypothetical assumption is considered improbable the representation would say so, for example, "... assuming [describe hypothetical assumption], which we consider to be highly unlikely."*

20.04 If the date of the signed representations is later than the date of the preparation of the forecast (see paragraph 8.11), the following representation would be added:

> We are not aware of any material changes in the information or circumstances from [*date*], the date of the forecast, to the present.

Chapter 21

The Practitioner's Report on the Results of Applying Agreed-Upon Procedures

> Because financial forecasts and projections are similar in many respects, separate guidance for projections is provided only to the extent that it differs from that for forecasts. *Italicized* paragraphs in this chapter that include a "P" in the paragraph number show how the guidance presented for forecasts should be modified for projections. Any plain-text paragraph not followed by an italicized paragraph applies to both forecasts and projections even though it uses only the term *forecast*.

21.01 The practitioner's report on the results of applying agreed-upon procedures should be in the form of procedures and findings. The practitioner's report should contain the following elements:

a. A title that includes the word *independent*

b. Identification of the specified users

c. Reference to the financial forecast covered by the practitioner's report and character of the engagement

d. A statement that the procedures performed were those agreed to by those specified users identified in the report

e. Identification of the responsible party and a statement that the financial forecast is the responsibility of the responsible party

f. A statement that the agreed-upon procedures engagement was conducted in accordance with attestation standards established by the American Institute of Certified Public Accountants

g. A statement that the sufficiency of the procedures is solely the responsibility of the specified parties and a disclaimer of responsibility for the sufficiency of those procedures

h. A list of the procedures performed (or reference thereto) and related findings (the practitioner should not provide negative assurance—see paragraph 21.02)

i. Where applicable, description of any agreed-upon materiality limits (see paragraph 21.03)

j. A statement that the practitioner was not engaged to, and did not, conduct an examination of the forecast; a disclaimer of opinion on whether the presentation of the forecast is in conformity with AICPA presentation guidelines and on whether the underlying assumptions provide a reasonable basis for the forecast, *or a reasonable basis for the projection given the hypothetical assumptions*; and a statement that if the practitioner had performed additional procedures, other matters might have come to his or her attention that would have been reported

k. A statement of restrictions on the use of the report because it is intended to be used solely by the specified parties

    l. Where applicable, reservations or restrictions concerning procedures or findings as discussed in paragraphs 19.20 and 21.07–.08

    m. A caveat that the forecasted results may not be achieved

    n. A statement that the practitioner assumes no responsibility to update the report for events and circumstances occurring after the date of the report

    o. Where applicable, a description of the nature of the assistance provided by a specialist as discussed in paragraphs 19.21–.23

    p. The manual or printed signature of the practitioner's firm

    q. The date of the report

Findings

21.02 A practitioner should present the results of applying agreed-upon procedures to specific subject matter in the form of findings. The practitioner should not provide negative assurance about whether the forecast is in conformity with AICPA presentation guidelines or on whether the underlying assumptions provide a reasonable basis for the forecast. Further, the practitioner should not provide negative assurance in his or her findings resulting from application of procedures to specific items in the forecast. For example, the practitioner should not include a statement in his or her report that "nothing came to my attention that caused me to believe that rental income should be adjusted."

21.03 The practitioner should report all findings from application of the agreed-upon procedures. The concept of materiality does not apply to findings to be reported in an agreed-upon procedures engagement unless the definition of materiality is agreed to by the specified parties. Any agreed-upon materiality limits should be described in the practitioner's report.

21.04 The practitioner should avoid vague or ambiguous language in reporting findings. For example, if the practitioner's procedure was to recalculate a forecasted amount based on the assumptions disclosed, it would be inappropriate to describe the findings as "the result approximated the amount of forecasted rental income." Instead, the findings would be described unambiguously such as, "no exceptions were found as a result of applying the procedure."

21.05 The following two examples illustrate reports that might be issued when the engagement is limited to applying agreed-upon procedures to a financial forecast.

Sample Report 1

Independent Accountant's Report on Applying Agreed-Upon Procedures

Board of Directors—XYZ Corporation

Board of Directors—ABC Company

At your request, we have performed certain agreed-upon procedures, as enumerated below, with respect to the forecasted balance sheet, statements of income, retained earnings, and cash flows of DEF Company, a subsidiary of ABC Company, as of December 31, 20XX, and for the year then ending. These procedures, which were agreed to by the Boards of Directors of XYZ Corporation and ABC Company, were performed solely to assist you in evaluating the forecast in connection with the proposed sale of DEF Company to XYZ Corporation. DEF Company's management is responsible for the forecast.

This agreed-upon procedures engagement was conducted in accordance with attestation standards established by the American Institute of Certified Public Accountants. The sufficiency of these procedures is solely the responsibility of the specified parties.

Consequently, we make no representation regarding the sufficiency of the procedures described below either for the purpose for which this report has been requested or for any other purpose.

    a. With respect to forecasted rental income, we compared the occupancy statistics about expected demand for rental of housing units used in the forecast to occupancy statistics for the following comparable properties. Comparable properties for this purpose are defined as [*describe characteristics of comparability, for example, those located in Sample City with between xxx and yyy rental units, rental prices within z percent of those used in the forecast.*]

            [*List comparable properties*]

    As a result of performing this procedure, we found occupancy statistics used in the forecast were [*describe findings*].

    b. We traced each amount in the forecast to underlying schedules prepared by management and tested the arithmetical accuracy of management's calculations of rental income, operating income, and income tax expense contained thereon.

We found no differences as a result of these procedures.

We were not engaged to, and did not, conduct an examination, the objective of which would be the expression of an opinion on the accompanying prospective financial statements. Accordingly, we do not express an opinion on whether the prospective financial statements are presented in conformity with AICPA presentation guidelines or on whether the underlying assumptions provide a reasonable basis for the presentation. Had we performed additional procedures, other matters might have come to our attention that would have been reported to you. Furthermore, there will usually be differences between the forecasted and actual results, because events and circumstances frequently do not occur as expected, and those differences may be material. We have no responsibility to update this report for events and circumstances occurring after the date of this report.

This report is intended solely for the information and use of the Boards of Directors of ABC Company and XYZ Corporation and is not intended to be and should not be used by anyone other than these specified parties.

[*Signature*]

[*Date*]

Sample Report 2

Independent Accountant's Report on Applying Agreed-Upon Procedures

ABC Trustee

XYZ Company

At your request, we performed the agreed-upon procedures, as enumerated below, with respect to the forecasted balance sheet, statements of income, retained earnings, and cash flows of XYZ Company as of December 31, 20XX, and for the year then ending. These procedures, which were agreed to by ABC Trustee and XYZ Company, were performed solely to assist you in evaluating the forecast in connection with the Loan Agreement dated February 2, 20XX. XYZ Company's management is responsible for the forecast.

This agreed-upon procedures engagement was conducted in accordance with attestation standards established by the American Institute of Certified Public Accountants. The sufficiency of these procedures is solely the responsibility of the specified parties. Consequently we make no representation regarding the sufficiency of the procedures described below either for the purpose for which this report has been requested or for any other purpose.

> *a.* We read the prospective financial statements and compared them in regard to format with the guidelines established by the American Institute of Certified Public Accountants for presentation of a financial forecast.

We found no exceptions as a result of this procedure.

> *b.* We tested the arithmetical accuracy of the totals and subtotals contained in the forecasted balance sheet and the related forecasted statements of income, retained earnings, and cash flows of XYZ Company. We also tested the arithmetical accuracy of management's calculations of net sales, cost of sales, and income tax expense shown thereon, based on the assumptions disclosed.

We found no differences as a result of these procedures.

We were not engaged to, and did not, perform an examination, the objective of which would be the expression of an opinion on the accompanying prospective financial statements. Accordingly, we do not express an opinion on whether the prospective financial statements are presented in conformity with AICPA presentation guidelines or on whether the underlying assumptions provide a reasonable basis for the presentation. Had we performed additional procedures, other matters might have come to our attention that would have been reported to you. Furthermore, there will usually be differences between the forecasted and actual results, because events and circumstances frequently do not occur as expected, and those differences may be material. We have no responsibility to update this report for events and circumstances occurring after the date of this report.

This report is intended solely for the information and use of the audit committees and managements of ABC Trustee and XYZ Company, and is not intended to be and should not be used by anyone other than these specified parties.

[*Signature*]

[*Date*]

Explanatory Language

21.06 The practitioner also may include explanatory language about matters such as the following:

- Disclosure of stipulated facts, assumptions, or interpretations (including the source thereof) used in the application of agreed-upon procedures

- Description of the condition of records, controls, or data to which the procedures were applied
- Explanation of sampling risk

Dating of Report

21.07 The date of completion of the agreed-upon procedures should be used as the date of the practitioner's report.

Restrictions on the Performance of Procedures

21.08 When circumstances impose restrictions on the performance of the agreed-upon procedures, the practitioner should attempt to obtain agreement from the specified parties for modification of the agreed-upon procedures. When such agreement cannot be obtained (for example, when the agreed-upon procedures are published by a regulatory agency that will not modify the procedures), the practitioner should describe any restrictions on the performance of procedures in his or her report or withdraw from the engagement.

Knowledge of Matters Outside Agreed-Upon Procedures

21.09 The practitioner need not perform procedures beyond the agreed-upon procedures. However, in connection with the application of agreed-upon procedures, if matters come to the practitioner's attention by other means that significantly contradict the financial forecast, the practitioner should include this matter in his or her report. For example, if, during the course of applying agreed-upon procedures, the practitioner becomes aware of a presentation deficiency by means other than performance of the agreed-upon procedures, the practitioner should include the matter in his or her report.

Chapter 22

Guidance on the Practitioner's Services and Reports on Prospective Financial Statements for Internal Use Only

Because financial forecasts and projections are similar in many respects, separate guidance for projections is provided only to the extent that it differs from that for forecasts. *Italicized* paragraphs in this chapter that include a "P" in the paragraph number show how the guidance presented for forecasts should be modified for projections. Any plain-text paragraph not followed by an italicized paragraph applies to both forecasts and projections even though it uses only the term *forecast*.

22.01 A practitioner may be engaged to provide services on financial forecasts that are restricted to internal use in a variety of circumstances. For example, the practitioner may assemble a financial forecast in connection with an evaluation of the tax consequences of future actions or in connection with advice and assistance to a client evaluating whether to buy or lease an asset. If the forecast is to be restricted to internal use,[1] a practitioner may perform a compilation, examination, or agreed-upon procedures engagement in accordance with AICPA standards[2] or any of a spectrum of "other services" on it. The practitioner need not report on such other services unless requested by the client.[3] This chapter also suggests procedural and reporting guidance that the practitioner might use in providing such other services on a financial forecast for internal use only.

22.02 In obtaining satisfaction that the forecast will be restricted to internal use, the practitioner may rely on either the written or oral representation of the responsible party, unless information comes to his or her attention that contradicts the responsible party's representation. If not satisfied that the financial forecast will be restricted to internal use only, the practitioner should follow the guidance in paragraph 10.02.

Procedures

22.03 The practitioner's procedures should be consistent with the nature of the engagement. Earlier chapters of this guide provide useful guidance on the type of procedures a practitioner would apply if the nature of the engagement is similar to a compilation, examination, or application of agreed-upon procedures.

---

[1] In deciding whether a potential use is *internal* use, the practitioner should consider the degree of consistency of interest between the responsible party and the user regarding the forecast. If their interests are substantially consistent (for example, both the responsible party and the user are employees of the entity about which the forecast is made), the use would be deemed internal use. On the other hand, where the interest of the responsible party and the user are potentially inconsistent (for example, the responsible party is a nonowner manager and the user is an absentee owner), the use would not be deemed internal use. In some cases, this determination will require exercise of considerable professional judgment.

[2] In this guide, see chapters 12–14 for guidance on compilations, chapters 15–17 for examinations, and chapters 19–21 for application of agreed-upon procedures.

[3] However, see paragraph 22.09.

22.04 If a practitioner provides other services on a financial forecast for internal use, he or she should establish an understanding with the client, preferably in writing, regarding the services to be performed and should specify in this understanding that the financial forecast and the report, if any, are not to be distributed to outside users.

Reporting

22.05 AT section 301, *Financial Forecasts and Projections* (AICPA, *Professional Standards*), does not require the practitioner to report on other services performed on a financial forecast for internal use only. Accordingly, a practitioner can submit a computer-generated or manually prepared financial forecast to a client without reporting on it when the forecast is for internal use only.

22.06 If the practitioner decides to issue a report and purports to have compiled, examined, or applied agreed-upon procedures to a financial forecast for internal use only in conformity with AICPA standards, he or she should follow the reporting guidance in other chapters of this guide.[4] If the practitioner decides to issue a report on other services performed with respect to a financial forecast for internal use only, the report's form and content are flexible. However, the practitioner should not report on financial forecasts that exclude a summary of significant assumptions.[5] The report preferably would

a. be addressed to the responsible party.

b. identify the statements being reported on.

c. describe the character of the work performed and the degree of responsibility taken[6] with respect to the financial forecast.

d. include a caveat that the prospective results may not be achieved.

e. indicate the restrictions as to the distribution of the financial forecast and report.

f. be dated as of the date of the completion of the procedures.

22.06P *In addition to the elements listed previously, the practitioner's report on a financial projection for internal use only preferably would include a description of the limitations on the usefulness of the presentation.*

---

[4] See chapters 14, "The Practitioner's Compilation Report;" 17, "The Practitioner's Examination Report;" and 21, "The Practitioner's Report on the Results of Applying Agreed-Upon Procedures," for guidance on reporting on a compilation, examination, or application of agreed-upon procedures, respectively.

[5] See paragraph 9.05 for guidance on presentation formats for disclosure of significant assumptions.

[6] The practitioner's report on the financial forecast should not be similar to that given for examination or agreed-upon procedures engagements unless he or she complies with the standards for such engagements. Paragraph .06 of AT section 101, *Attest Engagements* (AICPA, *Professional Standards*), states that "any professional service resulting in expression of assurance must be performed under AICPA professional standards that provide for expression of assurance. Reports issued by a practitioner in connection with other professional standards should be written to be clearly distinguishable from and not to be confused with attest reports. . . . a report that merely excludes the words, 'was conducted in accordance with attestation standards established by the American Institute of Certified Public Accountants' but is otherwise similar to an examination, a review, or an agreed-upon procedures attest report may be inferred to be an attest report."

22.07 In addition to the preceding, the practitioner's report would, if applicable, preferably

    a. indicate if the practitioner is not independent with respect to an entity on whose financial forecast he or she is providing services. A practitioner should not provide any assurance on a financial forecast of an entity with respect to which he or she is not independent.

    b. describe omitted disclosures that come to his or her attention (for example, the omission of the summary of significant accounting policies discussed in paragraph 8.06), or simply state that there are omissions of disclosures required under the guidelines for presentation of a financial forecast. For example, when a financial forecast is included in a personal financial plan, the description may be worded as follows:

> This financial forecast was prepared solely to help you develop your personal financial plan. Accordingly, it does not include all disclosures required by the guidelines established by the American Institute of Certified Public Accountants for the presentation of a financial forecast.

22.08 The following is an example report, for cases in which the practitioner chooses to issue a report, if he or she has assembled a financial forecast for which distribution is limited to internal use:

> We have assembled, from information provided by management, the accompanying forecasted balance sheet, statements of income, retained earnings, and cash flows of XYZ Company as of December 31, 20XX, and for the year then ending. (This financial forecast omits the summary of significant accounting policies.)[7] We have not compiled or examined the financial forecast and express no assurance of any kind on it. Further, there will usually be differences between the forecasted and actual results, because events and circumstances frequently do not occur as expected, and those differences may be material. In accordance with the terms of our engagement, this report and the accompanying forecast are restricted to internal use and may not be shown to any third party for any purpose.

22.08P *The following is an example report, for cases in which the practitioner chooses to issue a report, when a practitioner has assembled a financial projection for which distribution is limited to internal use:*

> *We have assembled, from information provided by management, the accompanying projected balance sheet, statements of income, retained earnings, and cash flows of XYZ Company as of December 31, 20XX, and for the year then ending. (This financial forecast omits the summary of significant accounting policies.)[8] The accompanying projection and this report were prepared for [state special purpose, for example, "presentation to the Board of Directors of XYZ Company for its consideration as to whether to add a third operating shift"] and should not be used for any other purpose. We have not compiled or examined the financial projection and express no assurance of any kind on it. Further, even if [state hypothetical assumption, for example, "the third operating shift is added"], there will usually be differences between the projected and actual results, because events*

---

[7] This sentence would be included, if applicable.

[8] *This sentence would be included, if applicable.*

and circumstances frequently do not occur as expected, and those differences may be material. In accordance with the terms of our engagement, this report and the accompanying projection are restricted to internal use and may not be shown to any third party for any purpose.

22.09 If a financial forecast for internal use only is included with a practitioner's written communication (for example, with a transmittal letter or report), a caveat that the prospective results may not be achieved and a statement that the financial forecast is for internal use only should be communicated in writing. Such caveat and statement should be included in the communication or in the prospective financial statements.

Part 4

Guidance for Practitioners Who Provide Services on Partial Presentations of Prospective Financial Information

Chapter 23

Partial Presentations of Prospective Financial Information

Because forecasted and projected information are similar in many respects, separate guidance for projected information is provided only to the extent that it differs from that for forecasted information. *Italicized* paragraphs that include a "P" in the paragraph number show how the guidance presented for forecasted information should be modified for projected information. Any plain-text paragraph not followed by an italicized paragraph applies to both forecasted and projected information even though it uses only the term *forecast*.

23.01 Much of the guidance presented in earlier chapters of this guide can be applied to partial presentations of prospective financial information. This chapter describes how that guidance applies to the unique aspects of partial presentations. It also discusses the standards that apply when the practitioner is engaged to examine, compile, or apply agreed-upon procedures to a partial presentation (see paragraph 23.16).

23.02 A partial presentation is a presentation of prospective financial information that excludes one or more of the items required for prospective financial statements as described in paragraph 8.06.[1] A partial presentation may include either forecasted or projected information and may either be extracted from a presentation of prospective financial statements or may be prepared to meet a specific need.[2] Examples of partial presentations include

- sales forecasts.

- presentations of forecasted or projected capital expenditure programs.

---

[1] Paragraph 8.06 indicates that a financial forecast may take the form of complete basic financial statements or may be limited to the following items (where such items would be presented for historical financial statements for the period):

    a. Sales or gross revenues
    b. Gross profit or cost of sales
    c. Unusual or infrequently occurring items
    d. Provision for income taxes
    e. Income from continuing operations
    f. Discontinued operations or extraordinary items
    g. Net income
    h. Basic and diluted earnings per share
    i. Significant changes in financial position

When the financial forecast takes the form of basic financial statements, the requirement to disclose significant changes in financial position in item (*i*) is accomplished by presenting a statement of cash flows and its related note disclosures in accordance with Financial Accounting Standards Board *Accounting Standards Codification* 230, *Statement of Cash Flows*.

If the omitted applicable item is derivable from the information presented, the presentation would not be deemed a partial presentation. Paragraph 8.08 states that a summary of significant assumptions and accounting policies and an appropriate introduction should accompany the forecast.

[2] Partial presentations do not include estimates in historical financial statements and related notes required by generally accepted accounting principles (GAAP) or an other comprehensive basis of accounting. Guidance on auditing accounting estimates is contained in AU-C section 540, *Auditing Accounting Estimate, Including Fair Value Accounting Estimates and Related Disclosures* (AICPA, *Professional Standards*).

- projections of financing needs.

- other presentations of specified elements, accounts, or items of prospective financial statements (for example, projected production costs) that might be part of the development of a full presentation of prospective financial statements.

- forecasts that present operating income but not net income.

- forecasts or projections of taxable income that do not show significant changes in financial position.

- presentations that provide enough information to be translated into elements, accounts, or items of a financial forecast or projection. Examples include a forecast of sales units and unit selling prices and a forecast of occupancy percentage, number of rooms, and average room rates for a hotel. In contrast, if the prospective information only presents units expected to be sold but excludes unit selling prices, it would not be considered a partial presentation.

Uses of Partial Presentations

23.03   Partial presentations may be appropriate in many limited-use circumstances.[3] For example, a responsible party may prepare a partial presentation to analyze whether to lease or buy a piece of equipment or to evaluate the income tax implications of a given election because it may only be necessary to assess the impact on one aspect of financial results rather than on the financial statements taken as a whole. However, partial presentations are not ordinarily appropriate for general use. Accordingly, a partial presentation ordinarily should not be distributed to third parties who will not be negotiating directly with the responsible party (for example, in an offering document for an entity's debt or equity interests). In this context, *negotiating directly* is defined as a third-party user's ability to ask questions of, and negotiate the terms or structure of, a transaction directly with the responsible party.

23.04   The responsible party should consider whether a presentation omitting one or more items required for prospective financial statements will adequately present the information given its special purpose. Unless there is agreement between the responsible party and potential users specifying the content of the partial presentation, a partial presentation is inappropriate if it is incomplete for what it purports to present. Examples of partial presentations that might be inappropriate include a statement of forecasted receipts and disbursements that does not include certain existing commitments of the entity or a forecast of net income that does not include disclosure of changes in financial position if such disclosures would indicate the need for additional capital to sustain operations. A presentation of prospective sales, however, is an example of a presentation that would be appropriate in circumstances in which its intended use is to negotiate the terms of a royalty agreement based on sales.

Preparation and Presentation of Partial Presentations

23.05   Partial presentations omit one or more of the minimum items required in paragraph 8.06 for prospective financial statements.[4] The guidance

---

[3] See paragraphs 3.13 and 4.04.

[4] As used here, prospective financial statements include complete basic financial statements or the minimum items described in paragraph 8.06 (see footnote 1).

in the following paragraphs describes matters to be considered in the preparation and presentation of partial presentations.

23.06 *Key factors.* If the responsible party prepares a partial presentation without preparing prospective financial statements, the responsible party should consider key factors affecting elements, accounts, or items of prospective financial statements that are interrelated with those presented. In a sales forecast, for example, a key factor to be considered is whether productive capacity is sufficient to support forecasted sales. If the prospective information included in the partial presentation is extracted from the prospective financial statements, the effects of interrelationships among elements of the prospective financial statements should have been previously determined.

23.07 *Titles.* Titles of partial presentations should be descriptive of the presentation and state whether the presentation is of forecasted or projected information. In addition, titles should disclose the limited nature of the presentation and should not state that it is a financial forecast or a financial projection. Examples of appropriate titles are "Forecast of Production Capacity" and "Projected Operating Income Assuming a New Plant Facility."

23.08 *Accounting principles and policies.* Significant accounting policies relevant to the information presented and its intended purpose should be disclosed.

23.09 Occasionally, a different basis of accounting is used for preparing a partial presentation than that expected to be used in preparing the historical financial statements covering the same period as the partial presentation. In such circumstances, the presentation should disclose the basis of accounting to be used to prepare the historical financial statements covering the prospective period. Differences resulting from the use of the different basis to prepare the partial presentation should be described but need not be quantified.

23.10 *Materiality.* The concept of materiality should be related to the partial presentation taken as a whole.

23.11 *Assumptions.* Assumptions that are significant to a partial presentation include those assumptions having a reasonable possibility of a variation that may significantly affect the prospective results. Such assumptions may be either directly or indirectly related to the presentation. The selling price of a product, for example, is an assumption that could directly affect a sales forecast, whereas a company's productive capacity is an example of an assumption that could indirectly affect the sales forecast. Frequently, the more indirectly related an assumption is to the partial presentation, the greater the potential variation would have to be to have a material impact on the prospective results presented.

23.12 In some situations, the disclosure of assumptions deemed to be significant to the partial presentation of prospective financial information would be virtually the same as those disclosures that would be necessary if a full presentation of prospective financial statements were to be made. For example, in a partial presentation of forecasted operating results, it is likely that most assumptions that would be significant with respect to a full presentation would also be significant with respect to the presentation of the forecasted operating results. Thus, those assumptions should be disclosed.

23.13 In other, more limited partial presentations of prospective financial information, however, there may be few assumptions having a reasonable possibility of a variation that would significantly affect the presentation. In a presentation of forecasted sales, for example, it would only be necessary to disclose those assumptions relating directly to the sales forecast, such as future demand and pricing, unless other assumptions—such as marketing and advertising programs, productive capacity and production costs, financial stability or working capital sufficiency—have a reasonable possibility of a variation significant enough to have a material impact on the sales forecast.

23.14 The introduction preceding the summary of assumptions for a partial presentation should include a description of the purpose of the presentation and any limitations on the usefulness of the presentation.

23.15 The following is an example of the introduction for a partial presentation of forecasted sales:

> This sales forecast presents, to the best of management's[5] knowledge and belief, expected sales during the forecast period. Accordingly, the sales forecast reflects management's judgment as of (date), the date of this forecast, of the expected conditions and its expected course of action. The sales forecast is for use in negotiating the Company's lease override provisions and should not be used for any other purpose. The assumptions disclosed herein are those that management believes are significant to the sales forecast. There will usually be differences between the forecasted and actual results because events and circumstances frequently do not occur as expected, and those differences may be material.

23.15P *The following is an example of the introduction preceding the summary of assumptions for a schedule of projected production at a maximum productive capacity:*

> *This projection of production by product line presents, to the best of management's[6] knowledge and belief, the Company's expected production for the period if management chooses to operate its plant at maximum capacity. Accordingly, the projection of production by product line reflects management's judgment as of [date], the date of this projection, of the expected conditions and its expected course of action if the plant were operated at maximum capacity. The projected statement is designed to provide information to the Company's board of directors concerning the maximum production that might be achieved and related costs if current capacity were expanded through the addition of a third production shift. Accordingly, this projected statement should not be used for any other purpose. The assumptions disclosed herein are those that management believes are significant to the projected statement; however, management has not decided to operate the plant at maximum capacity. Even if the plant were operated at maximum capacity, there will usually be differences between projected and actual results because events and circumstances frequently do not occur as expected, and those differences may be material.*

---

[5] If the responsible party is other than management, the references to management should ordinarily be replaced with the name of the party who assumes responsibility for the assumptions.

[6] *See footnote 5.*

Practitioner's Involvement With Partial Presentations

23.16 A practitioner who has been engaged to or does examine, compile, or apply agreed-upon procedures to a partial presentation should do so in accordance with the guidance in chapters 12–14 for compilations, chapters 15–17 for examinations, and chapters 19–21 for agreed-upon procedures, respectively. This chapter provides additional guidance for applying those standards to services on partial presentations.[7]

23.17 This chapter does not provide standards or procedures for engagements involving partial presentations used solely in connection with litigation services, although it provides helpful guidance for many aspects of such engagements and may be referred to as useful guidance in such engagements. *Litigation services* are engagements involving pending or potential formal legal or regulatory proceedings before a trier of fact in connection with the resolution of a dispute between two or more parties, for example, in circumstances in which a practitioner acts as an expert witness. This exception is provided because, among other things, the practitioner's work in such proceedings is ordinarily subject to detailed analysis and challenge by each party to the dispute.[8]

23.18 The practitioner should consider whether it is appropriate to report on a partial presentation.[9]

23.19 Occasionally, a practitioner may be engaged to prepare a financial analysis of a potential project in which the engagement includes obtaining the information, making appropriate assumptions, and assembling the presentation. In such circumstances, the practitioner makes the assumptions and the analysis is not, and should not be characterized as, forecasted or projected information as defined in paragraph 23.02. Such analysis would not be appropriate for general use[10] (paragraph .06 of AT section 301, *Financial Forecasts and Projections* [AICPA, *Professional Standards*]).

Compilation and Examination Procedures

23.20 The procedures for compilations and examinations of prospective financial statements are generally applicable to partial presentations.[11] However, the practitioner's procedures may be affected by the nature of the information presented. As described in paragraph 23.06, many elements of prospective financial statements are interrelated. The practitioner should give appropriate consideration to whether key factors affecting elements, accounts, or items that are interrelated with those in the partial presentation he or she has been engaged to examine or compile have been considered, including key factors that may not necessarily be obvious in the partial presentation (for example, productive capacity relative to a sales forecast), and whether all significant assumptions have been disclosed. The practitioner may find it necessary for the scope of the examination or compilation of some partial presentations to be

---

[7] When providing services on a partial presentation restricted to internal use only, the practitioner may apply the guidance in paragraphs 22.01–.09.

[8] See paragraph 10.03.

[9] See paragraphs 23.03–.04.

[10] If the responsible party reviews and adopts the assumptions and presentation, the presentation might be a partial presentation. See paragraphs 23.02–.03 for the definition and uses of partial presentations.

[11] See chapters 12, "Compilation Procedures," and 15, "Examination Procedures."

similar to that for the examination or compilation of a presentation of prospective financial statements. For example, the scope of a practitioner's procedures when he or she examines forecasted results of operations would likely be similar to that of procedures used for the examination of prospective financial statements because the practitioner would most likely need to consider the interrelationships of all accounts in the examination of results of operations.

Applying Agreed-Upon Procedures to Partial Presentations

23.21 The guidance in chapter 19, "Application of Agreed-Upon Procedures," is generally applicable to engagements to apply agreed-upon procedures to a partial presentation.

Standard Practitioner's Compilation, Examination, and Agreed-Upon Procedures Reports

23.22 The practitioner's standard report on a partial presentation should include the elements for standard reports on prospective financial statements described in the following chapters:

- Compilations: chapter 14, "The Practitioner's Compilation Report"
- Examinations: chapter 17, "The Practitioner's Examination Report"
- Agreed-upon procedures: chapter 21, "The Practitioner's Report on the Results of Applying Agreed-Upon Procedures"

Because partial presentations are generally appropriate only for limited use (see paragraph 23.03) reports on partial presentations of both forecasted and projected information should include a description of any limitations on the usefulness of the presentation.

23.23 Chapters 14, 17, and 21 describe circumstances in which the practitioner's standard report on a financial forecast may require modification. The guidance for modifying the practitioner's standard reports included in those sections is generally applicable to partial presentations. Also, depending on the nature of the presentation, the practitioner may decide to disclose that the partial presentation is not intended to be a forecast of financial position, results of operations, or cash flows. The following are the forms of the practitioner's standard report when he or she has compiled, examined, or applied agreed-upon procedures to a partial presentation.[12]

Compilation Report on a Partial Presentation of Forecasted Information

Board of Directors—AAA Hotel

Board of Directors—ABC Bank

We have compiled the accompanying forecasted statement of net operating income before debt service, depreciation, and income taxes of AAA Hotel for the year ending December 31, 20X1 (the forecasted statement), in accordance with attestation standards established by the American Institute of Certified Public Accountants. The accompanying forecasted statement was prepared for the purpose of negotiating a proposed construction loan to be used to finance expansion of the hotel.

---

[12] These report forms are appropriate whether the presentations are based on GAAP or on an other comprehensive basis of accounting.

A compilation is limited to presenting forecasted information that is the representation of management and does not include evaluation of the support for the assumptions underlying such information. We have not examined the forecasted statement and, accordingly, do not express an opinion or any other form of assurance on the accompanying statement or assumptions. Furthermore, there will usually be differences between forecasted and actual results because events and circumstances frequently do not occur as expected, and those differences may be material. We have no responsibility to update this report for events and circumstances occurring after the date of this report.

The accompanying forecasted statement and this report are intended solely for AAA Hotel and XYZ Bank and are not intended to be and should not be used by anyone other than these specified parties.

[Signature]

[Date]

Compilation Report on a Partial Presentation of Projected Information

Board of Directors—XYZ Company

We have compiled the accompanying sales projection of XYZ Company for each of the years in the three-year period ending December 31, 20X1, in accordance with attestation standards established by the American Institute of Certified Public Accountants. The accompanying sales projection was prepared for the purpose of considering a new marketing program.

A compilation is limited to presenting projected information that is the representation of management and does not include evaluation of the support for the assumptions underlying such information. We have not examined the sales projection and, accordingly, do not express an opinion or any other form of assurance on the accompanying sales projection or assumptions. Furthermore, even if the Company attained the 15-percent market share of the electric toaster market, there will usually be differences between projected and actual results because events and circumstances frequently do not occur as expected, and those differences may be material. We have no responsibility to update this report for events and circumstances occurring after the date of this report.

The accompanying sales projection and this report are intended solely for the information and use of the Board of Directors of XYZ Company and are not intended to be and should not be used by anyone other than these specified parties.

[Signature]

[Date]

Examination Report on a Partial Presentation of Forecasted Information

Independent Accountant's Report

Board of Directors—AAA Hotel

Board of Directors—ABC Bank

We have examined the accompanying forecasted statement of net operating income before debt service, depreciation, and income taxes of AAA Hotel for the year ending December 31, 20X1 (the forecasted statement). AAA Hotel's management is responsible for the forecasted statement, which was prepared for the purpose of negotiating a proposed construction loan to be used to finance expansion of the hotel. Our responsibility is to express an opinion on the forecasted statement based on our examination.

Our examination was conducted in accordance with attestation standards established by the American Institute of Certified Public Accountants and, accordingly, included such procedures as we considered necessary to evaluate both the assumptions used by management and the preparation and presentation of the forecasted statement. We believe our examination provides a reasonable basis for our opinion.

In our opinion, the accompanying forecasted statement is presented in conformity with the guidelines for presentation of forecasted information established by the American Institute of Certified Public Accountants, and the underlying assumptions provide a reasonable basis for management's forecasted statement. However, there will usually be differences between forecasted and actual results because events and circumstances frequently do not occur as expected, and those differences may be material. We have no responsibility to update this report for events and circumstances occurring after the date of this report.

The accompanying forecasted statement and our report are intended solely for the information and use of AAA Hotel and XYZ Bank and are not intended to be used and should not be used by anyone other than these specified parties.

[*Signature*]

[*Date*]

Examination Report on a Partial Presentation of Projected Information

Independent Accountant's Report

Board of Directors—XYZ Company

We have examined the accompanying sales projection of XYZ Company for each of the years in the three-year period ending December 31, 20X1. XYZ Company's management is responsible for the sales projection, which was prepared for the purpose of considering a new marketing program. Our responsibility is to express an opinion on the sales projection based on our examination.

Our examination was conducted in accordance with attestation standards established by the American Institute of Certified Public Accountants and, accordingly, included such procedures as we considered necessary to evaluate both the assumptions used by management and the preparation and presentation of the sales projection. We believe our examination provides a reasonable basis for our opinion.

In our opinion, the sales projection referred to above is presented in conformity with the guidelines for presentation of projected information established by the American Institute of Certified Public Accountants, and the underlying assumptions provide a reasonable basis for management's projection of expected sales during the period assuming the Company were to achieve a 15-percent market share of the electric toaster market. However, even if the Company achieves a 15-percent market share, there will usually be differences between projected and actual results because events and circumstances frequently do not occur as expected, and those differences may be material. We have no responsibility to update this report for events and circumstances occurring after the date of this report.

The accompanying sales projection and this report were prepared solely for the information and use of the Board of Directors of XYZ Company and are not intended to be and should not be used by anyone other than these specified parties.

[Signature]

[Date]

Agreed-Upon Procedures Report on a Partial Presentation of Forecasted Information

Independent Accountant's Report on Applying Agreed-Upon Procedures

Board of Directors—XYZ Company

Board of Directors—ABC Corporation

At your request, we have performed certain agreed-upon procedures, as enumerated below, with respect to the sales forecast of XYZ Company for the year ending December 31, 20X2. These procedures, which were agreed to by the Boards of Directors of XYZ Company and ABC Corporation, were performed solely to assist you in evaluating the forecasted information in connection with the XYZ Company Royalty Agreement dated March 15, 20X1.

This agreed-upon procedures engagement was conducted in accordance with attestation standards established by the American Institute of Certified Public Accountants. The sufficiency of these procedures is solely the responsibility of the specified parties. Consequently, we make no representation regarding the sufficiency of the procedures described below either for the purpose for which this report has been requested or for any other purpose.

  a. We read the sales forecast and compared it in regard to format with the guidelines established by the American Institute of Certified Public Accountants for presentation of a partial presentation of forecasted information.

We found no exceptions as a result of this procedure.

  b. We proved the arithmetical accuracy of the totals and subtotals contained in the sales forecast. We also traced each amount in the sales forecast to underlying schedules prepared by management and proved the arithmetical accuracy of management's calculations of sales contained thereon.

We found no differences as a result of these procedures.

We were not engaged to and did not perform an examination, the objective of which would be the expression of an opinion on the accompanying forecasted information. Accordingly, we do not express an opinion on whether the sales forecast is presented in conformity with AICPA presentation guidelines or on whether the underlying assumptions provide a reasonable basis for the presentation. Had we performed additional procedures, other matters might have come to our attention that would have been reported to you. Furthermore, there will usually be differences between the forecasted and actual results, because events and circumstances frequently do not occur as expected, and those differences may be material. We have no responsibility to update this report for events and circumstances occurring after the date of this report.

The accompanying sales forecast and this report are intended solely for the information and use of the Boards of Directors of XYZ Company and ABC Corporation and are not intended to be and should not be used by anyone other than these specified parties.

[*Signature*]

[*Date*]

23.24 The illustrative partial presentations of prospective financial information included in exhibits 23-1 and 23-2 are presented in conformity with the presentation guidelines in chapter 8, "Presentation Guidelines," although other presentation formats could also be consistent with those guidelines. For example, it may be appropriate to present the summary of significant assumptions and accounting policies in a less formal manner than that illustrated, such as computer-printed output (indicating data and relationships) from "electronic worksheets" and general purpose financial modeling software, as long as the responsible party believes that the disclosures and assumptions presented can be understood by users. The following is a brief summary of the illustrative partial presentations presented in exhibits 23-1 and 23-2:

    a. Exhibit 23-1 illustrates a sales forecast prepared for the purpose of negotiating a retail company's lease override provisions.

    b. Exhibit 23-2 illustrates a forecasted statement of net operating income before debt service and depreciation in connection with the contemplated construction of a new sports arena.

Exhibit 23-1

ABC Retail Company
Statement of Forecasted Sales
For Each of the Three Years Ending December 31, 20X3[13]

	Years Ending December 31,		
	20X1	*20X2*	*20X3*
Forecasted sales	$629,000	$679,000	$726,000

This sales forecast presents, to the best of management's knowledge and belief, expected sales during the forecast period. Accordingly, the sales forecast reflects management's judgment as of February 14, 20X1, the date of this forecast, of the expected conditions and its expected course of action. The sales forecast is for use in negotiating the Company's lease override provisions and should not be used for any other purpose. The assumptions disclosed herein are those that management believes are significant to the sales forecast. There will usually be differences between the forecasted and actual results because events and circumstances frequently do not occur as expected, and those differences may be material.

This sales forecast is based on an expected average rate of overall increase in market demand for the Company's products, sporting goods equipment, of 3 percent per year. During the past 5 years, market demand for sporting goods equipment has increased approximately 3 percent per year, and the Company expects this rate of industry growth to remain steady throughout the forecast period. The sales forecast is also based on an expected increase in the Company's market share in its geographical selling region to 23 percent by 20X3, which represents a 6 percent to 7 percent increase in market share over the forecast period. The Company's market share during the past 3 years has increased 1 to 2 percentage points each year, and the Company expects this rate of increase to continue during the forecast period. The sales forecast is also based on an expected 4 percent to 5 percent increase in the rate of inflation for each of the next 3 years. The Company expects that it will be able to increase the prices of its products to cover increased costs due to inflation.

The Company plans to maintain its advertising and marketing programs at current levels and has retail floor space available to provide for the increase in the number of products it expects to sell.

---

[13] *Note:* The summary of significant accounting policies is not illustrated.

Exhibit 23-2

MARS Arena
Forecasted Statement of Net Operating Income
Before Debt Service and Depreciation
For Years Ending December 31, 20X1 and 20X2
(in thousands)

	Reference	20X1	20X2
Operating revenues	C	$ 2,700	$ 2,600
Operating expenses			
Salaries and wages	D	1,050	1,100
Office and general	E	700	650
Utilities	F	500	510
Operations and maintenance	G	150	160
Total operating expenses		2,400	2,420
Net operating income before debt service and depreciation		$ 300	$ 180

See accompanying Summary of Significant Forecast Assumptions and Accounting Policies.

MARS Arena
Summary of Significant Forecast Assumptions and Accounting Policies
For Years Ending December 31, 20X1 and 20X2

The accompanying forecasted statement presents, to the best of management's knowledge and belief, Mars Arena's expected net operating income before debt service and depreciation for the two-year period ending December 31, 20X2. Accordingly, the forecasted statement reflects management's judgment as of August 29, 20X0, the date of this forecasted statement, of the expected conditions and its expected course of action. This presentation is intended for use by the City of Mars in evaluating financing alternatives in connection with the contemplated construction of the new arena and should not be used for any other purpose. The assumptions disclosed herein are those that management believes are significant to the forecasted statement. There will usually be differences between the forecasted and actual results because events and circumstances frequently do not occur as expected, and those differences may be material.

The forecasted statement presents net operating income before debt service and depreciation. Accordingly, it is not intended to be a forecast of financial position, results of operations, or cash flows.

A—Description of the Project

The City of Mars plans to build a new 10,000-seat arena at the southeast intersection of Maxwell Road and Rugby Road to replace their existing 8,000-seat arena (the City's existing arena). Mars Arena will have 3,000 available parking spaces.

B—Summary of Significant Accounting Policies

[*not illustrated*]

C—Operating Revenues

There are four basic types of events forecasted to generate operating income: sporting events, family shows (for example, circus, ice shows), concerts, and exhibitions. The significant sources of revenue for each type of event include arena rental, parking fees, food and beverage concessions, novelty and souvenir income, and advertising. Attendance during the initial year of operations is forecasted to be greater than the second year based on the "bonus" a new arena can enjoy as patrons come to see the new facility as well as to see the event. A summary of operating revenue by type of event follows.

Year 1	Event Days	Average Attendance	Total Attendance	Total Revenue
Sporting events	70	4,000	280,000	$ 860,000
Family shows	45	4,500	202,500	515,000
Concerts	30	8,500	255,000	1,025,000
Exhibitions	25	2,500	62,500	180,000
Advertising	—		—	120,000
Totals	170		800,000	$2,700,000

Year 2	Event Days	Average Attendance	Total Attendance	Total Revenue
Sporting events	70	3,900	273,000	$ 835,000
Family shows	45	4,300	193,500	490,000
Concerts	30	8,200	246,000	990,000
Exhibitions	25	2,200	55,500	160,000
Advertising	—		—	125,000
Totals	170		768,000	$2,600,000

The bases for the significant income assumptions are discussed in the following paragraphs.

Arena rental. Management estimates that the new arena will schedule approximately 170 event days in a representative year consisting of seventy sporting events, 45 family shows, 30 concerts, and 25 exhibitions. Event days were forecasted based on discussions with users (such as sporting teams and event sponsors) and on market research and analysis performed by an independent consultant. Also, the City of Mars recently obtained a commitment from the local minor-league hockey team to play their home games in Mars Arena.

Mars Arena will be rented out on the basis of a percentage of the dollars generated by ticket sales (called a "percentage of gross receipts") or a fixed rent (called a "flat rate"). The percentages of gross gate receipts accruing to the facility are based on current average percentages retained by the City's existing arena. These percentages range from 10 percent to 50 percent depending on the type of event. Management expects ticket prices to increase between 5 percent and 15 percent over prices at the City's existing arena, depending on the type of event, as a result of the new modernized facility. Ticket prices forecasted for each type of event have been compared with those received by other facilities for similar events. Flat rate rentals are usually negotiated by users who do not charge an admission price or have a series of events. The flat rate rental for Mars Arena is forecasted to be between $1,000 and $4,000 and is based on an analysis of rates charged by other comparable arenas for the types of events forecasted. Management does not anticipate an increase in ticket prices or flat rate rentals during the second year of operations.

Parking fees. Management will operate and maintain the parking facility and, accordingly, all revenues accrue to Mars Arena. Consistent with experience at the City's existing arena, management estimates that 75 percent of all patrons will arrive by car for each event. The forecasted information assumes each car will carry an average of 2.7 persons and average parking rates will be $3.50 per car.

Food and beverage concessions. Management has negotiated a contract with ABC Company to supply and manage the food and beverage concessions. Concession income is forecasted to be 30 percent of gross concession revenue generated at each event, based on the contractual agreement with ABC Company. Mars Arena will provide all equipment and personnel necessary to operate the concessions. Patron's forecasted average expenditure per type of event ranges from $0.75 to $3.00 and is based on an analysis of data for comparable events and facilities, including the City's existing arena.

Novelty and souvenir income. Similar to food and beverage concessions, management has negotiated a contract with ABC Company to supply and manage the novelty and souvenir concessions. Novelty and souvenir income is forecasted to be 30 percent of gross novelty revenue based on the contractual agreement. Mars Arena will provide all equipment and personnel necessary to operate the novelty and souvenir stands. Patron's forecasted average expenditure per type of event ranges from $0.00 to $5.25 and is based on an analysis of data for comparable events and facilities.

Advertising. Advertising income will be generated primarily from signage on the interior and exterior of Mars Arena. Revenues included in the forecasted information are based on the signage capacity of Mars Arena, contract negotiations to date, and advertising revenues at the City's existing arena.

D—Salaries and Wages

The forecasted information assumes that management will make maximum use of full-time staff rather than subcontract out services, such as facility management and security. Personnel requirements are based on staffing organizations at similar sports arenas and public assembly facilities. Pay for hourly workers is based on local wage levels and wage rates being paid to employees of the City's existing arena. Wage levels are expected to increase approximately four percent in the second year.

Salaries are forecasted on an individual basis using expected salary rates during the forecast period. Part-time salaries and wages are assumed to be event-related expenses and passed through to tenants, except for 15 percent, which is absorbed by Mars Arena.

E—Office and General Expenses

Office and general expenses consist of insurance, advertising, fees for services, and other office and general expenses. Insurance expense is based on costs at the City's existing arena and on a review of insurance coverage proposals that include estimates of general liability, fire, workers' compensation, auto-business, liquor liability and boiler-machinery coverage. Advertising expenses are based on costs incurred by the City's existing arena, the number and type of forecasted events, and expected price increases from advertising agencies. Advertising expenses are expected to be higher in the first year of operations in order to promote the new facility. Fees for services include, but are not limited to, consulting fees, legal fees, and accounting and auditing fees. These fees are estimated based on expenses of the City's existing arena and on plans by management to engage consultants to assist in starting up operations. Other office and general expenses are based on experience at comparable facilities and on costs incurred by the City's existing arena.

F—Utility Expenses

Utility expenses have been estimated by the project team architects and engineers. Utility expenses include fuel and gas, electricity, water, and sewer costs.

G—Operations and Maintenance Expenses

Operations and maintenance expenses were estimated based on the requirements of facilities similar in construction and design, age, and intended use.

Appendixes

Appendix A

SEC Policy on Projections

REGULATION S-K

Title 17 of U.S. Code of Federal Regulations, Part 229, STANDARD INSTRUCTIONS FOR FILING FORMS UNDER SECURITIES ACT OF 1933, SECURITIES EXCHANGE ACT OF 1934 AND ENERGY POLICY AND CONSERVATION ACT OF 1975—REGULATION S-K, Subpart .10, "General."

(b) *Commission policy on projections.* The Commission encourages the use in documents specified in Rule 175 under the Securities Act and Rule 3b-6 under the Exchange Act of management's projections of future economic performance that have a reasonable basis and are presented in an appropriate format. The guidelines set forth herein represent the Commission's views on important factors to be considered in formulating and disclosing such projections.

(1) *Basis for projections.* The Commission believes that management must have the option to present in Commission filings its good faith assessment of a registrant's future performance. Management, however, must have a reasonable basis for such an assessment. Although a history of operations or experience in projecting may be among the factors providing a basis for management's assessment, the Commission does not believe that a registrant always must have had such a history or experience in order to formulate projections with a reasonable basis. An outside review of management's projections may furnish additional support for having a reasonable basis for a projection. If management decides to include a report of such a review in a Commission filing, there also should be disclosure of the qualifications of the reviewer, the extent of the review, the relationship between the reviewer and the registrant, and other material factors concerning the process by which any outside review was sought or obtained. Moreover, in the case of a registration statement under the Securities Act, the reviewer would be deemed an expert and an appropriate consent must be filed with the registration statement.

(2) *Format for projections.* In determining the appropriate format for projections included in Commission filings, consideration must be given to, among other things, the financial items to be projected, the period to be covered, and the manner of presentation to be used. Although traditionally projections have been given for three financial items generally considered to be of primary importance to investors (revenues, net income (loss) and earnings (loss) per share), projection information need not necessarily be limited to these three items. However, management should take care to assure that the choice of items projected is not susceptible of misleading inferences through selective projection of only favorable items. Revenues, net income (loss) and earnings (loss) per share usually are presented together in order to avoid any misleading inferences that may arise when the individual items reflect contradictory trends. There may be instances, however, when it is appropriate to present earnings (loss) from continuing operations, or income (loss) before extraordinary items in addition to or in lieu of net income (loss). It generally would be

misleading to present sales or revenue projections without one of the foregoing measures of income. The period that appropriately may be covered by a projection depends to a large extent on the particular circumstances of the company involved. For certain companies in certain industries, a projection covering a two or three year period may be entirely reasonable. Other companies may not have a reasonable basis for projections beyond the current year. Accordingly, management should select the period most appropriate in the circumstances. In addition, management, in making a projection, should disclose what, in its opinion, is the most probable specific amount or the most reasonable range for each financial item projected based on the selected assumptions. Ranges, however, should not be so wide as to make the disclosures meaningless. Moreover, several projections based on varying assumptions may be judged by management to be more meaningful than a single number or range and would be permitted.

(3) *Investor understanding.*

(i) When management chooses to include its projections in a Commission filing, the disclosures accompanying the projections should facilitate investor understanding of the basis for and limitations of projections. In this regard investors should be cautioned against attributing undue certainty to management's assessment, and the Commission believes that investors would be aided by a statement indicating management's intention regarding the furnishing of updated projections. The Commission also believes that investor understanding would be enhanced by disclosure of the assumptions which in management's opinion are most significant to the projections or are the key factors upon which the financial results of the enterprise depend and encourages disclosure of assumptions in a manner that will provide a framework for analysis of the projection.

(ii) Management also should consider whether disclosure of the accuracy or inaccuracy of previous projections would provide investors with important insights into the limitations of projections. In this regard, consideration should be given to presenting the projections in a format that will facilitate subsequent analysis of the reasons for differences between actual and forecast results. An important benefit may arise from the systematic analysis of variances between projected and actual results on a continuing basis, since such disclosure may highlight for investors the most significant risk and profit-sensitive areas in a business operation.

(iii) With respect to previously issued projections, registrants are reminded of their responsibility to make full and prompt disclosure of material facts, both favorable and unfavorable, regarding their financial condition. This responsibility may extend to situations where management knows or has reason to know that its previously disclosed projections no longer have a reasonable basis.

(iv) Since a registrant's ability to make projections with relative confidence may vary with all the facts and circumstances, the responsibility for determining whether to discontinue or to resume making projections is best left to management. However, the Commission encourages registrants not to discontinue or to resume projections in Commission filings without a reasonable basis.

Appendix B

SEC Safe Harbor Rule for Projections

Title 17 of U.S. Code of Federal Regulations, Part 230, GENERAL RULES AND REGULATIONS, SECURITIES ACT OF 1933, Subpart .175, "Liability for certain statements by issuers."

(a) A statement within the coverage of paragraph (*b*) of this section which is made by or on behalf of an issuer or by an outside reviewer retained by the issuer shall be deemed not to be a fraudulent statement (as defined in paragraph (*d*) of this section), unless it is shown that such statement was made or reaffirmed without a reasonable basis or was disclosed other than in good faith.

(b) This rule applies to the following statements:

    (1) A forward-looking statement (as defined in paragraph (c) of this section) made in a document filed with the Commission, in Part I of a quarterly report on Form 10-Q, (§ 249.308a of this chapter), or in an annual report to security holders meeting the requirements of Rule 14a-3(b) and (c) or 14c-3(a) and (b) under the Securities Exchange Act of 1934 (§§ 240.14a-3(b) and (c) or 240.14c-3(a) and (b) of this chapter), a statement reaffirming such forward-looking statement after the date the document was filed or the annual report was made publicly available, or a forward-looking statement made before the date the document was filed or the date the annual report was publicly available if such statement is reaffirmed in a filed document, in Part I of a quarterly report on Form 10-Q, or in an annual report made publicly available within a reasonable time after the making of such forward-looking statement; *Provided*, that

        (i) At the time such statements are made or reaffirmed, either the issuer is subject to the reporting requirements of section 13(a) or 15(d) of the Securities Exchange Act of 1934 and has complied with the requirements of Rule 13a-1 or 15d-1 (§§ 239.13a-1 or 239.15d-1 of this chapter) thereunder, if applicable, to file its most recent annual report on Form 10-K, Form 20-F, or Form 40-F; or if the issuer is not subject to the reporting requirements of Section 13(a) or 15(d) of the Securities Exchange Act of 1934, the statements are made in a registration statement filed under the Act, offering statement or solicitation of interest, written document or broadcast script under Regulation A or pursuant to sections 12(b) or (g) of the Securities Exchange Act of 1934; and

        (ii) The statements are not made by or on behalf of an issuer that is an investment company registered under the Investment Company Act of 1940; and

    (2) Information that is disclosed in a document filed with the Commission, in Part I of a quarterly report on Form 10-Q (§ 249.308a of this chapter) or in an annual report to shareholders meeting the requirements of Rules 14a-3 (b) and (c) or 14c-3 (a)

and (b) under the Securities Exchange Act of 1934 (§§ 240.14a-3(b) and (c) or 240.14c-3(a) and (b) of this chapter) and that relates to:

    (i) The effects of changing prices on the business enterprise, presented voluntarily or pursuant to Item 303 of Regulation S-K (§ 229.303 of this chapter), "Management's Discussion and Analysis of Financial Condition and Results of Operations," Item 5 of Form 20-F (§ 249.220(f) of this chapter), "Operating and Financial Review and Prospects," Item 302 of Regulation S-K (§ 229.302 of this chapter), "Supplementary Financial Information," or Rule 3-20(c) of Regulation S-X (§ 210.3-20(c) of this chapter); or

    (ii) The value of proved oil and gas reserves (such as a standardized measure of discounted future net cash flows relating to proved oil and gas reserves as set forth in FASB ASC paragraphs 932-235-50-29 through 932-235-50-36 (Extractive Activities—Oil and Gas Topic) presented voluntarily or pursuant to Item 302 of Regulation S-K (§ 229.302 of this chapter).

(c) For the purpose of this rule, the term *forward-looking statement* shall mean and shall be limited to:

    (1) A statement containing a projection of revenues, income (loss), earnings (loss) per share, capital expenditures, dividends, capital structure or other financial items;

    (2) A statement of management's plans and objectives for future operations;

    (3) A statement of future economic performance contained in management's discussion and analysis of financial condition and results of operations included pursuant to Item 303 of Regulation S-K (§ 229.303 of this chapter) or Item 9 of Form 20-F; or Item 5 of Form 20-F.

    (4) Disclosed statements of the assumptions underlying or relating to any of the statements described in paragraphs (c) (1), (2), or (3) of this section.

(d) For the purpose of this rule the term *fraudulent statement* shall mean a statement which is an untrue statement of a material fact, a statement false or misleading with respect to any material fact, an omission to state a material fact necessary to make a statement not misleading, or which constitutes the employment of a manipulative, deceptive, or fraudulent device, contrivance, scheme, transaction, act, practice, course of business, or an artifice to defraud, as those terms are used in the Securities Act of 1933 or the rules or regulations promulgated thereunder.

Appendix C

IRS Regulations Regarding Tax Shelter Opinions (Circular 230)

Department of the Treasury

Internal Revenue Service

31 CFR Part 10

Regulations Governing the Practice of Attorneys, Certified Public Accountants, Enrolled Agents, and Enrolled Actuaries Before the Internal Revenue Service

AGENCY: Department of the Treasury.

ACTION: Final rule.

SUMMARY

This document contains final regulations governing practice before the Internal Revenue Service (IRS) to set standards for providing covered opinions used in the promotion of tax shelter offerings. The final and amended regulations reflect the Treasury Department's concern about the proliferation of abusive tax shelters in recent years and the role of the IRS practitioner's opinion in the promotion of such shelters. The regulations address the problem by imposing duties upon IRS practitioners who furnish covered opinions for use in connection with tax shelter offerings.

§10.35 Requirements for covered opinions.

(a) A practitioner who provides a covered opinion shall comply with the standards of practice in this section.

(b) *Definitions.* For purposes of this subpart—

    (1) A *practitioner* includes any individual described in 10.2(a)(5).

    (2) *Covered opinion—*

        (i) *In general.* A *covered opinion* is written advice (including electronic communications) by a practitioner concerning one or more Federal tax issues arising from—

            (A) A transaction that is the same as or substantially similar to a transaction that, at the time the advice is rendered, the Internal Revenue Service has determined to be a tax avoidance transaction and identified by published guidance as a listed transaction under 26 CFR 1.6011-4(b)(2);

            (B) Any partnership or other entity, any investment plan or arrangement, or any other plan or arrangement, the principal purpose of which is the avoidance or evasion of any tax imposed by the Internal Revenue Code; or

            (C) Any partnership or other entity, any investment plan or arrangement, or any other plan or arrangement, a significant purpose of which is the avoidance or evasion of any tax imposed by the Internal Revenue Code if the written advice—

    (1) Is a *reliance opinion*;

    (2) Is a *marketed opinion*;

    (3) Is subject to *conditions of confidentiality*; or

    (4) Is subject to *contractual protection.*

  (ii) *Excluded advice.* A *covered opinion* does not include—

    (A) Written advice provided to a client during the course of an engagement if a practitioner is reasonably expected to provide subsequent written advice to the client that satisfies the requirements of this section;

    (B) Written advice, other than advice described in paragraph (b)(2)(i)(A) of this section (concerning listed transactions) or paragraph (b)(2)(i)(B) of this section (concerning the principal purpose of avoidance or evasion) that—

      (1) Concerns the qualification of a qualified plan;

      (2) Is a *State or local bond opinion*; or

      (3) Is included in documents required to be filed with the Securities and Exchange Commission.

    (C) Written advice prepared for and provided to a taxpayer, solely for use by that taxpayer, after the taxpayer has filed a tax return with the Internal Revenue Service reflecting the tax benefits of the transaction. The preceding sentence does not apply if the practitioner knows or has reason to know that the written advice will be relied upon by the taxpayer to take a position on a tax return (including for these purposes an amended return that claims tax benefits not reported on a previously filed return) filed after the date on which the advice is provided to the taxpayer;

    (D) Written advice provided to an employer by a practitioner in that practitioner's capacity as an employee of that employer solely for purposes of determining the tax liability of the employer; or

    (E) Written advice that does not resolve a Federal tax issue in the taxpayer's favor, unless the advice reaches a conclusion favorable to the taxpayer at any confidence level (for example, not frivolous, realistic possibility of success, reasonable basis or substantial authority) with respect to that issue. If written advice concerns more than one Federal tax issue, the advice must comply with the requirements of paragraph (c) of this section with respect to any Federal tax issue not described in the preceding sentence.

  (3) A *Federal tax issue* is a question concerning the Federal tax treatment of an item of income, gain, loss, deduction, or credit, the existence or absence of a taxable transfer of property, or the value of

property for Federal tax purposes. For purposes of this subpart, a *Federal tax issue* is significant if the Internal Revenue Service has a reasonable basis for a successful challenge and its resolution could have a significant impact, whether beneficial or adverse and under any reasonably foreseeable circumstance, on the overall Federal tax treatment of the transaction(s) or matter(s) addressed in the opinion.

(4) *Reliance Opinion—*

   (i) Written advice is a *reliance opinion* if the advice concludes at a confidence level of at least more likely than not (a greater than 50 percent likelihood) that one or more significant Federal tax issues would be resolved in the taxpayer's favor.

   (ii) For purposes of this section, written advice, other than advice described in paragraph (b)(2)(i)(A) of this section (concerning listed transactions) or paragraph (b)(2)(i)(B) of this section (concerning the principal purpose of avoidance or evasion), is not treated as a *reliance opinion* if the practitioner prominently discloses in the written advice that it was not intended or written by the practitioner to be used, and that it cannot be used by the taxpayer, for the purpose of avoiding penalties that may be imposed on the taxpayer.

(5) *Marketed opinion—*

   (i) Written advice is a *marketed opinion* if the practitioner knows or has reason to know that the written advice will be used or referred to by a person other than the practitioner (or a person who is a member of, associated with, or employed by the practitioner's firm) in promoting, marketing or recommending a partnership or other entity, investment plan or arrangement to one or more taxpayer(s).

   (ii) For purposes of this section, written advice, other than advice described in paragraph (b)(2)(i)(A) of this section (concerning listed transactions) or paragraph (b)(2)(i)(B) of this section (concerning the principal purpose of avoidance or evasion), is not treated as a *marketed opinion* if the practitioner prominently discloses in the written advice that—

   (A) The advice was not intended or written by the practitioner to be used, and that it cannot be used by any taxpayer, for the purpose of avoiding penalties that may be imposed on the taxpayer;

   (B) The advice was written to support the promotion or marketing of the transaction(s) or matter(s) addressed by the written advice; and

   (C) The taxpayer should seek advice based on the taxpayer's particular circumstances from an independent tax advisor.

(6) *Conditions of confidentiality.* Written advice is subject to *conditions of confidentiality* if the practitioner imposes on one or more recipients of the written advice a limitation on disclosure of the tax treatment or tax structure of the transaction and the limitation on disclosure protects the confidentiality of that practitioner's tax strategies, regardless of whether the limitation on disclosure is legally binding. A

claim that a transaction is proprietary or exclusive is not a limitation on disclosure if the practitioner confirms to all recipients of the written advice that there is no limitation on disclosure of the tax treatment or tax structure of the transaction that is the subject of the written advice.

(7) *Contractual protection.* Written advice is subject to *contractual protection* if the taxpayer has the right to a full or partial refund of fees paid to the practitioner (or a person who is a member of, associated with, or employed by the practitioner's firm) if all or a part of the intended tax consequences from the matters addressed in the written advice are not sustained, or if the fees paid to the practitioner (or a person who is a member of, associated with, or employed by the practitioner's firm) are contingent on the taxpayer's realization of tax benefits from the transaction. All the facts and circumstances relating to the matters addressed in the written advice will be considered when determining whether a fee is refundable or contingent, including the right to reimbursements of amounts that the parties to a transaction have not designated as fees or any agreement to provide services without reasonable compensation.

(8) *Prominently disclosed.* An item is *prominently disclosed* if it is readily apparent to a reader of the written advice. Whether an item is readily apparent will depend on the facts and circumstances surrounding the written advice including, but not limited to, the sophistication of the taxpayer and the length of the written advice. At a minimum, to be prominently disclosed an item must be set forth in a separate section (and not in a footnote) in a typeface that is the same size or larger than the typeface of any discussion of the facts or law in the written advice.

(9) *State or local bond opinion.* A *state or local bond opinion* is written advice with respect to a *Federal tax issue* included in any materials delivered to a purchaser of a State or local bond in connection with the issuance of the bond in a public or private offering, including an official statement (if one is prepared), that concerns only the excludability of interest on a State or local bond from gross income under section 103 of the Internal Revenue Code, the application of section 55 of the Internal Revenue Code to a State or local bond, the status of a State or local bond as a qualified tax-exempt obligation under section 265(b)(3) of the Internal Revenue Code, the status of a State or local bond as a qualified zone academy bond under section 1397E of the Internal Revenue Code, or any combination of the above.

(10) *The principal purpose.* For purposes of this section, the principal purpose of a partnership or other entity, investment plan or arrangement, or other plan or arrangement is the avoidance or evasion of any tax imposed by the Internal Revenue Service Code if that purpose exceeds any other purpose. The principal purpose of a partnership or other entity, investment plan or arrangement, or other plan or arrangement is not to avoid or evade Federal tax if that partnership, entity, plan or arrangement has as its purpose the claiming of tax benefits in a manner consistent with the statute and Congressional purpose. A partnership, entity, plan or arrangement may have a significant purpose of avoidance or evasion even though it does not have the principal purpose of avoidance or evasion under this paragraph (b)(10).

(c) *Requirements for covered opinions.* A practitioner providing a *covered opinion* must comply with each of the following requirements.

(1) *Factual matters*

(i) The practitioner must use reasonable efforts to identify and ascertain the facts, which may relate to future events if a transaction is prospective or proposed, and to determine which facts are relevant. The opinion must identify and consider all facts that the practitioner determines to be relevant.

(ii) The practitioner must not base the opinion on any unreasonable factual assumptions (including assumptions as to future events). An unreasonable factual assumption includes a factual assumption that the practitioner knows or should know is incorrect or incomplete. For example, it is unreasonable to assume that a transaction has a business purpose or that a transaction is potentially profitable apart from tax benefits. A factual assumption includes reliance on a projection, financial forecast or appraisal. It is unreasonable for a practitioner to rely on a projection, financial forecast or appraisal if the practitioner knows or should know that the projection, financial forecast or appraisal is incorrect or incomplete or was prepared by a person lacking the skills or qualifications necessary to prepare such projection, financial forecast or appraisal. The opinion must identify in a separate section all factual assumptions relied upon by the practitioner.

(iii) The practitioner must not base the opinion on any unreasonable factual representations, statements or findings of the taxpayer or any other person. An unreasonable factual representation includes a factual representation that the practitioner knows or should know is incorrect or incomplete. For example, a practitioner may not rely on a factual representation that a transaction has a business purpose if the representation does not include a specific description of the business purpose or the practitioner knows or should know that the representation is incorrect or incomplete. The opinion must identify in a separate section all factual representations, statements or findings of the taxpayer relied upon by the practitioner.

(2) *Relate law to facts*

(i) The opinion must relate the applicable law (including potentially applicable judicial doctrines) to the relevant facts.

(ii) The practitioner must not assume the favorable resolution of any significant Federal tax issue except as provided in paragraphs (c)(3)(v) and (d) of this section, or otherwise base an opinion on any unreasonable legal assumptions, representations, or conclusions.

(iii) The opinion must not contain internally inconsistent legal analyses or conclusions.

(3) *Evaluation of significant Federal tax issues—*

    (i) *In general.* The opinion must consider all significant Federal tax issues except as provided in paragraphs (c)(3)(v) and (d) of this section.

    (ii) *Conclusion as to each significant Federal tax issue.* The opinion must provide the practitioner's conclusion as to the likelihood that the taxpayer will prevail on the merits with respect to each significant Federal tax issue considered in the opinion. If the practitioner is unable to reach a conclusion with respect to one or more of those issues, the opinion must state that the practitioner is unable to reach a conclusion with respect to those issues. The opinion must describe the reasons for the conclusions, including the facts and analysis supporting the conclusions, or describe the reasons that the practitioner is unable to reach a conclusion as to one or more issues. If the practitioner fails to reach a conclusion at a confidence level of at least more likely than not with respect to one or more significant Federal tax issues considered, the opinion must include the appropriate disclosure(s) required under paragraph (e) of this section.

    (iii) *Evaluation based on chances of success on the merits.* In evaluating the significant Federal tax issues addressed in the opinion, the practitioner must not take into account the possibility that a tax return will not be audited, that an issue will not be raised on audit, or that an issue will be resolved through settlement if raised.

    (iv) *Marketed opinions.* In the case of a *marketed opinion*, the opinion must provide the practitioner's conclusion that the taxpayer will prevail on the merits at a confidence level of at least more likely than not with respect to each significant Federal tax issue. If the practitioner is unable to reach a more likely than not conclusion with respect to each significant Federal tax issue, the practitioner must not provide the marketed opinion, but may provide written advice that satisfies the requirements in paragraph (b)(5)(ii) of this section.

    (v) *Limited scope opinions.*

        (A) The practitioner may provide an opinion that considers less than all of the significant Federal tax issues if—

            (1) The practitioner and the taxpayer agree that the scope of the opinion and the taxpayer's potential reliance on the opinion for purposes of avoiding penalties that may be imposed on the taxpayer are limited to the Federal tax issue(s) addressed in the opinion;

            (2) The opinion is not advice described in paragraph (b)(2)(i)(A) of this section (concerning listed transactions), paragraph (b)(2)(i)(B) of this section (concerning the principal purpose of avoidance or evasion) or paragraph (b)(5) of this section (a *marketed opinion*); and

(3) The opinion includes the appropriate disclosure(s) required under paragraph (e) of this section.

(B) A practitioner may make reasonable assumptions regarding the favorable resolution of a Federal tax issue (an assumed issue) for purposes of providing an opinion on less than all of the significant Federal tax issues as provided in this paragraph (c)(3)(v). The opinion must identify in a separate section all issues for which the practitioner assumed a favorable resolution.

(4) *Overall conclusion.*

(i) The opinion must provide the practitioner's overall conclusion as to the likelihood that the Federal tax treatment of the transaction or matter that is the subject of the opinion is the proper treatment and the reasons for that conclusion. If the practitioner is unable to reach an overall conclusion, the opinion must state that the practitioner is unable to reach an overall conclusion and describe the reasons for the practitioner's inability to reach a conclusion.

(ii) In the case of a *marketed opinion,* the opinion must provide the practitioner's overall conclusion that the Federal tax treatment of the transaction or matter that is the subject of the opinion is the proper treatment at a confidence level of at least more likely than not.

(d) *Competence to provide opinion; reliance on opinions of others.*

(1) The practitioner must be knowledgeable in all of the aspects of Federal tax law relevant to the opinion being rendered, except that the practitioner may rely on the opinion of another practitioner with respect to one or more significant Federal tax issues, unless the practitioner knows or should know that the opinion of the other practitioner should not be relied on. If a practitioner relies on the opinion of another practitioner, the relying practitioner's opinion must identify the other opinion and set forth the conclusions reached in the other opinion.

(2) The practitioner must be satisfied that the combined analysis of the opinions, taken as a whole, and the overall conclusion, if any, satisfy the requirements of this section.

(e) *Required disclosures.* A covered opinion must contain all of the following disclosures that apply—

(1) *Relationship between promoter and practitioner.* An opinion must prominently disclose the existence of—

(i) Any compensation arrangement, such as a referral fee or a fee-sharing arrangement, between the practitioner (or the practitioner's firm or any person who is a member of, associated with, or employed by the practitioner's firm) and any person (other than the client for whom the opinion is prepared) with respect to promoting, marketing or recommending the entity, plan, or arrangement (or a substantially similar arrangement) that is the subject of the opinion; or

(ii) Any referral agreement between the practitioner (or the practitioner's firm or any person who is a member of, associated with, or employed by the practitioner's firm) and a person (other than the client for whom the opinion is prepared) engaged in promoting, marketing or recommending the entity, plan, or arrangement (or a substantially similar arrangement) that is the subject of the opinion.

(2) *Marketed opinions.* A *marketed opinion* must prominently disclose that—

(i) The opinion was written to support the promotion or marketing of the transaction(s) or matter(s) addressed in the opinion; and

(ii) The taxpayer should seek advice based on the taxpayer's particular circumstances from an independent tax advisor.

(3) *Limited scope opinions.* A *limited scope opinion* must prominently disclose that—

(i) The opinion is limited to the one or more Federal tax issues addressed in the opinion;

(ii) Additional issues may exist that could affect the Federal tax treatment of the transaction or matter that is the subject of the opinion and the opinion does not consider or provide a conclusion with respect to any additional issues; and

(iii) With respect to any significant Federal tax issues outside the limited scope of the opinion, the opinion was not written, and cannot be used by the taxpayer, for the purpose of avoiding penalties that may be imposed on the taxpayer.

(4) *Opinions that fail to reach a more likely than not conclusion.* An opinion that does not reach a conclusion at a confidence level of at least more likely than not with respect to a significant Federal tax issue must prominently disclose that—

(i) The opinion does not reach a conclusion at a confidence level of at least more likely than not with respect to one or more significant Federal tax issues addressed by the opinion; and

(ii) With respect to those significant Federal tax issues, the opinion was not written, and cannot be used by the taxpayer, for the purpose of avoiding penalties that may be imposed on the taxpayer.

(5) *Advice regarding required disclosures.* In the case of any disclosure required under this section, the practitioner may not provide advice to any person that is contrary to or inconsistent with the required disclosure.

(f) *Effect of opinion that meets these standards*—

(1) *In general.* An opinion that meets the requirements of this section satisfies the practitioner's responsibilities under this section, but the persuasiveness of the opinion with regard to the tax issues in question and the taxpayer's good faith reliance on the opinion will be determined separately under applicable provisions of the law and regulations.

(2) *Standards for other written advice.* A practitioner who provides written advice that is not a covered opinion for purposes of this section is subject to the requirements of §10.37.

(g) *Effective date.* This section applies to written advice that is rendered after June 20, 2005.

Appendix D

Private Securities Litigation Reform Act of 1995

(Title I, Reduction of Abusive Litigation)

SEC. 102. SAFE HARBOR FOR FORWARD-LOOKING STATEMENTS.

(a) AMENDMENT TO THE SECURITIES ACT OF 1933.—Title I of the Securities Act of 1933 (15 U.S.C. 77a et seq.) is amended by inserting after section 27 (as added by this Act) the following new section:

SEC. 27A. APPLICATION OF SAFE HARBOR FOR FORWARD-LOOKING STATEMENTS.

(a) **APPLICABILITY.**—This section shall apply only to a forward-looking statement made by—

(1) an issuer that, at the time that the statement is made, is subject to the reporting requirements of section 13(a) or section 15(d) of the Securities Exchange Act of 1934;

(2) a person acting on behalf of such issuer;

(3) an outside reviewer retained by such issuer making a statement on behalf of such issuer; or

(4) an underwriter, with respect to information provided by such issuer or information derived from information provided by the issuer.

(b) **EXCLUSIONS.**—Except to the extent otherwise specifically provided by rule, regulation, or order of the Commission, this section shall not apply to a forward-looking statement—

(1) that is made with respect to the business or operations of the issuer, if the issuer—

(A) during the 3-year period preceding the date on which the statement was first made—

(i) was convicted of any felony or misdemeanor described in clauses (i) through (iv) of section 15(b)(4)(B) of the Securities Exchange Act of 1934; or

(ii) has been made the subject of a judicial or administrative decree or order arising out of a governmental action that—

(I) prohibits future violations of the antifraud provisions of the securities laws;

(II) requires that the issuer cease and desist from violating the antifraud provisions of the securities laws; or

AAG-PRO APP D

                (III) determines that the issuer violated the antifraud provisions of the securities laws;

      (B) makes the forward-looking statement in connection with an offering of securities by a blank check company;

      (C) issues penny stock;

      (D) makes the forward-looking statement in connection with a roll-up transaction; or

      (E) makes the forward-looking statement in connection with a going private transaction; or

(2) that is—

      (A) included in a financial statement prepared in accordance with generally accepted accounting principles;

      (B) contained in a registration statement of, or otherwise issued by, an investment company;

      (C) made in connection with a tender offer;

      (D) made in connection with an initial public offering;

      (E) made in connection with an offering by, or relating to the operations of, a partnership, limited liability company, or a direct participation investment program; or

      (F) made in a disclosure of beneficial ownership in a report required to be filed with the Commission pursuant to section 13(d) of the Securities Exchange Act of 1934.

(c) SAFE HARBOR.—

(1) IN GENERAL.—Except as provided in subsection (b), in any private action arising under this title that is based on an untrue statement of a material fact or omission of a material fact necessary to make the statement not misleading, a person referred to in subsection (a) shall not be liable with respect to any forward-looking statement, whether written or oral, if and to the extent that—

      (A) the forward-looking statement is—

            (i) identified as a forward-looking statement, and is accompanied by meaningful cautionary statements identifying important factors that could cause actual results to differ materially from those in the forward-looking statement; or

            (ii) immaterial; or

      (B) the plaintiff fails to prove that the forward-looking statement—

            (i) if made by a natural person, was made with actual knowledge by that person that the statement was false or misleading; or

            (ii) if made by a business entity; was—

                (I) made by or with the approval of an executive officer of that entity, and

(II) made or approved by such officer with actual knowledge by that officer that the statement was false or misleading.

(2) ORAL FORWARD-LOOKING STATEMENTS.—In the case of an oral forward-looking statement made by an issuer that is subject to the reporting requirements of section 13(a) or section 15(d) of the Securities Exchange Act of 1934, or by a person acting on behalf of such issuer, the requirement set forth in paragraph (1)(A) shall be deemed to be satisfied—

(A) if the oral forward-looking statement is accompanied by a cautionary statement—

(i) that the particular oral statement is a forward-looking statement; and

(ii) that the actual results could differ materially from those projected in the forward-looking statement; and

(B) if—

(i) the oral forward-looking statement is accompanied by an oral statement that additional information concerning factors that could cause actual results to differ materially from those in the forward-looking statement is contained in a readily available written document, or portion thereof;

(ii) the accompanying oral statement referred to in clause (i) identifies the document, or portion thereof, that contains the additional information about those factors relating to the forward-looking statement; and

(iii) the information contained in that written document is a cautionary statement that satisfies the standard established in paragraph (1)(A).

(3) AVAILABILITY.—Any document filed with the Commission or generally disseminated shall be deemed to be readily available for purposes of paragraph (2).

(4) EFFECT ON OTHER SAFE HARBORS.—The exemption provided for in paragraph (1) shall be in addition to any exemption that the Commission may establish by rule or regulation under subsection (g).

(d) DUTY TO UPDATE.—Nothing in this section shall impose upon any person a duty to update a forward-looking statement.

(e) DISPOSITIVE MOTION.—On any motion to dismiss based upon subsection (c)(1), the court shall consider any statement cited in the complaint and cautionary statement accompanying the forward-looking statement, which are not subject to material dispute, cited by the defendant.

(f) STAY PENDING DECISION ON MOTION.—In any private action arising under this title, the court shall stay discovery (other than discovery that is specifically directed to the applicability of the exemption provided for in this section) during the pendency of any motion by a defendant for summary judgment that is based on the grounds that—

(1) the statement or omission upon which the complaint is based is a forward-looking statement within the meaning of this section; and

(2) the exemption provided for in this section precludes a claim for relief.

(g) EXEMPTION AUTHORITY.—In addition to the exemptions provided for in this section, the Commission may, by rule or regulation, provide exemptions from or under any provision of this title, including with respect to liability that is based on a statement or that is based on projections or other forward-looking information, if and to the extent that any such exemption is consistent with the public interest and the protection of investors, as determined by the Commission.

(h) EFFECT ON OTHER AUTHORITY OF COMMISSION.—Nothing in this section limits, either expressly or by implication, the authority of the Commission to exercise similar authority or to adopt similar rules and regulations with respect to forward-looking statements under any other statute under which the Commission exercises rulemaking authority.

(i) DEFINITIONS.—For purposes of this section, the following definitions shall apply:

    (1) FORWARD-LOOKING STATEMENT.—The term "forward-looking statement" means—

        (A) a statement containing a projection of revenues, income (including income loss), earnings (including earnings loss) per share, capital expenditures, dividends, capital structure, or other financial items;

        (B) a statement of the plans and objectives of management for future operations, including plans or objectives relating to the products or services of the issuer;

        (C) a statement of future economic performance, including any such statement contained in a discussion and analysis of financial condition by the management or in the results of operations included pursuant to the rules and regulations of the Commission;

        (D) any statement of the assumptions underlying or relating to any statement described in subparagraph (A), (B), or (C);

        (E) any report issued by an outside reviewer retained by an issuer, to the extent that the report assesses a forward-looking statement made by the issuer; or

        (F) a statement containing a projection or estimate of such other items as may be specified by rule or regulation of the Commission.

    (2) INVESTMENT COMPANY.—The term "investment company" has the same meaning as in section 3(a) of the Investment Company Act of 1940.

    (3) PENNY STOCK.—The term "penny stock" has the same meaning as in section 3(a)(51) of the Securities Exchange Act of 1934, and the rules and regulations, or orders issued pursuant to that section.

    (4) GOING PRIVATE TRANSACTION.—The term "going private transaction" has the meaning given that term under the rules or regulations of the Commission issued pursuant to section 13(e) of the Securities Exchange Act of 1934.

(5) SECURITIES LAWS.—The term "securities laws" has the same meaning as in section 3 of the Securities Exchange Act of 1934.

(6) PERSON ACTING ON BEHALF OF AN ISSUER.—The term "person acting on behalf of an issuer" means an officer, director, or employee of the issuer.

(7) OTHER TERMS.—The terms "blank check company," "roll up transaction," "partnership," "limited liability company," "executive officer of an entity" and "direct participation investment program," have the meanings given those terms by rule or regulation of the Commission.

Appendix E

Schedule of Changes Made to the Text From the Previous Edition

As of November 1, 2012

This schedule of changes identifies areas in the text and footnotes of this guide that have been changed from the previous edition. Entries in the table of this appendix reflect current numbering, lettering (including that in appendix names), and character designations that resulted from the renumbering or reordering that occurred in the updating of this guide.

Reference	Change
General	The use of footnotes denoted with a symbol instead of a number (referred to as *temporary footnotes*) has been discontinued. All content in such footnotes has been added to chapter text, converted to a numbered footnote, or deleted.
General	Guidance related to the clarified auditing standards (Statement on Auditing Standards Nos. 122–126 [AICPA, *Professional Standards*]) has been incorporated throughout this guide.
Preface	Revised for clarification and the passage of time.
Paragraph 1.14	Revised to reflect the issuance of Statement on Standards for Attestation Engagements (SSAE) No. 17, *Reporting on Compiled Prospective Financial Statements When the Practitioner's Independence Is Impaired* (AICPA, *Professional Standards*, AT section 301 par. .23).
Paragraph 3.07 and footnote 5 in paragraph 8.06	Revised for clarification.
Paragraphs 8.14–.15, 10.15, and 10.22 and footnote 11 in paragraph 10.21	Revised for clarification.
Footnote 1 to chapter 11 title	Added.
Paragraphs 11.02, 11.05, and 11.07; footnote 1 in paragraph 14.02; and footnote 5 in paragraph 14.05	Revised for clarification.
Paragraph 14.05	Revised to reflect the issuance of SSAE No. 17.

(continued)

Reference	Change
Former footnote 2 to heading before paragraph 15.05	Deleted for clarification.
Footnote 3 in paragraph 15.11	Revised for clarification.
Paragraphs 15.52, 18.04, and 18.09 and footnote 4 in paragraph 18.08	Revised for clarification.
Former footnote 4 to heading before paragraph 19.11	Deleted.
Paragraph 21.04	Revised for clarification.
Appendix A	Revised for clarification.
Appendix B	Revised for clarification.
Appendix E	Updated.
Index	Added.

Index

Printed in the United States
By Bookmasters